What people are saying about
The Prophet's Way

"This is the most important book I have ever read. . . . Now I can do no less than give my remaining years to its message."
—JOSEPH CHILTON PEARCE, AUTHOR OF
THE CRACK IN THE COSMIC EGG AND
THE BIOLOGY OF TRANSCENDENCE

"*The Prophet's Way* produces its own butterfly effect: the simple act of reading it can change your life."
—MICHAEL HUTCHISON, AUTHOR OF
MEGA BRAIN POWER AND *THE BOOK OF FLOATING*

"*The Prophet's Way* draws you in like a novel, keeping you on the edge waiting to see what happens next, yet is a true story.

"Like a painting by a great master that was painted over and hidden for centuries, Thom Hartmann peels away the layers of distortion heaped on original visions of religion and faith which existed 2,000 years ago, revealing once again the essence of humanity, spirituality, and mysticism.

"This book helped me make a major change in my life for the better."
—ROB KALL, COAUTHOR OF
BIOFEEDBACK THEORY & PRACTICE; FOUNDER OF
FUTUREHEALTH, INC.

"Thom Hartmann is an absolutely original mind, with an original way of looking at the world: he has made an enormous contribution to our culture."
—OWEN LIPSTEIN, FORMER EDITOR IN CHIEF OF
PSYCHOLOGY TODAY AND *MOTHER EARTH NEWS*

"This book represents the path of a spiritual initiate and the signposts he met along the way. We Coptics are honored that Thom's path included Hamid Bey and Master Stanley, two great lights of the 20th century."

—JOHN DAVIS, DIRECTOR OF THE COPTIC FELLOWSHIP

"Thom Hartmann exposes many of the ugly truths hiding beneath the surface of contemporary 'civilization.' Hartmann's book masterfully combines autobiography, science, and Christian spirituality and shows us how to rehabilitate our world with acts of compassion rooted in spiritual humility and faith in the Creator of all creatures and cultures.
"Easy to read, hard to practice."

—JAY FIKES, PH.D., AUTHOR OF CARLOS CASTANEDA: ACADEMIC
OPPORTUNISM AND THE PSYCHEDELIC SIXTIES AND
REUBEN SNAKE, YOUR HUMBLE SERPENT

"Thom Hartmann is one of the great adventurers of our time, both in the world at large and the world of ideas."

—JILL NEIMARK,
JOURNALIST AND AUTHOR OF BLOODSONG

The Prophet's Way
A Guide to Living in the Now

Thom Hartmann

Park Street Press
Rochester, Vermont

Park Street Press
One Park Street
Rochester, Vermont 05767
www.InnerTraditions.com

Park Street Press is a division of Inner Traditions International

Library of Congress Cataloging-in-Publication Data
Hartmann, Thom, 1951–
  The prophet's way : a guide to living in the now / Thom Hartmann.
    p. cm.
  ISBN 978-0-89281-198-4 (pbk.)
  1. Spiritual life. I. Title.

BL624.H342 2004
204'.4—dc22

                                                                    2004007501

Printed and bound in the United States at Lake Book Manufacturing, Inc.

10 9 8 7 6 5 4

This book was typeset in Sabon

*This book is dedicated to the memory
of Oakley and Nelle Hammond and
Carl and Esther Hartmann.
It is also offered in loving appreciation
to Gottfried and Ursula Müller,
who made possible its contents.*

From the time of the origins of the Judeo-Christian tradition, and continuing to the present, some people have considered the name of the Creator so holy that it should not be spoken or written completely except in the most extraordinary of circumstances.

In respect of this tradition, this book follows the custom of using a dash in place of the vowel ("G-d") in the word we most often use in English to replace the name of the Creator.

Contents

Acknowledgments

Special thanks are deserved by many people. In particular, I owe a great debt of gratitude to my wife and children: Louise, Kindra, Justin, and Kerith; and my editors, in particular Dave deBronkart, Susan Burgess, Brad Walrod, and Kyle Roderick. Thanks go to Jon Graham, Ehud Sperling, and Jeanie Levitan for believing in this book and helping to make its publication and distribution possible. To Jane Shumway and Tim Englemann for their insights and thoughts. To Rob Kall for his quotes. To those who started before me in our spiritual work: John Davis, Hal and Shelley Cohen, Grace Felton, Gerhard and Gerda Lipfert, Father Ben Carreon, Bernie Cooper, Don Haughey, Bob and Millie DusSault, Vern Phillips, Louise Richards, Manfred Olzewski, Neva Hite, Lee Hite.

Also special thanks to those friends and acquaintances who helped me along my various paths which indirectly made this book possible: Raun Melmed, John Ratey, Edward Hallowell, John and Veronica Deane, Nigel and Corrinne Peacock, Luise Stössel, Michael Popkin, Bob Koski, Scott and Julie Cress, Skye and Jane Lininger, Scott Berg, Andi, Rick and Wanda Bogin, Rochel Haigh Blehr, Jerry Schneiderman, Michael Kurland, Michael Hutchison, Carla Nelson, Elisa Davis, Kathy Daya, Kathy Lynch, Judy Ybarra, Ken Kiyoshi, Horst Von Heyer, Jay Fikes, Jane and Clare Shumway, Michael and Heidi Garnatz, Jack and Norma Vance, Jack Reiley, Jaye, George Lynn, Dick Gregory, Brian Savory, Wilson Harrell, Will Krynen, Paul and Marilyn Nosie, Jane Merrithew, Rick Bogin, Peg Hopper, Patty Merrill, Maureen O'Hara, Leif Roland, Masanobu Taniguchi, Terry ("Baba Rum Raisin") O'Connor, Richard Zmijewski, J. Tevere MacFadyen, Kate Kelley, Peggy Ramundo, Owen Lipstein, Tom Allen, Gwynne Fisher, Tom Larsen, and all the people who made Salem New Hampshire happen.

Introduction

He who is swimming against the stream comes to the Source.

—GOTTFRIED MÜLLER

There's a mountainside path in northern Bavaria that's walked every Saturday by a friend of mine who's also my teacher. The path leads to a stone on which he has carved the tetragrammaton, the four letters of the name of G-d. The man is Herr Gottfried Müller, and he calls the path his "prophet's way."

He calls his path the prophet's way because along this path he can call out to, and feel the presence of, the ancient prophets. In both the physical and the spiritual world, it's his path for meeting divinity.

He has invited me many times to share his prophet's way, as you'll learn in this book. I've traveled the world with him, seeing it now through different eyes and hearing it with different ears as a result of his instruction.

On this path, I've learned some powerful lessons and transformational techniques that I feel an obligation to share.

I know, for example, that it is possible for all of us—ordinary, mortal humans—to know divinity, if we, too, will follow the prophet's way. And we can use this knowledge to transform the world. "But," as Herr Müller is so fond of saying, "you must *do* it!"

When I was a child, I read a story in which a spiritual teacher said that there are always "saints" or holy people on the Earth, and that they hold the world together. Decades later, Gottfried Müller told me that Abram Poljak, his spiritual mentor—an Hasidic Jew and scholar of Kabbalah who'd survived the Holocaust to become a Christian mystic—was of the same opinion.

But Poljak (and Müller) took it a huge step further, saying that we *all* can become keepers of the flame of life on Earth, and both steadfastly refused to participate in or with any organized religion that may want to place itself between them and Spirit. There are no special entry requirements to spiritual awakening, they say, other than desire and willingness. Given that permission, I've walked into their world, and invite you to join me.

So this book is a chronicle of my travels along the prophet's way, both spiritually and physically, touching the lives of people on four continents. In here, you'll find specific teachings and techniques you can use to change yourself and your world.

I invite you to walk with me along the prophet's way, in the hopes that together we can globally touch the power of life, and thus re-create and transform ourselves, our planet, and our children's future.

ATLANTA, DECEMBER 1996

Meeting Master Stanley

If the cask is to hold the wine, its water must first be poured out.

—Meister Eckhart

Around 1969 I went to hear a lecture given by a "Coptic Minister" named Lee who traveled from Detroit to give speeches every week in Lansing, Michigan. Lee taught about meditation, prayer, the subtle or etheric body, and the return of the Messiah. He was a fascinating man with extraordinary piercing brown eyes and a contagious laugh; I began to attend his speeches every week, often taking friends.

My spiritual seeking had moved out of the Hippie culture (although I still had shoulder-length hair) and into the subcultures of Christian mysticism. My experiences living at the anti-war center of the underground *The Paper* tabloid in East Lansing, and in San Francisco's Haight-Ashbury area, and even briefly in the military culture, had convinced me that there was something we were all missing. It was right in front of us, and we weren't seeing it.

Or perhaps it was within us.

Lee told us of his mentor and teacher, a man named Kurt Stanley (Lee referred to him as "Master Stanley"), who conducted a weekly service at the Coptic Temple in Detroit. Lee told amazing stories about Master Stanley healing people with his hands, reading minds, and showing his aura and seeing those of others.

As a person with a traditional Methodist upbringing, I thought this sounded both odd and heretical, but I was also constantly driven by an all-consuming curiosity. In my earlier years I'd visited enough extraordinary inner worlds to know that simply going through the motions of religion wasn't where I personally would find Father G-d or Mother Holy Spirit or Son the Christ. I was on a Hunt.

So one afternoon I drove to Detroit to hear Master Stanley.

3

There was quite a crowd at the door of the building, a huge old house in downtown Detroit. A large, three-story, red-brick building in a disintegrating part of town, the Temple had once been the Governor's Mansion for the state of Michigan during that brief period in the nineteenth century when the state capital was in Detroit. It had then passed through several hands and ended up with the Coptics in the 1950s.

A woman with an officious glare, graying hair, and what appeared to be a short temper guarded the door, letting in people she knew and examining the rest of us as if we were potential carriers of disease. I had hair down past my shoulders at the time, and was wearing jeans and a blue work shirt: typical garb for a college student in the late 1960s. Grace, it turned out her name was, eyed me harshly and said, "You can't come in."

"Why?" I asked, perplexed.

"No drugs or hippies," she said.

"Is Lee here?" I asked.

Her eyes narrowed. "You know Lee?"

"I'm a student of his from Lansing."

She was still shaking her head, looking again at my hair and clothes, when Lee appeared in the door. "Let him in, Grace," he said.

She stepped back from the door without a word. I walked in.

Inside, the building smelled of old wood, wax, dust, and incense. To the right was a large staircase with a thick oak banister, and to my left was the entrance to the main room, which at one time was probably a formal ballroom.

I stepped into the main room, and saw perhaps two hundred people sitting on folding chairs. At the front of the room was a raised platform, a lectern with flowers and lit candles to either side, and behind the stage a large banner of an aunch, the Egyptian Christian cross with a circle at the top, and the symbol of an eye in the center of it. The eye looked familiar and Lee, who was standing beside me, noticed me staring at it. "Look on a dollar bill and you'll see it," he whispered. I dug one out of my pocket; sure enough, there it was, on top of the Egyptian pyramid, a design handed down by our Christian-mystic founding fathers.

I sat down and waited for a half hour or so until the room became dark and suddenly silent. An old man, the right half of his lower lip missing so you could see his gums and teeth, wearing a long, white robe trimmed in gold, walked into the room and nodded at us. He held a white handkerchief over his mouth, but kept seeming to forget it, exposing his injury.

"That's Master Stanley," Lee whispered.

Everybody stood up, and the old man led us in a prayer and song. Then he gave an hour's lecture in thickly-accented English.

Master Stanley's real name was Kurt Stanley, and he was from Switzerland; his mentor, the man who'd founded the Coptics in the United States, was Master Hamid Bey, a renegade Orthodox Coptic Christian priest from Egypt who started Coptic Temples in the western United States, in Los Angeles and other cities.* Hamid Bey had ordained Kurt Stanley in 1937.

The lecture was interesting, but mostly stuff I'd heard before from Lee: the importance of not judging others, of giving selflessly, of having compassion for all living things even to the point of not eating meat, and of always striving to be conscious of the presence of the Holy Spirit.

"It is this Spirit which fills and animates the world," Master Stanley said. "It is the breath and voice of G-d. It interpenetrates each of us, and gives us life, separating a living person from a corpse, even though both are chemically identical." He paused for a moment, as if considering something, holding the white handkerchief over the lower part of his mouth. (I later learned he'd been a chemist in Switzerland and was injured in an explosion which included radioactive materials. Some became embedded in his lower jaw and ate away the tissues.)

Then he stepped around the front of the lectern and said, "Jesus said that it was when people saw that they believed. Watch."

He closed his eyes and seemed to stop breathing. A soft, golden light began to surround his body. I looked up and around the room for

---

*There is a possibility of some confusion between this Coptic church, founded by Hamid Bey, and the Orthodox Coptic Church. The Orthodox Coptic Church is very similar to the Roman Catholic Church, even to the point of having a Pope, and is the largest Christian church in Egypt. Hamid Bey broke away from the Orthodox Coptics sixty years ago and founded a separate church, which Hamid Bey said was more true to the "secret and mystical" teachings only available to priests of the Orthodox church. This new organization is what is now the Coptic Fellowship.

the source of the light: there was none. Nor was there any shadow behind or around him, as you'd see if somebody was shining a spotlight on him. And the glow was perfectly even, surrounding his entire body, extending out perhaps an inch or two everywhere except his head, where it seemed to extend out several inches. It looked like a soft, golden mist, yet was perfectly transparent.

I was stunned. Was I hallucinating? Perhaps a remnant experience from some drug I'd taken years earlier?

He took a breath and the glow shimmered. "What color do you see?" he said softly.

A hundred voices said, "Gold."

We can't all be hallucinating identically, I thought. It was both reassuring and frightening: this was *real*.

Eyes still closed, he nodded, then stopped breathing again. A long minute passed and the glow slowly changed from gold to blue. My heart was racing; everybody in the room could see this transition, too. It had to be a trick! Yet nowhere could I see the light source.

If this was real, physically real, the implications were even harder to deny.

"What color do you see now?" he said.

"Blue," everybody said. Lee leaned over and whispered to me, "This is nothing. You should see how bright he gets when we're meditating."

"How does he do it?" I whispered, but Lee shook his head as the man behind me poked me in the back. I said nothing more.

Master Stanley continued his aura demonstration for another few minutes, moving through red, yellow, and white. When he was finished, he seemed drained, but continued his speech. "That was not the Holy Spirit," he said. "It was merely the life force of a human. It's within each of you; I am not special. Only you must learn to control and project your life force, as it is your gift, one of your many gifts, from the Holy Spirit, which the Bible refers to as the Amen, the faithful and true witness, the beginning of the manifestation of G-d."

After the speech and a long chant of "Amen," Master Stanley left the room and climbed the stairs as the congregation sang a final song.

Lee nudged me. "Want to go meet him?"

"You bet!" I said.

TOUCHED BY THE MAN WITH THE AURA

Lee led me up the stairs, to the end of a long line of people, most in their fifties and sixties. At least half the people who'd attended the service were lined up down the long hall on the second floor that led to Master Stanley's office. Grace guarded his door, arms crossed over her chest and a skeptical look on her face as people told her why they wanted in. A few she turned away, but most she let in, one at a time. The people coming out seemed to stagger, as if the light in the dim hallway was startlingly bright.

Two people ahead of us in line were a man in his sixties, a crutch under one arm, and a younger man who looked enough like him that I concluded it was his son holding up his other shoulder. The older man's legs seemed withered and he dragged them as if they were dead branches.

When they got up to Grace, I heard the young man say to her in a choked voice, "My father was wounded in the war in Europe, and has been paralyzed from the waist down since 1944. Can Master Stanley do anything for him?"

"We'll see," she said, opening the door to let them in.

Five minutes later the old man and his son walked out. The old man's legs were wobbly, but he carried his crutch in his right hand and had a huge smile on his tear-streaked face, and his son was sobbing uncontrollably.

Having seen the light show downstairs, and now seeing this man walk out after he'd hobbled in, I was torn apart emotionally. The rational scientist in me was screaming "hoax!" while the part of me that had grown up reading these same types of stories about Jesus glowing as he walked on the water and healing lame people was staggered by the possibility that Jesus's final words to his disciples, when he told them that the things he'd done they would do also, might be true.

And, whether or not it wanted to acknowledge it, the scientist in me knew I couldn't deny what I'd seen. I could question it, but I couldn't deny it.

Thus, as the old man and his son passed us, a huge lump welled up in my throat. I looked at the door and felt both afraid and excited. Lee, sensing my emotional turmoil, reached over and squeezed my arm. "It's OK," he said in a whisper.

At last, Lee opened the door to Master Stanley's office and led me in.

◆

The room was dark other than a few candles on his large oak desk, and he sat in a straight-backed chair in the middle of the room, an identical empty chair facing him.

"Master Stanley, this is Thom Hartmann, one of my students from Lansing," Lee said.

Master Stanley looked at me with pale blue eyes but said nothing. I had the odd feeling that he was looking through me.

Lee motioned to the empty chair. "Sit down," he said to me.

I sat, my knees just touching Master Stanley's. It was a culturally uncomfortable closeness, but I was afraid to move the chair back and Master Stanley seemed unconcerned by it.

Lee walked to the door, opened it, and left us alone.

Master Stanley looked at me for a long time; it must have been at least three or four minutes, staring directly into my eyes. It seemed that he didn't blink or breathe, although I was so consumed with inner questions that he could have done both and I may have missed it. In my mind I was reciting the Lord's Prayer, something I'd done since I was a child when I was frightened.

Finally he spoke, his voice thin and soft. "What do you want from me?"

"I don't know," I said, thinking that to ask for a healing would be unnecessary, and to say that I wanted to know G-d would sound pretentious. He could create and read auras; I'd leave it to him to know what was best for me.

"Let's meditate," he said. "Close your eyes, look to the center of your forehead, and recite the name of Jesus Christ."

I did that for a few minutes, and began to feel very hot, as if I had a fever.

His voice came out of the darkness in front of me, so soft it was almost a whisper, in his thick German accent. "People who approach spiritual work have an important destiny," he said. "They are members of Christ's army of light."

I opened my eyes; he was staring at me again and I was whipping back and forth between thinking he was just a crazy old man playing a role and feeling, frankly, frightened by the situation. (Among other things, nobody had ever told me I had a destiny—much less a man who had just done things I never thought I'd see.)

He coughed several times, a deep rattling in his lungs, then stood up. I started to stand, but he put out his hand. "I have been told to do this for you. You would ultimately do it yourself, but time is short. You cannot wait 60 years, as I did, for it to open."

"What?"

"Shhhhhh . . ."he whispered as he walked around beside my chair. "Close your eyes again, and look at the center of your forehead."

I did so, and felt him put a soft, dry, warm hand on my forehead. His other hand pressed against the base of my spine. "Take a deep breath in through your nose," he said. "And relax as you do it."

I took in the breath, and a third of the way into it suddenly felt a searing hot sensation, bright, and yellow as if it were liquid steel, rush up my spine, along with a roaring sound in my ears. His hand burned my lower back, and the hand on my forehead was now ice cold.

As I finished the breath, the darkened screen of the inside of my forehead exploded in bright, golden light, as if I had thrown open my eyes and looked directly into the sun. His hand on my forehead was now hot as well, and I felt like I might throw up.

The sensation was like nothing I'd ever experienced: the electric shock that ran up the inside of my spine was sharp and cutting, the light more startling than painful, and yet as the light exploded and then seemed to pour over the top of my head, I was left with an ecstatic feeling, an over-whelming sensation of love in my chest, and the breathless tingle of an orgasm that had gone through my mind rather than my genitals.

Master Stanley returned to his chair. "That light you now see in your forehead is your entry point into the world of the Holy Spirit. Always seek it out and one day you may even see there the throne of G-d Himself. Then you will find your destiny."

I tried to say something; I'd heard Lee talk about kundalini (the rising of the body's most elemental energy up through the spine) and the spiritual eye and all that, but I'd never expected to experience it without years of tortuous yoga and pranayama* practice.

---

*Pranayama is a system of breathing exercises that are most often part of yoga. One purpose is to move around energy in the body, particularly the primary spiritual energy stored at the base of the spine.

Instead of being able to speak, though, I started sobbing. Tears of joy, grief, pain, happiness—it was all intermingled. A wall of some sort broke down. All through high school I was a self-proclaimed agnostic, having turned my back on the church of my parents as I studied science with a fierce fascination. During my hippie days I'd had many extraordinary out-of-body and other paranormal experiences, but could easily dismiss many of them as being drug-induced. Now I realized, deep down in my guts and for the first time since my childhood, that the world of spirit was real.

After a few moments, I caught my breath and got myself under control. The room was still dim, but Master Stanley was now glowing again, his body enveloped in a golden light, far brighter than it had been downstairs. "I am not the one who will give you your final work," he said softly. "You are far too young and inexperienced, and that man will come into your life later. But I have been ordered to open your eyes and to teach you. You may become one of my students, if you choose."

I nodded and said, "OK"

He smiled and his glow receded. "Now you must leave. There are others to see before this body turns to ash."

I walked unsteadily to the door and stepped out into the bright light of the hallway where Lee met me. As we left, Grace said to him in a stage whisper: "We don't want hippies here." He glared at her, but I could only smile. My heart was so full, I wanted to hug and kiss her. And everybody else in the building!

During the drive back to Lansing, I kept reviewing my experiences. The empirical, rational, scientist part of me wanted to know if it was all some kind of trick. Maybe he had some kind of electric shock device? A Van de Graaff generator that whipped up a huge static field to make him glow?

But the part of me that had been fascinated since childhood with issues of consciousness and spirituality intuited that it was all real, that there were no tricks, and that Master Stanley had no hidden agenda and wasn't trying to power-trip me. I was leaning heavily toward the conclusion that everything I'd assumed about reality up to that moment might, in fact, just be a thin shaving, peeled from the trunk of the tree of life.

THE DRIVE TO DISCOVER WHAT REALLY MATTERS

It was an issue I'd pondered for years, but my meeting with Master Stanley was the first time something outside of my own control had been entirely paranormal. What he had done was something I'd read about and heard about, but never really expected to experience firsthand.

As I drove home, I became even more certain: what most people call consciousness is really only a shadow, or a mechanistic manifestation of brain cells and stimulus-response. It's only the brain's interpretation of sensory inputs. And I saw and felt in that moment that "real" consciousness is something far deeper; that real consciousness is anchored in the very *nature* of reality and creation.

I made the firm decision during that drive home that I would devote the rest of my life to finding what was "real."

That night I awoke from a sound sleep and sat up in my bed. I was living in a small, rented room over a storefront across the street from Michigan State University, and there were people coming and going at all hours. I figured a noise in the hall had awakened me, but I could hear nothing.

Then, in the air a few feet in front of me, a globe materialized, slowly spinning, the size of a beach ball. I immediately recognized it as the Earth, as seen from space. The blue oceans, green and brown land masses, and white patterns of clouds and storms. It was both real and not-real: like a hologram projected into the air.

As I watched, the land masses began to darken at various points. Small black pustules formed, like little blisters or cancers on the Earth. The blue of the oceans became brown and muddy around these areas. The cancers slowly expanded, blackening the Earth and cracking it in places, until they covered virtually all the land of the planet. The clouds turned a death-like yellow-gray, and the waters no longer sparkled blue but were a dull and putrid green-brown.

A thought came into my mind as if a voice were speaking to me: "The Earth is a living thing. It is infected."

Then the Earth shuddered as it spun. It jerked to one side, as if the spin were changing, and the blackened areas split open. The Earth shuddered again, and the black areas cracked and shattered into fragments, falling off into the air around the image and vanishing. The

Earth was once again clear and clean, spinning gracefully, displaying oceans the color of lapis lazuli and land richly covered with green.

The voice in my mind said, "The Earth has healed itself."

The image vanished and I lay back in my bed, realizing that the infection in my vision was humankind; the Earth was as much a living organism as I was, a single and complete entity in its own right, perhaps even with its own unique consciousness., and it would respond to a toxic infection by throwing it off, as my body would shed a bacterial invasion or a scab.

I couldn't sleep, so I pulled out a Bible from the stack of books next to my bed. I flipped it open to a random page toward the end, and my eyes looked down at the words of the Book of Revelation (11:18): ". . . and I shall destroy them which destroy the Earth."

Stunned, I closed the Bible and put it on the bookshelf as if it were hot. I slept fitfully the rest of that night, knowing intuitively that every major change—be it in the world or in individual human life—was preceded by signs and markers. There are always warnings, and I'd just seen a vivid one.

THE BEGINNING OF THE NEW AGE

This vision, and then opening the Bible to that quote, upset me so much that the next week I brought it up with Master Stanley.

"What you have seen is not unique," he said. "We humans *are* an infection on the Earth. It shall heal itself. This will be the beginning of the new times, what some would call the new age."

"As in the biblical Revelation?" I said. "Wars, plagues, famines, earthquakes. . ."

"Perhaps," he said. "It depends on the choices we make in the next thirty years. But in either case, it will be a time of great renewal and spiritual energy.

"Dark and light are always in balance. There cannot be a shadow without a light, and the strongest light will create the darkest shadow.

"Everything will accelerate and intensify. People will feel this, they'll know that the world is moving faster, that time is moving faster, that there is a spiritual pressure like a wind to their backs, but most won't understand its nature. They'll wonder why they have no time, why the world is moving so fast, why life is slipping through their fingers like dry sand. Those who don't understand the meaning of this time will be swept away by it. That's why we must teach them."

"But why all the disasters? Why all the deaths?"

He pushed his handkerchief to his mouth and said, "These are the mysteries. Perhaps one day you will unravel them. In any case, we all chose to be on the Earth at this time to experience them, and we therefore have an important work to do."

WHY DO WE TEACH THAT MYSTICS ONLY LIVE IN PLACES AND TIMES WE CAN'T SEE?

Before meeting Master Stanley, I'd read books about remarkable spiritual persons: Yogananda, Gurdjieff, Ramana Maharshi, Edgar Cayce, St. John of the Cross, St. Teresa of Avila, Terese Neumann, and, of course, the stories in the Bible. I'd read them with both skepticism and hope—skeptical that people with such powers and insights could even be real (much less alive in our world today), and yet hopeful that they were, and that someday I would have an opportunity to meet such a person.

Thus, meeting Master Stanley presented me with conflicting feelings, thoughts, and sights. I recognized in him a spiritual power that was positive and loving. But there were also parts of me that doubted what I'd seen with my own eyes and what I'd felt in my own body. I thought it may be simply an anomaly: one of those things you genuinely see, even though you know you'll never understand *how* it could be so—like the work of a good stage magician—yet you know on a factual level it's an illusion.

So, on one level, like most people raised in our culture, I was skeptical of the whole thing. The prevalent story of Western culture is that all those things happened "back then," but can't happen "now."

But the skepticism didn't make me disbelieving. Rather, it raised in me an old, subtle conflict that I'd never resolved, a conflict that perhaps I'd never even put my finger on:

Modern religion is an odd mixture of belief and non-belief.

We are told: "Believe that this *did* happen, but don't believe anybody who says they can do this kind of stuff today."

We are told: "This is right; this is so; but this over here is wrong.

Remember these answers *we* give *you*." In sharp contrast to this tradition, Master Stanley, who gave a more powerful demonstration of spirituality than I'd ever seen anywhere, never said "Behold!" and never demanded that any of us believe everything he taught. "Take what is useful," he often said.

This spoke volumes to me.

Skepticism and doubt have always been both my strengths and my weaknesses. I was taught in school that they were strengths—the scientific method—and in my youth I believed totally in the religion of modern science. (I call it a religion because it's a set of values that people accept and pursue, believing in them even though they can't *prove* that their belief is correct.) Nuclear power would mean free electricity for everybody, we could feed the world's population no matter what it became, doctors were priests who had the power of life and death because of their understanding of medical technology, and all problems had solutions *if only we could know enough.*

Ironically, decades later science itself would disprove the "religion" of "if only we could know enough." Chaos theory, born out of weather forecasting, put a rather heartless end to that belief. The scientists proved that no matter how much information you collect about most natural processes, an even tinier deviation can throw off your predictions.

That's when the National Weather Service gave up trying for certainty: they stopped predicting "It'll rain tomorrow" and switched to the now-familiar "*probability* of precipitation."

Their computers had proven that *we can't figure it all out.*

But I didn't know that at the time; nobody did. As far as we knew, science was the only true light in the darkness: as a child I worshipped knowledge, but didn't yet understand wisdom.

So I tried to understand Master Stanley's teachings, and to put them into perspective.

IN SEARCH OF EXPLANATIONS

I read the New Testament thoroughly for the first time, read books of prophecy concerning the return of the Messiah, and sought within myself the insights and knowledge that would answer my doubts.

But my strongest identification in the Bible was still with my namesake Thomas, the doubter. And even though Master Stanley had done "miracles" in front of me, they were also things that I thought I could explain with science, albeit the science of metaphysics, homeopathy, and the farthest reaches of Einstein's and Bohm's physics. They were all things that I discovered others had done or seen, and were all in the realm of phenomena—which must ultimately be explainable.

But the strongest parts of me wanted to learn more, to come to know spiritual reality in a positive and loving way, and I could see, feel, and hear that emanating from Master Stanley.

So, setting my doubts aside (but keeping them available for if/when they'd be necessary), and deciding not to argue about those things where I was truly skeptical, I chose to study with him.

I knew that the worst that could happen would be that I'd learn some interesting lessons, and the best might be that I'd achieve those spiritual states and insights I'd read and heard about for years.

To explain to you how I experienced this learning, I first have to back up and share with you the major questions I brought with me, and the thoughts I'd had in the preceding years.

Why Are We Here?
And Other Mysteries

G-d dwells in the nothing-at-all that was prior to nothing.
—Meister Eckhart

Life is temporal. We're born, we live, and we die. This is pretty obvious, although it's sometimes surprising how many people (and I, myself) live as if they didn't know it.

One of the big problems with this, for me, was that the religious tradition in which I'd been raised said that, essentially, *this temporal life was our One Chance to succeed or fail* spiritually, and if we succeeded we would be rewarded with eternity in heaven, and if we failed, an angry god would get his revenge on us, or at least punish us, with eternal pain and torment.

Both of these options seemed less than pleasant to me.

My inborn nature of always being interested in new things and easily bored made the prospect of spending even a week sitting on a cloud playing a harp sound ultimately unpleasant. I became tired and bored with even the things I liked most after a while, and that was usually a matter of hours, days, weeks, or months. But eternity? I couldn't imagine *anything* I'd want to do for eternity. So heaven didn't sound all that exciting.

And then there was the alternative: hell. But what sort of god would set up his subjects by throwing them into a world filled with temptation, give them an innate desire to succumb to that temptation, and then not only zap them but *brutally torment them for eternity* if they gave in to those very temptations? It reminded me of a kid I knew when I was eight years old who used to capture bugs, put them in a bottle, and then poke them with a pencil lead if and when they tried to get to the water in a bottle cap he'd put in there.

Such a god seemed inconceivably brutal to me, and I concluded that this story of my religion's god couldn't be entirely true.

I didn't doubt the existence of G-d, but couldn't imagine He or She would behave in such a petty fashion.

But humans I knew, *are* capable—easily capable—of such brutality.

So, I concluded, these stories of how this god would treat us if we strayed from the orders of "his" priests must be something that humans had largely devised.

And that made sense; that held water. From observing particularly incompetent and power-tripping parents with their children, yelling things in the supermarket like "If you continue doing that, I'll tell your father!" I concluded that the kind of humans who'd come up with this "power through threat of consequences" interpretation were those types (largely male) who wanted to exercise control over others.

So for years I had suspected that the "You've only got one chance, don't screw it up" school of religion had been devised by men trying to gain control over others.

My mind was still open, but no other explanation to date had made sense.

In my search for truth and meaning, I'd visited scores of churches and checked out dozens of religions, from the Mormons to the Seventh Day Adventists to Catholicism to Judaism to the fundamentalist Protestant sects to the Unitarians. What I'd seen confirmed this for me: those churches whose pastors were the most insecure and the most eager to control their subjects dwelled the most (both personally and denominationally) on this "vengeful god" aspect of the Bible.

I'd even read (and memorized a few of) the writings of Cotton Mather* and other early Puritans, and found, again, that these men (always men, it seemed) who wanted to set up essentially theocratic governments (among the early Puritans in America, and, today, little semi-theocratic kingdoms in their own churches) were people whose primary motivation was power and the control of others. And I naturally rebelled against the idea of any sort of control of me by others, be

---

*Cotton Mather's *Sinners in the Hands of an Angry God* is his archetypical sermon. Even today it's taught in many high schools to illustrate the vengeful climate in seventeenth century Puritan life.

they humans or even a mean and vengeful god with the power to torment me for all of eternity.

So, I concluded during my teenage years, there had to be a basic flaw here. I believed that much of the Bible was divinely inspired, since so much of the writing felt spirit-connected and was consistent with my own personal experiences of reality and Spirit. But there was that other stuff in there, too: somebody must have, somehow and at some time, twisted things that were true and pure and spiritual around in order to use the very power of Spirit to control and dominate other humans.

NEW TRADITIONS?

During those early years I dove into scholarship, purchasing dozens of books on the history of Christianity, including one eight-volume scholarly work (denominationally unaffiliated) titled *The History of the Christian Church* and written in 1909 by David Schaff in Switzerland which was, at the best, startling. In that book and others, I found more and more evidence that the modern religion into which I was born was an amalgam of things past.

I learned about the transformation of the Roman Empire from its own "pagan" religion into Christianity, when the Jewish followers of Yeshua (Jesus in Hebrew) had grown in numbers and power to the point where Rome could no longer simply continue to kill them off or use them for sport (feeding them to lions). So the leaders of Rome proclaimed a new, non-Jewish but *Roman* Christianity as their own, baptized the Roman army en-masse, and, to make this new Official State Religion palatable to the Roman masses, incorporated their old practices into it, while vigorously discarding the remnants of Judaism that had been practiced by the Jewish Jesus and his Jewish followers.

The Icthar Bunny

One of their first steps was to change the Jewish Passover that Jesus and His followers observed.* In doing so, they created a modified version

---

*Many say the Last Supper was a Passover celebration; others think it was a typical Friday-night Sabbath meal.

of the Romans' spring equinox worship of their fertility goddess Icthar (pronounced "Easter" in English). Traditional springtime fertility rituals had included eating eggs and sprinkling the soil with the blood of small, highly-fertile animals, such as rabbits. In taking control of the new religion, the Roman leaders integrated these rituals into the story of the resurrection.

Restricted Access to "The Rulebook"

The Bible—the history and principles of these people's new religion—was taken away from them. To keep people ignorant of their own violations of the Jewish history of this new religion (such as not worshipping idols ["Don't pray to statues"] and Jesus's instruction to "Call no man 'Father'"), the leaders in Rome made it unlawful for any person but a priest to read the Bible.

They claimed that the information was too sacred for everydy people to know. But this made no sense to me; why would this god say we're supposed to follow the rules but we're not allowed to know them?

This rule held until around the time of the Protestant Reformation and Martin Luther, just a few hundred years ago.

Brightly Lit Evergreens on the Shortest Day

I learned of the later adoption, in Europe, of an old Celtic tradition: burning a pine tree on the highest hill the local priest could find, on the evening of the shortest day of the year (the winter solstice).

At that time, the average person didn't understand the tilting angle and sun-bound rotation of the Earth and how this caused the seasons to change and the days to lengthen and shorten. So people naturally became nervous every year as the length of the days became shorter and shorter.

The Celtic priests (and those of many other "primitive" religions of northern Europe), knowing about seasonal cycles, would promise that they could use their "power" to re-ignite the sun, to bring it back to full brilliance, and so around December 25 every year they'd have all the people bring the biggest pine tree they could find up to the top of the hill and, with great pomp and ceremony designed to show the priest's control over the sun, the high priest would light the tree on fire and command the sun to return to full brilliance and the days to lengthen.

Sure enough, over the next few weeks nature would comply with the priest's demand and the days would begin to get longer. "He did it again!" the people would all say in amazement, and that priest would be confident of his power for another year. After all, if anybody defied him, he could simply threaten to extinguish the sun, over which he obviously had a pretty substantial measure of control.*

I'd always wondered why Christmas is in December, when I knew from other studies that the most likely historical date of the birth of Jesus is placed by some scholars in March or April. That's the season when all of Rome was taxed that year, and that's when travel from Nazareth to Bethlehem would have been possible. In any case, Jesus's birth was not at all celebrated by His early followers; but now it was proclaimed by Rome to be the date, by coincidence, when most of the residents of Europe were burning trees on mountaintops. And thus Christmas was born, centuries after the death of Christ's early disciples.

Changing the day of Worship

The most radical change of all was totally dumping the Sabbath Day (Saturday), which was mandated in the Ten Commandments as a day of rest, and replacing it with the day that the Romans had traditionally worshipped *their* god of the Sun, Sunday, and making that the day of worship.

By changing the "weekly holy day" from a restful Sabbath/Saturday, which ran from sunset Friday night to sunset Saturday night (the Jews considered a new day to have started when the sun set from the old day to the point where you could see three stars in the sky) to the midnight-to-midnight of Sunday (the Romans divided each day in the middle of the night), the removal of Jesus's Jewishness from the new Christianity was well underway.

WHAT TO MAKE OF THESE FINDINGS?

At first these discoveries were disillusioning to me, as was learning that this same Church had tortured people, something I know Jesus

---

*A similar story is told in Mark Twain's *A Connecticut Yankee in King Arthur's Court*. In it the Yankee, knowing the date of a coming eclipse, "proves" his power by "making the sun go away" at just the time he said it would.

would never have endorsed. Obviously, something had gone astray.

But then I realized that they were simply the history of *political and human* institutions—organized religions.* They didn't in any way diminish what had been there in the first place: the underlying truths and realities of the teachings of Jesus and those who had preceded him. Instead, adopting the "Icthar bunny" and other rituals were culturally expedient things humans did to perpetuate and grow a human, political institution which uses religion to claim its power.

And I quickly overcame my initial reaction to these discoveries: I still am moved by a Christmas Eve mass, and an outdoor sunrise Easter service brings into vivid relief the sacrifice that Jesus made and the agony He must have gone through, as we can read in the story of His final evening in the Garden of Gethsemane. I also am moved by the Passover Seder and by Buddhist ceremonies of prostration, even though these are not traditions in which I grew up. One of the wonderful things about humans is our adaptability: even if the history of a ritual is less than holy, if we invest it with spirit and love, then it can become holy.

But these discoveries also led me to question many of the assumptions that I'd previously thought to be absolute infallible truths, such as the biblical teachings about sin, the purpose of ritual, and the "dominion" of humankind over nature, which makes people think it's perfectly acceptable to kill animals and destroy nature simply for fun, or to please their palate, or for profit.

Take, for example, sin.

Human nature is essentially in opposition to the way most organized religions say we *should* live, a fact that works out quite well for organized religion. Our nature is to sin, as sin is defined by many of the world's great religions. We live in a state of "hunger," hungry for experience (play, variety, good food), knowledge (defined, it seems, by the cultural milieu in which one is born: some are hungry for knowledge of

---

*The Spanish Inquisition, and 300 years of witch hunts in which millions of women were tortured and murdered, were works of the Church of Rome. Particularly informative is the *Malleus Maleficarium,* which was published by the Church as their official doctrine on how to hunt "witches" and torture them into confession (or kill them if they wouldn't confess).

batting averages, others for answers about the meaning of life), love (nurturing, affection, sex, recognition, attachment), and many more. Virtually all of these hungers are recognized, or have been recognized, by major religions as running the risk of sin, and therefore often "wrong."

The explanation given for this by the religious tradition I'd grown up in is that man's sinful nature is the result of a Big Mistake made years ago, in the Garden of Eden, by Eve. This story of a woman being responsible for the flaws in humankind's nature is echoed in the myths and histories of other male-dominated religions and cultures as well (Pandora's box, etc.)

But my studies of psychology and physiology taught me that humans, when acting out these "sins," were merely doing the same things that most of the rest of animal creation did. "Hunger" was built into the species as a survival mechanism, to perpetuate Homo sapiens, and was put there by evolution or the Original Creator but certainly not by a woman eating an apple.

The story of Eve, it seemed to me at the time, probably came from a male power structure developing yet another rationalization for the oppression of women: females were, after all, responsible for the predicament we were all in, by that story. So, according to that story, they deserve to be oppressed, right? Certainly, these awful women— who that story says are responsible for all our misery and the fact that this god is always standing around with a stick waiting to poke us— could never qualify for something "holy" or "pure" such as, for example, becoming a priest.

There was also the problem, for me, of "fire" and "cults."

In a frankly selfish way, I *wanted* fire in my religious experience. When I was young, perhaps seven or eight years old, I spent some time on a farm in Michigan with an elderly farm couple who were fervent Christian mystics. They introduced me to the idea of sitting outside and praying eyes-open, remaining conscious of the world around me, seeing the presence of the Creator in the trees and clouds and soil, and feeling the presence of the Creator's incarnated consciousness— Christ-consciousness in my definitions—within me as I sat there in a plastic lawn-chair, awe-struck by the Presence around me.

I wanted to find a church filled with people as committed to, and eager for, that mystical experience as I was. It seemed, however, that most of the Christian churches I attended were more social or political institutions, concerned with how people dressed and providing an opportunity for social interaction, or pushing a political agenda from the pulpit instead of reaching out for the presence of Christ.

On the other hand, the few churches I visited where the people seemed to be afire with spiritual energy also qualified, in my mind, as cults.

While most people think of cults as simply being religions that haven't yet achieved popular status, or as some sort of murky "them" with unorthodox religious beliefs, I developed a different definition that I think works better. I saw a cult as any institution that stole free will by threatening people if they left, or—in the worst of the cults—if they even *thought* about leaving. The form of the threat could be overt ("You'll burn in hell. . ." or outright threats of contemporary physical violence) or subtle (peer pressure or financial pressure), but in a cult, by my definition, there was always that threat.

Given this definition, a cult doesn't even need to be a religion: I know of some companies that are run as cults, particularly those involved in multi-level-marketing (which also involves the evangelistic component often found in cults). There are also physicians and psychotherapists who run their practices as cults, creating dependency and disempowering their patients. Some families operate as cults, as do some political movements. Many of the self-help groups I've come across also look like cults to me, threatening both implicitly and explicitly that if people leave the group they'll inevitably fall, fail, and lapse back into their old miseries. Even many of our contemporary and well-accepted religious institutions are run as cults, by my definition.

Cults are always, ultimately, about stealing personal power from individuals and giving it to the cult and the cult's leaders. They operate on the principle of "weak individual, stronger group, strongest leadership" and have as a prime directive to keep people under control. Sometimes they're astoundingly blunt about this, with openly disempowering slogans telling people exactly what they are and aren't allowed to do, such as "a woman's place is. . ." (a popular phrase in many modern religious and social cults).

Cults are "soul stealers."

And so I was left with this weird paradox. The churches I could find that seemed most filled with fire were also run as cults, their preachers shouting great proclamations of hellfire and damnation to anybody who dared step away from their particular point of view.

Thus I discovered, early on, that the modern day organized Christian church, in most of its versions, wasn't for me.

Yet there were the teachings of Jesus in the Sermon on the Mount, which I very much did believe were truthful and pure. And He said that even looking at a woman with thoughts of lust was the same as having sex with her; that even being angry was tantamount to murder.

This was a tough one. I originally interpreted it to mean He was saying thought precedes action, and, as Master Hamid Bey said, "What a man thinks about, he can do; what a man thinks about constantly, he cannot help but do." But later I was to realize that Jesus's teaching in that story was far deeper and more profound than such a simple explanation. That contrary to the way it was presented to me in church, it had nothing to do with the wrath of G-d. And that the organized religions of the world were right about how destructive "sin" could be to spiritual development, but only very few (primarily the Kabbalists in Judaism, and the Christian mystics like St. John of the Cross and Herr Müller) understood why and how.

I realized as I read the writings of the mystics and listened to Master Stanley and Lee that our highest purpose and highest abilities are those of Spirit. Before we came into this world we chose our life, our parents, our situations, and even this moment as I am writing this or you are reading it, so that we could do specific spiritual work here that we can't do elsewhere. Our mission is to let go of our entanglements to the world and to re-connect our "consciousness" to that of the *"I Am That I Am,"* the uncreated before creation, the source of all. And wallowing in those "hungers," in "sin," slows that process down.

This understanding of what sin really is became a key for me to understanding what happens when we die, what our work here may be, and why I have devoted so much of my life to spiritual search.

And it led me, at first, to a period of intense and solitary self-examination and contemplation.

Life in a Tipi

Every day people are straying away from church
and going back to God.

—LENNY BRUCE

My best friend through school was Clark Stinson. We met when we were 13, and instead of pursuing the normal pastimes of teenagers we spent our time studying Sanskrit (we had an old study-guide book I found in my father's library), reading the Tibetan Book of the Dead, and arguing minutiae of the Bible. Clark's mother was interested in metaphysics and shared a book called *Autobiography of a Yogi* with us. Years later, when I went to Detroit with her and Clark to attend an initiation in Kriya Yoga by Yogacharia Oliver Black, the oldest living disciple of Yogananda, I recognized Yogananda's Kriya technique as identical to an ancient Coptic exercise Master Stanley had taught us years earlier, called the Cobra Breath.

I introduced Clark to Master Stanley and Lee, and Clark and I began a serious study of spirituality. We were both in our late teens by then, and Clark had recently married. I was recovering from a painful breakup with a girlfriend, and we agreed that to do our spiritual work best we should seek isolation.

So Clark and his wife bought a tipi, and I bought one, and we three gave away everything else we owned in the world except some clothes and our spiritual books. We bought a hundred pounds of wheat, a hundred pounds of dried fruit, some basic camping equipment, and got a ride up into Michigan's Upper Peninsula, where an old trapper led us on a three-day trek back into the Chippewa National Forest to a small lake that isn't on most maps.

We spent the summer there, Clark and his wife on one side of the lake, me on the other. Three days of each week we practiced silence, and did meditation and prayer every day for hours.

I had a pet tachnid fly: a small insect that looks like a honeybee but is actually a fly. When I'd meditate in the morning on my blanket outside my tipi, he'd come and hover just above my right hand, as if he were drawing nourishment from me. Sometimes he'd hover there for as much as twenty minutes; occasionally he'd land and walk around with careful steps like an astronaut exploring a distant but friendly planet. I also shared my tipi with a large and furry brown-and-black wolf spider, who came out at night as the sun set and picked the sleeping mosquitoes off the canvas on the west side of my tipi; I watched the play of life and death, predator and prey.

(Here's an odd synchronicity that Carl Jung would have appreciated: I haven't seen a tacbnid fly in years, but, as I'm typing these words into a laptop computer on my back porch in Atlanta, one just hovered over my left hand for a few moments and then landed. She's here with me as I'm typing, sitting on my hand.)

One cold and rainy afternoon, Clark and I were walking through the woods looking for berries and edible plants. We'd gotten pretty skilled at identifying what was safe and what wasn't, and were filling a bag with leaves and fruits.*

"This must be what our ancestors lived like," Clark observed. "Hunting and gathering."

"Except that we're vegetarians, so we're just gathering," I said, joking.

But to Clark it wasn't a joke. "Seriously. What we call civilization started when humans started farming. But humans like us were around for tens and maybe hundreds of thousands of years before that. Fully conscious, awake and aware, thinking and feeling just like us. But they were hunters and gatherers instead of farmers."

"Without agriculture there would be no civilization?" I said. It was an interesting thought.

"Remember Miss Hemmer?" Clark said. Miss Hemmer had been

---

*This early interest later led me to study wild plant taxonomy at Wayne State University, and then to get C.H., M.H., and Ph.D. degrees from Emerson College, Dominion Herbal College, and Brantridge Forest School (UK) in herbal and homeopathic medicine. In the mid-1970s I started The Michigan Healing Arts Center, and in the 1980s studied and practiced acupuncture in the world's largest acupuncture teaching hospital in Beijing, China.

our eighth grade biology teacher, and one of the best teachers I've ever known in my life. Clark and I conspired to make her life difficult, but we also loved her and learned more from her each month than from any of our other teachers in a year. And she was a huge fan of Margaret Mead. "She said that in primitive societies there isn't suicide, depression, drug addiction, all that stuff."

"The noble savage," I said, shivering. "I'm skeptical. And cold. And the Indians who once lived here were probably cold, too."

He shrugged and said, "This life seems much more natural to me."

At least I had to agree with that.

A few days later, Clark came running over to my tipi with his Bible, all excited. "Look at this!" he said, pointing out Genesis 4:2. "It says, 'Cain was a tiller of the ground.' The Bible is talking about how the first murderer was also the first farmer. And in the twenty-fifth verse, it makes it clear that Abel, the brother who was not the farmer, was the one who G-d loved the most."

"So what? It's a classic archetype of the oldest child being the most beloved but also the one who screws up; it's all over, from Greek mythology to Shakespeare."

"Don't you see? Adam and Eve were gatherers, like we are now. They walked around the Garden of Eden and picked up food. But then they tasted of the knowledge of good and evil, of life and death. That's your food supply—you live or die by it. When you live as a gatherer, you live by the whim of nature: if there's no food you die. When you begin to store up food, you can defy nature and survive a drought. You then have the power to control life: the knowledge of life and death, or good and evil. So the tasting of the apple must mean that Adam and Eve experimented with agriculture, that they defied the god of nature. It's a warning! It's saying that the primitive life of hunting, gathering, and herding was more in accord with nature's way than is agriculture.*

Clark dove deep into the issue, but I didn't consider it all that important at the time. I couldn't see how when people started farming after the end of the Ice Age it could have been a bad thing—after all, it brought us modern society and science. Clark, however, was totally

---

*Reading Daniel Quinn's novel *Ishmael* in 1995 brought Clark's personal obsession into a clearer light for me.

certain that agriculture and what he called "the organized ones" (who I'd later call, in writing about Attention Deficit Disorder, the farmers) were responsible for the coming death of the Earth. I wasn't to seriously consider the issue again, though, for over twenty years.

I was also told during that time, quite clearly and directly in several dreams and strong intuitions, that my ultimate spiritual teacher would not be a yogi from India or any of the other Eastern religions (even though I was studying these, too), but a Christian from Europe. I was amazed by this, as the Maharishi and all the other teachers seemed to be coming out of India, but the message was unmistakable. And ever since I'd first read Carl Jungs writings (particularly his autobiography), I'd paid careful attention to my dreams, and took seriously their content.

At the time, I assumed it must have meant Master Stanley, as he was Swiss. But I later learned that, as Master Stanley had said, he was not my ultimate teacher.

That summer in the tipi was profoundly transformational for me, a time of preparation for what would come next. It taught me that I should never be afraid to lose or give away everything (as I've done more than once since then), that possessions can be meaningless, and that there is great peace in solitude. As a "gifted but hyperactive" young adult, I learned for the first time how to truly and profoundly relax and get control over the wild racing of my mind. I learned to look within for strength and discovered that the forest is afire with life. I felt truly alive, truly connected to my creator, in a more real and visceral way than I'd ever before experienced.

The Question of the Soul

O Lord my God, I have trusted in thee;
O Jesu my dearest one, now set me free.
In prison's oppression, in sorrow's obsession,
I weary for thee.
With sighing and crying bowed down as dying,
I adore thee, I implore thee, set me free!

—MARY STUART (MARY, QUEEN OF SCOTS)
WRITTEN IN HER BOOK OF DEVOTION BEFORE HER EXECUTION

One of the issues I have been struggling with throughout my life is that of the soul. What or where was the soul, and, perhaps more important, *who* is the soul? And how does that relate to my earlier questions about the nature of consciousness?

Is the soul the personality? Does this mean that, if I were to go to some sort of afterlife, I'd be there as Thom Hartmann, walking around in something resembling this body with these same thoughts, feelings, and opinions? That people would recognize me and say, "Oh, hi there! You're Thom Hartmann, aren't you?"

Jesus seemed to imply that this might not be the case when he was asked about whose husband a wife would have in heaven if she'd been handed from brother to brother during life, wedding each in turn as the older ones died, as was a common custom in His times. He replied that she wouldn't be any of their wives, and added the cryptic comment that in heaven people didn't marry.

Does that mean that the trappings of person-ness—the personality and all the relationships developed throughout a lifetime with it, all our hopes and desires, dreams and fears, likes and dislikes—would not carry through to heaven? It seemed to.

Yet the thought of the personality not enduring past the end of life is terrifying. If "I" don't endure—either to go to an afterlife or even to

29

reincarnate—then what's the point of it all? Are we just ambulatory meat, merely sentient animals, roaming around on the Earth and making up quaint stories to palliate ourselves and deal with our fears of death? Freud, at least, largely took this view, as did many of the philosophers and early teachers of psychology I'd studied in my childhood. Yet such a cynical and secular world-view seemed untenable to me.

I couldn't accept the idea that we just ended at death, not only because it was an unpleasant notion, but also because there was plenty of evidence to contradict it.

Back in the late 1960s, stories of Near Death Experiences (NDE) were filtering into the popular media, and by the mid-1970s some truly scholarly examinations had been made of them, the most famous being by Elisabeth Kübler-Ross. My own father-in-law had "died" of a massive bee-sting attack and been revived after his heart stopped, and he told Louise (my wife and his daughter) and me of his NDE which was so similar to those of others—the light, the tunnel, the feeling of ineffable bliss. Prior to that, he'd been a lifelong alcoholic, even throughout his career as Assistant Attorney General for the State of Michigan. When he finally stopped drinking, however, he didn't need AA or any other organization or institutionalized help to do it: he'd literally "seen the light," and often discussed his experiences on "the other side" with us.

My teachers Master Stanley and Master Hamid Bey responded to my questions about the nature of the soul and personality by saying that the ancient Christian Coptic teachings indicated that the soul survived and reincarnated, and that the purpose of these reincarnations was to "become perfect, even as your Father in heaven is perfect." The Orthodox Coptic Church believes it is the oldest of all the Christian denominations, having been started by St. Mark just after the crucifixion, and the sect of it that Master Hamid Bey was raised in traces its roots back to the Essenes. (He taught us that the Essenes were the Jewish sect which "produced the pure vessels of Mary and Elizabeth, who produced John the Baptist and Jesus." The Essenes, who left some scrolls near the Dead Sea and Mount Carmel, were destroyed by the Romans in the years following Jesus's crucifixion, but their messianic mission was preserved down through the years by a mystical and largely underground Coptic sect of the Orthodox Egyptian [Coptic] Church.) Hamid Bey said, therefore, that they had access to the most ancient and "true" teachings of Jesus. He pointed to several veiled references to reincarnation in the Bible, and they made a lot of sense to me. The idea of life continuing on after death, of multiple chances to "get it right," of karma and consequences for our actions on Earth being played out on Earth appealed to my sense of justice and logic. And I'd always had intuitions that this wasn't my first time on the Earth. For example, when the disciples asked Jesus, "Who sinned, that this man was born blind, him or his parents?" Jesus didn't reply by saying, "What a stupid question—how could he have sinned before his birth?" Instead, He calmly replied that neither was the case in the instance of this particular man, but that he was born blind only so that Jesus could heal him and therefore show the world that He was the Messiah (and then, of course, He gave the man his sight). But the question itself, Hamid Bey said, showed that Jesus and his disciples considered the idea of reincarnation to be a rather normal possibility. (Some would say that the "sin before birth" might have been a reference to "original sin," but if that were the case, then logic would indicate that everybody must be born blind if being born blind is the logical result of that universal sin. So it's unlikely they were referring to original sin.)

And, of course, there are the many places in the Bible where it simply comes right out and discusses reincarnation:

> And his disciples asked him, saying, "Why then say the scribes that Elijah must first come [before the arrival of the Messiah]?" And Jesus answered and said unto them, "Elijah truly shall first come, and restore all things. But I say unto you, That Elijah is come already, and they knew him not, but have done unto him whatsoever they listed. Likewise shall also the Son of man suffer of them." Then the disciples understood that he spoke unto them of John the Baptist.
>
> —MATTHEW 17:10–13

It made sense to me.

My studies of the Edgar Cayce readings, Kaballah, mystical Christianity, as well as the teachings of ancient religions like Hinduism and Buddhism, impelled me to consider the possibility that reincarnation was real. It would, first off, mean that the nasty god who I'd been told by the preachers of my childhood was out to get me might really not be so nasty after all, but instead was interested in giving me multiple chances, or even a specific path or journey in my soul's evolution toward its ultimate goal. Secondly, it put in context many of the experiences I'd had in my own life.

But the possibility of reincarnation also raised for me the question of *which* personality was enduring?

And what about the non-normal situations, such as, for example, if a person had had multiple personality disorder (MPD)?

People with MPD don't just have different emotional states: they actually have different personalities, different people, as it were, living within them. These different personalities are so vivid and disparate that physical conditions such as asthma, adult-onset diabetes, and warts will actually come and go as the various personalities take over the body. Could it be that these people are inhabited by more than one soul?

Or is the soul independent of the personality?

The most common theory of MPD is that it usually comes about as the result of extremely severe childhood abuse. As children, we only have embryonic or nascent personalities. Our "I-ness" develops slowly throughout childhood and adolescence, eventually manifesting as a full-blown adult personality. The prevailing theory of MPD is that the developing child/personality has to create a second, "Observer" personality in order to dissociate itself from the abuse and therefore not be destroyed by it. This leads to two separate people developing in the same brain, and these two sometimes even split into three, four, or more, particularly if the child shifts into the presumably safe observer personality during an experience of abuse. Being in the Observer personality during a period of abuse necessitates the creation of a *new* Observer, and therefore another new personality is formed.

Even more baffling are the studies done on severe epileptics. It was found that if the brain of a person were severed in half (the nerves connecting the two hemispheres, the corpus callosurn, being cut), then the person was left with a situation where the left half of the person literally did not know what the right half was doing (leading to some odd coordination problems), and when one eye and ear was covered/plugged and a question asked, and then the process repeated in the other ear/eye, the opposite parts of the brain would give different answers. Two different people, sometimes with quite different attitudes, likes, and opinions (but both claiming the same name, body, and personality), would come to occupy the one brain.

Similarly, some rare individuals are born with only one hemisphere of the brain intact. Oddly, these people are capable of growing up in a fairly natural fashion, and often only a trained observer can tell that they had this birth defect. The flip side of that is that when people with MPD are subjected to brain scans, different parts of their brains light up when their different personalities emerge.

Apparently the brain has enough redundancy, enough excess capacity, that it can even support the consciousness and personality of several different people at once. But does this mean it can sustain multiple souls?

And what about young children who die before their personality is formed? Without reincarnation, does that mean that heaven is filled with blithering babies? Or is the soul and personality fixed before birth, only waiting to emerge as the body ages and the brain is capable of handling it? Certainly many parents (including Louise and me) would argue that a child's developing personality is evident even before birth—some children kick and squirm *in utero* while others are quiet and passive, and these behaviors persist into adulthood.

My experience owning several golden retriever dogs over the years would also argue that there's a strong genetic component to the personalities of dogs. All grew up to be uncannily identical, and were also very similar to other retrievers I've met owned by other people. Different breeds have different behaviors (personalities), but within the same breed, all dogs seem quite similar. Setting aside metaphysics, then, one could argue that at least some component of personality is genetic, the result of DNA programming, as much in people as in dogs. (And studies of human identical twins lend support to that direction of thought.) Some have used this fact to support notions of eugenics (racial hygiene) or to argue that there is no such thing as the soul. Others, stretching points made by Carl Jung or scientist Rupert Sheldrake, would say that there's a consciousness or morphic field associated with the organism which emerges from that particular DNA combination which leads entirely to the personality.

But assuming there is a soul, and it's somehow associated with personality, then what about those people who are born with profoundly crippling forms of mental retardation? Can they sin? Who and where is their soul? Is some angry god going to punish them because they failed to perform the requisite rituals of confession and testimony (or because their relatives failed to)? And, in heaven, who or what would they be?

And, even more fascinating, how does this relate to the various ancient and modern cultures which have evolved among humans on the Earth, from the early hunter/gatherers to the farmers, to the industrial and information era? Could they tie into both an evolutionary path for, and the mistakes of, the human race? Could it be that the human race might even be an expression of the consciousness of the Earth and this part of the universe as some Native American religions imply? And how would this relate to Western culture spirituality, and what psychologist Abraham Maslow called "self-actualization"?

The sciences of psychology and biology that I'd so vigorously studied earlier offered only anti-religious answers. Decades later I would find possible answers to all these questions. And the answers would lead me to a profound reassurance and confidence that G-d indeed is real, as is the soul, and that possible answers to the questions of heaven and hell, reincarnation and past lives, and even the purpose of life on Earth may be found right there in the words of Jesus and other religious figures and philosophers, yet are so well hidden that in this Cartesian culture it takes the most elegant science devised to illuminate their reality.

But before I was to discover that, I had more work to do, more lessons to learn. Most important, I had not yet met the teacher I'd been told to expect.

Meeting Herr Müller

All greatness is unconscious, or it is little and naught.
—THOMAS CARLYLE,
ON BOSWELL'S LIFE OF JOHNSON

During the next few years I became one of Master Stanley's students, and was ordained as a Coptic minister. The certificate of ordination signed by his teacher, Master Hamid Bey, is one of my most treasured possessions, and the brown robe he presented to me still hangs in my closet.

Many more marvelous things happened with Master Stanley, like when he instantly healed my then-girlfriend of hepatitis,* and numerous other things that he'd make jokes about and call "little miracles."

I learned techniques for prayer, breathing, and meditation that Master Stanley said Saint Mark (author of the Gospel of Mark) had taught when he founded what Coptics believe is the oldest and first of the Christian churches, the Orthodox Coptic Church in Egypt, when Mark traveled to that country after Jesus' crucifixion. I don't know to what extent these were really St. Mark's teachings, but my experience is that they brought a stillness to my mind and soul.

These teachings were brought to the U.S. by Master Hamid Bey, who was given over to the mystical sect of the Coptic church by his parents when he was five years old and there learned the "inner secrets" of these techniques in preparation for priesthood. He detailed these in his autobiography *My Life Preceding 5,000 Burials.*

The title of Master Hamid Bey's book referred to his ability to use his meditative abilities to stop his heart and breathing for hours at a time (or at least slow them down to the point where they were imperceptible).

---

*The diagnosis was confirmed the next day by her father, who was an M.D. and had done the original diagnosis and had sent out the blood tests. This event caused her father to begin attending the weekly services in Detroit.

In the 1930s, when he first came to the United States, he'd get crowds to come hear him teach by doing "demonstrations," where a local under-taker would put him into a coffin, lower it into a grave, cover it with dirt, and leave it all day or overnight, guarded by the local police. The next morning they'd dig him up and open the coffin. Apparently dead, he'd then come back to life to the amazement of the crowd.

The 1950s TV show "You Asked For It" featured him on one of its segments. He was put into a glass box, with a small candle burning next to his head, and then the glass box was sealed and lowered into a glass tank of water. As the camera and millions of people watched (this was in the days of live television, although I saw a film of it years later at a Coptic conference), after a few minutes the candle went out from lack of oxygen. Hamid Bey lay motionless, and the host began to get nerv-ous. Hamid Bey's assistant calmed him, and they left the box underwa-ter. A half hour later, they hoisted out the glass box, and a horrified doctor certified that Hamid Bey had no heartbeat. Then Hamid Bey opened his eyes and sat up, eliciting a shriek from the doctor.

To many people this was a mystery, almost a miracle. "Latent form is the master of obvious form," Heraclitus wrote 2,500 years ago, and, "The nature of things is in the habit of concealing itself." Hamid Bey agreed: it's an eternal truth that in all teachings there are multiple lev-els of meaning. And over the centuries the question of whether Jesus's most important teachings were intended for the masses or only for his "little flock" has been hotly debated. For over 1,500 years of Church history, the view prevailed that the mysteries were not for the masses, and therefore it was deemed a sin worthy of punishment that anybody other than a priest or monk would even possess or read the Bible. This only changed after the Protestant Reformation, and even now most Catholics (and most Protestants, too) have never been encouraged by a priest to read their entire Bible all the way through, but instead are fed weekly excerpts, sanctioned by the Church.

"There are many mysteries in the Bible," Hamid Bey once told a small group of us. "They are there but most people cannot see them. Jesus referred to them in Luke 8:9,* and there have been many sects

---

*The disciples asked Jesus what this parable might mean, and he said, "The mysteries of the kingdom of G-d are revealed to you, but for the rest there are only parables, so that they might see but not perceive, listen but not understand."

over the years, from the Jesuits to the Brotherhood of the Rose Cross to the Essenes who were committed to finding and living them. But in the temple, that most ancient part of the Coptic church, we were directly taught these mysteries as Jesus taught them to His disciple Mark, who founded our church."

During these years, Master Stanley referred to each of our destinies, often tying it to his favorite theme, the return to the Earth of Jesus Christ. Many of his comments seemed cryptic and abstruse; now they have a more precise meaning as I see how rapidly the deterioration of our planet is accelerating, new diseases are emerging, and our oil-based civilization is beginning to come unraveled.

Lee was part of Master Stanley's original little group, and I soon joined it. (I got a haircut, and Grace, who was Master Stanley's assistant and driver, finally decided she liked me. I liked her, too—she was only trying to protect Master Stanley, and as I got to know her she turned out to be a kind and loving person who was one of the pillars of the Coptic church.)

Master Stanley encouraged each of us to go out into the world and give weekly lectures, talking about the coming changes in the Earth, particularly in the consciousness of humankind. He often referred to "the ancient ones" and "the older knowledge," but I didn't understand fully what he meant until later, looking back on it from a different context. At the time, I thought that he was talking about lost metaphysical knowledge, although on the other hand most of it didn't seem particularly lost: it was in any number of books available with only a small amount of effort. The Bible is probably the most conspicuous of them.

TRANSITION: MASTER STANLEY DIES

Lee, the minister who'd taken me to my first Coptic lecture, was already teaching in Lansing, where I lived. In early 1972, about the time I was to begin teaching, Master Stanley died. It was not altogether unexpected, and he in fact had told us many times that he would soon leave the Earth, but it was still a painful loss for those of us who knew him. For me it was a startling confrontation with mortality, and I felt a profound sense of loss.

Yet it was also a signal for me, a time of transition. Many changes were happening in my life. A few months after Master Stanley's death, I married the woman I'd been dating on and off since I was 17, Louise Goussy. Lee performed the ceremony at the Coptic Temple in Detroit at 11:11 A.M. on November 11, 1972, a date and time Master Stanley had thought significant. We picked them because of their symbolic significance to us and as a final gift to him.

When Master Stanley died, John Davis was appointed by Hamid Bey as head of the Midwestern Coptics, and he still runs the organization from his offices in Wyoming, Michigan (near Grand Rapids). John asked me if I'd take over the temple in Detroit, and I did that for several years, conducting the weekly services that Master Stanley had done for nearly thirty years, and performing a half-dozen weddings. Our oldest daughter, Kindra Theresa Hartmann, was born the day before Christmas, 1973, and Louise began bringing her every week to sit and listen to the sermons. By the time she was three, she could sit and meditate with Louise and me for a half hour without distraction.

One of my most vivid memories from that time is of an old man named Richard, who came every single week to the services. He always slept through my sermons, and always left a fifty dollar bill in the plate. And at least once a month, as he was leaving, he'd shake my hand and say, "Master Stanley healed my legs." I'd nod, remembering with a lump in my throat the time when he and his son were in front of me in that line before Master Stanley's office. I'd say, "I remember, Richard," and he'd sigh and say, "I wish he was still alive." I'd agree, thinking of Master Stanley's ashes which were in a small shrine in a private room upstairs.

After a few years in Detroit, Louise and I moved back to Lansing. There, I started a twice-weekly Coptic study group; Lee had left the organization shortly after Master Stanley's death. With Louise, we also opened the Michigan Healing Arts Center and sponsored monthly vegetarian potluck dinners and regular courses and talks on holistic medicine, herbology, and homeopathy. We had a masseuse, chiropractor, and medical doctor who all worked with us part-time, both teaching and offering services, and I taught the chiropractor and masseuse herbology and homeopathy in exchange for their giving me introductory instruction in their disciplines. Louise largely ran those programs, which steadily grew in parallel with the Coptic group.

After four or five years of this, we had a substantial-sized group. Every Tuesday night I'd give a lecture on one of the many things I'd learned from Master Stanley and Master Hamid Bey, and every Friday night we'd have a simple meditation service, no speech or talking, just sitting quietly for an hour in prayer and meditation. The importance of interior experience, of the mystical rather than institutional spiritual reality, was of overarching importance to me. For example, while publishing and editing the national Coptic magazine *The Coptic Journal,* I wrote this introduction for the Winter 1977 edition:

> Autumn is a quiet and gentle time of transition for the earth. The cycle of growth and expansion swings into a contemplative retreat as the ground is covered first by leaves and then a soft carpet of white, muting the echoes of summer's frantic activity.
>
> Yet transition is with us and about us always. In the coarse grain of the leafless tree we can see His shimmering activity of atoms, cells, structure, and growth. In the deep silence of the nighttime snowfall He beckons us to seek His peace, His protective comfort. The power of a billion cosmic explosions, heaving the universe into being and igniting our sun, is reflected in the bright whiteness of snow-covered fields. The pulse of the earth at rest is felt in the steady flow of water under ice-laden rivers. In all activity, in all rest, His presence is unmistakable.
>
> The greatest joy in life is to find His constant presence, His comforting love, in every moment of every day. Waking, sleeping, working, eating, dreaming, talking with others, meditating, simply watching the world, as we seek His nearness, He is always with us.
>
> Even now.

But something was missing in my relationship to the organization. I felt that I had stagnated, and that the death of Master Stanley had cut me off from a window into the future, an insight into that destiny he'd so often mentioned. It could be that—like so many—I needed or wanted an authority figure in my life. But on reflection, I believe it was that I wanted a living spiritual mentor, somebody who'd already walked the ground I still needed to pass over and could therefore help me along the path, much as a Ph.D. candidate or craftsman carefully picks his or her mentors.

I'd also started attending local churches, from Unity to Baptist to the Seventh Day Adventists, getting spiritual insights nearly everywhere I went. In every church or institution, I discovered people who were seeking a personal and mystical experience of Spirit, wanting more than the weekly hymn-singing and palliative words.

And I was still assailed by doubt, still unwilling to talk in my lectures about Master Stanley's more apocalyptic visions of the close of the Old Age and the coming of the Messiah and the New Age, which he often said would be accompanied by the revelation of "the most ancient of spiritual wisdom and knowledge" and would have to do with the discovery of a secret room under the Sphinx. Some of this stuff was just too far out for me, and other of it I thought may be possible (the Sphinx, for example), but my knowledge and belief of it wasn't sufficiently personal that I felt comfortable teaching it to others.

Then one week I went to a Pentecostal church in Lansing, the North Lansing Church of God. That Wednesday night there was an evangelist visiting from South Africa, a Jew who'd converted to Christianity and now was traveling the world with a convert's zeal.

Such people fascinate me: some, it seems, are sharing their own very real experience, and can thus teach from a place of quiet confidence and absolute assurance. You can see, hear, and feel the genuineness of their spirituality, and they radiate love and forgiveness. Others, I believe, are still trying to convince themselves of what they're teaching, and the more people they can "convert," the less uncertain they feel about their own teachings. The majority of the "evangelists" I've met in my life have been the latter, whereas the former are usually far less aggressive and often even wait for others to seek them out. Curious to discover what kind of person this traveling evangelist was, I sat in the very back row on the aisle.

Hymie Rubenstein (the evangelist) had worked himself up into a lather. He was running back and forth across the front of the church, microphone in hand, exhorting people to give their lives to Jesus and the normal Pentecostal stuff, occasionally pausing to speak in tongues. As he was making one of his turns on the stage, though, he suddenly spun about, so violently it nearly threw him to the ground, looked down the aisle directly into my eyes, lifted his arm and pointed a trembling finger at me. His voice dropped an octave: it was as if another person were speaking. He shouted a few things, including something to the effect of: "How can you teach the things of the spirit when you have not yet fully learned your own lessons and met your true teacher?!"

As I watched, shocked, my heart racing, he began to choke. He turned bright red and dropped the microphone to the floor, and took a quick step back, coughing.

After a moment, he picked up the microphone and tried to pick up his sermon where he'd left it off before he'd been "overcome," but he was not the same: apparently he believed the "message" was intended for him, and perhaps it was. Or perhaps he was in ecstasy and the words were meant for everyone in the church. There were more people than just me and Hymie there. Perhaps his sermon never regained its former fire because of his exhaustion from touching an ecstatic state.

But I believe it was for me (and that he thought it was for him). I can still see the image of the look in his eyes as he stared down that aisle and pointed his trembling finger at me. My stomach felt upside down, my throat was tight, and my eyes filled with tears. After a few moments, I got up and left the church.

That Friday night I announced to the people in my meditation class that I would no longer be teaching. People demanded to know why, but I couldn't tell them about the evangelist: it was frankly too embarrassing to admit I was so uncertain about my own teachings that Hymie's words had moved me to action. So I just said that my work there was finished: it was time to move on.

While most of the people who were coming to my classes were interested in learning from me, there were also those who were there because they wanted to have a guru or spiritual leader to follow: a savior, if you will. The longer I taught, the more often these types of people showed up, and it was disconcerting to me. I usually managed to challenge or shock or confront them in the first few weeks to the point where they didn't return.

At first it was flattering in an odd sort of way, as I imagine it would be for many people. But given a moment's serious thought, I knew that I wasn't prepared to take on other people's lives and be responsible for their spiritual destiny. I was a teacher, I knew, but not a guru or savior.

Hymie's message was a strong validation to me of thoughts I

already had: the message may even have been, as he obviously thought, meant for him, and just resonated so strongly within me that I took it to heart. In any case, I knew I had to break myself from those who wanted to be my students, rebuild my inner strength, and learn more before I could return to teaching.

I also had an intuitive knowledge that it was time to move on. Master Stanley was dead and Lee had left the Coptics. John Davis was doing a great job running the organization, but my herbal tea company, which sold a mixture named "Volupté" that contained ginseng, had drawn the ire of a woman in the Coptic organization who wanted me drummed out because my company "sold an aphrodisiac," and John was having a tough time with the conflict. I was writing and publishing *The Coptic Journal,* and traveling around the country speaking at Coptic conferences, but something had changed within me. It was a familiar feeling, and one that restless people can identify with: while I had (and have) great love and respect for John and the others in the Coptics, I knew that I had to go in another direction.

But where?

A PRAYER AND AN ANSWER

A week or two before Christmas, I was sitting in my meditation chair about 3 A.M. on a snowy night. There was a huge window in front of me, more than six feet square, and it looked out on trees covered with a thick blanket of snow; wet flakes fell to the moonlit ground. The snow was coming and going, clouds breaking, and the moonlight became bright and dim as the clouds moved. I could smell the old house and the clean freshness of air that leaked from outside around the window frame. I'd been meditating for a few hours, and now was just sitting in the chair, looking out at the snow, feeling quite peaceful. I said a prayer of thanks, my favorite prayer. Then the walls of the room started to shimmer. I could see through the trees in front of me, and for miles around. My consciousness was liquid and filled with light, streaming out of me like light from a star, yet bringing back to my mind everything it touched. My heart was filled with an ecstatic joy, but there was also a small and remote part of my mind that knew that I wasn't breathing.

I wondered if I was having a heart attack, if I was dying. I could feel the snow even though it was outside and I was indoors, could taste its cold moistness, could smell the trees, the distant exhaust of cars. It was as if I was everywhere in the world all at the same moment, with the things closest to me closer than those far away. Most vividly, I could feel the *life* in everything around me. And that rational part of my mind whispered at me again that my heart wasn't beating.

I turned my attention to my inert body, and suddenly the entire world collapsed into a single bright point, then I was back in my body looking out the window. My heart raced, I gasped for breath, and I clutched the arms of the chair.

"What was that?" I asked the air, although I intuitively knew that I'd finally found the answer to my lifelong question about the true nature of consciousness: I had just touched it.

A wave of peace flowed over me, something close to the heart of G-d.

"What should I do?" I said out loud;

"Wait," came the answer, a voice deep within my mind.

"I want to share this with others," I said. "I should sell my business and go out and teach again."

"Wait," came the answer a second time.

And so I waited, meditating daily and going on with my life and business, for the next three months.

A dream presaged the next event. In it, Paramahansa Yogananda (author of *Autobiography of a Yogi* and founder of The Self-Realization Fellowship) appeared to me and invited me to come with him to some place a short distance away which I somehow knew was a monastery. We were sitting in straight-back wooden chairs, facing each other, in the courtyard or parking lot of a large commercial area. Over his right shoulder, I noticed an arcade, which included a place showing XXX-rated movies. Thinking I'd get one last thrill before embarking on a monastic life, I said to him, "I'll be right back," and stood up to walk toward the arcade. As I walked past him, he vanished. I ran to his chair, yelling out his name, but he was gone, and I woke up sobbing.

A few days later, on March 7, 1978, I was in the middle of my morning prayers and meditation in a walk-in closet I'd converted into a prayer room in our home. I had a candle and a cushion to sit on, and a few quotes from various saints pinned to the walls, and was sitting and thinking, my mind just wandering. I remembered the evangelist, and a feeling of inner emptiness washed through me. What was next? What was my next lesson? What was my mission, and who was the teacher that seven years earlier Master Stanley had said I would one day meet when I was ready to understand his message? And how was I supposed to do something to change, improve, or even help save the world?

I closed my eyes, bowed my head, and said out loud, "G-d, please tell me what to do next. Give me a work that is Your work." (At the time I co-owned an herbal products company and an advertising agency, and wrote on natural medicine for a few national magazines: hardly spiritual work. But it paid the bills, often very well.) A sudden burst of emotion filled me—grief over Master Stanley's death, fear and hope for the future, the pain of the spiritual emptiness of my life and work in the business world, or the presaging of what would follow—and I fought back tears for a moment.

I reflected that it was the seventh day of the month, and seven had always been an important number for me. Perhaps that meant the day would have special significance.

I blew out the candle, stood up, and walked out of my little mom.

As I walked past the phone, it rang, and I turned and picked it up. The voice on the other end sounded distant, but was familiar.

"Thomas?" It was Don Haughey, one of Master Stanley's students, who to this day is the pastor of a small church in southern Michigan and runs a holistic healing center near Coldwater. At that time he was also a senior executive with the Holiday Inn chain, and he said he was calling from Germany.

"What's up, Don?"

"I can't tell you over the phone," he said. "It would just sound too crazy, and there isn't time. But your face just appeared in front of me not five minutes ago, and I knew I had to call you. There's a man here you have to meet and a place you have to see. We need you and you need this: trust me."

"Where?"

"It's a little town in the middle of nowhere in Germany. Called Stadtsteinach. I'll pick you up tomorrow morning in Nuremberg; there's a flight you can catch tonight out of Detroit."

I started to tell Don how busy I was, and then remembered the prayer I'd just uttered. "I'll be there," I said.

GOTTFRIED MÜLLER

Don met me the next morning at the airport, and as we drove the two-hour trip from Nuremberg to Stadtsteinach, he tried to tell me why he'd demanded I come.

"There's this man here," he said. "His name is Gottfried Müller, and he's the most extraordinary human I've ever met. If it's true that at any one time there are always a few saints on Earth, he must be one of them."

"Why?" I said. "How do you know?"

"You'll see," Don said. "You'll feel it when you meet him."

"How'd you meet him?"

"I was in Boston visiting Dr. Ann Wigmore at the Hippocrates Health Institute a few months ago when he came to visit and gave a short talk about his work. I was so impressed that I flew over here to hear his orchestra play in Stuttgart, then took the bus with him and the children back to Stadtsteinach."

"An orchestra?"

"Thom, I met the children before they played. They were practicing. It was obvious that many of them were retarded, deformed, or damaged in some way. All were homeless. And their music didn't sound like anything special when they were practicing. But when they came into that crowded hall and began to play, it was beautiful. And the most amazing thing happened . . . ." his voice trailed off.

"What, Don?"

"I know it sounds crazy, but as they were playing, I was sitting there, and the face of Jesus Christ appeared above them on the stage. It was absolutely real and totally vivid, although I imagine I'm the only one who saw Him."

"Wow." I didn't know what to think, but I was moved to believe him.

"And afterwards," Don continued, "Herr Müller got up on the stage and gave some sort of a speech in German that I didn't understand a word of, but I knew, right then, that I had to get to know him better. So afterwards I came to Stadtsteinach."

"Which is?"

"The world headquarters of Salem, pronounced like sah-lem. It's from the Hebrew and Arabic words for peace, Shalom and Salaam. He has a community here for abused or orphaned kids, and two others in Germany, and there's one starting in the United States, and he has programs in a few other countries. But it's not just that. It's one of the most spiritually powerful places I've ever visited on Earth."

We arrived in Stadtsteinach, a little town in the mountains of the Frankenwald. The side of one hill was covered with buildings, houses, an orchard, a soccer field, a covered riding arena, and a large pasture filled with horses. Kids of all ages ran in every direction: the place was alive with activity. Yet there was an odd sense of peace, a groundedness that I'd only once before experienced in relation to a place: when I'd spent that summer in my tipi. After a few months of meditation, the tipi became invested with a certain spirit: it became a holy place. This was what the Salem children's village in Stadtsteinach felt like.

A German man in his 60s, dressed in a businessman's suit and tie, balding with a graying beard, ran up to our car and threw out his arms to hug Don. "Welcome back, Don!" he said, then turned to me. "And you are Thomas Hartmann?" He used the German pronunciation for my first name.

"Yes," I said, as he pumped my hand. I felt a warm energy flow up my arm and into my heart: it was both pleasant and startling. His eyes twinkled; his face was creased in a smile.

"Welcome to Salem," he said, then grabbed my bag and began to haul it up the hill toward the guest houses.

I caught up with Don, just behind Herr Müller, and whispered, "Well, he's certainly one of the most enthusiastic people I've ever met."

Don grinned.

During the three days I was in Stadtsteinach, I learned that Herr Müller had a children's orchestra, and he wanted them to perform a fund-raiser that summer for the new American Salem program that was being started in Maryland by a young American woman who'd lived at Salem in Stadtsteinach for a year and a half. Don had told him I knew the advertising business, and could make it all happen.

We sat in his office, a modern painting of Jerusalem on one wall, an old clock and a hand-lettered, framed paper that looked like part of an illuminated manuscript on the other. It said, in German, Genesis 14:18:

And Melchizedek, king of Salem, brought forth bread and wine: and he was the priest of the most high JHWH.

"I want you to help Louise Sutermeister, the woman who runs the new Salem Children's Village in Maryland, to rent the best halls and publicize the event," Herr Müller said, raising a finger in the air to make his point. "Lincoln Center in New York, the Kennedy Center in Washington, the Berkeley Performance Center in Boston."

"For when?" I asked.

"August," he said without a second's hesitation.

"Of this year? 1978?"

"Yes, of course!"

"This is March. You can't book those halls for August in March. You have to book them at least a year in advance. Particularly during the summer: that's peak tourist time! And even if you got them, you don't have the time to properly do the publicity."

"You can do it," he said, staring at me in a way I hadn't experienced since the last time I'd seen Master Stanley.

"How?" I said, feeling uncomfortable under his stare.

"You and Louise Sutermeister can do it," he said. "G-d will help you."

I shrugged, not wanting to get into an argument. Obviously he had no idea what was involved in scheduling and promoting an event at Lincoln Center. "I'll try," I said.

He shot forward as if he'd been poked. "No, you will do it or you will not," he said, his voice now soft.

"Well, I'll try my best."

He pointed to a book on the table in front of me. "Try to pick up that book." His voice was a command.

I reached over and picked it up.

"Did I say, 'Pick it up'? Try to pick it up."

I put it back down and hesitated, unsure of what to do.

"Now you see," he said, waving a finger at me. "Stop lying to us and tell me if you will or will not help rent those halls and promote this event."

"I'll do it," I said, finally understanding his point, but knowing in my heart that it would be impossible. I was already planning the wording for the letter of regrets I'd send him.

Don, who'd suffered from sinus problems his whole life, was sniffling. "I need something to clear my nose," he said.

"Thomas will try to get you something for it," Herr Müller said, then laughed as if at his own joke. Even though it seemed that it was at my expense, I smiled. After a moment he grew serious. "Go for a walk," he said.

"Do you have any herbs or medications here?" I asked. "Perhaps some peppermint tea, or garlic, or horseradish?"

Herr Müller shrugged. "Go for a walk. And keep your eyes open." He pointed to his own eyes, wiggled his eyebrows in a Groucho Marx gesture, and laughed again.

Herr Müller walked us to the front door of the guest house's restaurant and pushed us out onto the sidewalk, saying, "Go! Hurry!" So Don and I went for a walk, away from Salem, down through the little town of Stadtsteinach, and then up into the mountains on the far side of town. We talked and walked for at least an hour, taking odd turns and twists, winding among little farmhouses and clusters of residential homes. Twice, we thought we were lost, but eventually found a landmark in the distant mountains we could orient ourselves by.

As we walked, Don told me of the things he'd learned from Herr Müller and how he saw Salem as being under a "dome of light." His descriptions were punctuated, though, by his sniffling. "I wish I had some horseradish," Don said. "That really is the best thing for me. It'll clean out my sinuses and get this stuff all draining out. I should have asked the cook at Salem if she had any."

"Herr Müller said we should keep our eyes open," I said, joking. "Maybe that's an exercise to clear your sinuses while you walk."

"I doubt it," Don said, although he tried wiggling his eyebrows. "No luck."

"Tell me more about Salem," I said.

"They're trying to re-create a healthy family for kids who've never known a family," Don said. "Each house has mixed boys and girls, of mixed ages, and two parents who the children call the German equivalent of 'Mom' and 'Dad.' They eat a vegetarian, whole-foods diet . . . ."

"That sounds good," I interjected. I'd become a vegetarian in 1969, and Master Stanley was a big promoter of vegetarianism. His rationale was that it was a "lighter way to walk on the Earth," healthier, and that it was very difficult for any person carrying around dead animal parts in their intestines to fine-tune their brain to "spiritual frequencies." He also said people were affected by both the "spiritual vibration" and the hormones (such as adrenaline) that animals generate in huge quantities when they know they're about to be slaughtered, and that ingesting the hormones and taking the vibrations of fear and death into our bodies makes people more aggressive and less able to calm their minds to "listen for the voice of G-d."

It had certainly been my experience: when I quit eating meat in the late 1960s, I noticed several dramatic shifts in my states of consciousness within the first year.

"You'll like it," Don said. "They grow all their own food on organic farms and in greenhouses, grind their own wheat into fresh bread the day it's baked, the whole thing. Herr Müller became a vegetarian during World War II as a statement of nonviolence."

"That's where I started, during the Vietnam war, initially for the same reason."

"Well, Herr Müller has taken it a good bit further. He wanted to stop vivisection, so he opened a research institute here and published hundreds of papers and did original research showing the value of testing on tissue cultures instead of animals. And he works to stop the mass slaughter of birds every year in Italy. And on and on."

"So it's a home with a good diet . . ."

"More than just a home. An extended family, really. They have a grandparents house with old people in it, who interact with the kids. When one dies they lay him or her out and the children come to say goodbye, as was normally done in German families over the past thousand years. And they have pottery and carpentry shops where the kids can learn trades, and an Olympic-sized riding hall for what they call "horseback riding therapy," and an indoor swimming pool and sauna, and it goes on and on. It's amazing." He sniffed hard. "Wish I had some horseradish."

"A family is an important thing."

"He had an insight that startled me," Don said. "You and I always took it for granted that if we got in trouble we could 'go home' to our parents or family. But that's not the case for most of these kids. So Herr Müller tells them that if they ever, at any time in their lives, need to come home, there is always a room for them at Salem."

"What if they just wanted to come back, goof off, and veg out in front of the TV?"

Don laughed. "Well, first, there's no TV at Salem. Beyond that, I don't know how they'd handle it, but I'm sure it would be with compassion and love."

We turned a corner and there, on the shoulder of the road, was a pile of recently-dug white roots. Each was the size of a large carrot, and the pile would have filled at least three or four bushel-baskets.

"What's that?" I said, not wanting to give voice to my suspicions.

"Dunno," said Don, an odd tone to his voice. He walked over to the pile, which was on the corner of some farmer's field, his steps careful and slow as if he couldn't believe what he was seeing. He picked up one of the roots and broke off a tip, then sniffed it. "Horseradish," he said, his eyes shining.

"Maybe he just knew it was horseradish harvest time," I said.

Don shook his head. "Could be. But I suspect that it's not as simple as that."

I was to soon discover that he was right, although not before I struggled through my own personal doubts and revelations with Herr Müller.

The Salem Pin and the Curve of Time

True light not only lights, but also warms.

—ABRAM POLJAK*

The second night I was at Salem in Germany was a Friday night, and Herr Müller was quite emphatic that we should get together and have some red wine with him, but that we shouldn't discuss business that night or at all the following day until sundown.

"You follow the Jewish Sabbath?" I said.

"I follow the Sabbath of Jesus" he said. "Of course, Jesus was Jewish, and so if we follow Him we must keep the Sabbath that He kept. But the Sabbath came before there were any separate races or religions or even people. It is for all humankind."

I noticed that he was wearing a small, blue, rectangular pin with a white circle in it. "What is that?" I asked.

"The logo of Salem," he replied, pronouncing it as sah-lem with the emphasis on the first syllable.

"And Salem means?"

"Peace," he said. "Salem is from *shalom* and *salaam,* the Hebrew and Arabic words for 'peace.' Like *Jerusalem,* which means 'City of Peace.' We are an instrument for peace in the world."

"And the meaning of the logo?"

He smiled and shrugged. "You will find your own meaning. For me it means Salem."

---

*For more writings of Abram Poljak, Herr Müller's teacher, see Appendix 2.

He took his pin off his jacket and looked at it thoughtfully for a moment, then looked directly into my eyes. "Thomas, I feel that you are one of our little flock. You are one chosen by G-d from before the beginning of time and you are here for a good and positive purpose. This is no accident. Do you understand?"

I felt a shock in my heart, as if somebody had punched me there, but not painful. In fact, it felt somewhat ecstatic. "Yes," I said. "I understand." Somewhere in my mind was a rational little voice telling me that this was all crazy, but in my heart, in my soul, I knew he spoke the truth.

"Wear this emblem," he said, handing it to me. "It is special for you."

I took the pin and looked at it carefully. The front was white and blue enamel around gold. On the back, just above the pin, were four raised letters in a sans-serif typeface: JHWH.* I put on the pin, and felt as if a spiritual shield had just gone up all around me.

"What are the letters on the back of the pin?" I asked.

"The tetragrammaton," he said. "The four letters of the holiest name of G-d. It is so holy it is almost unspeakable, which is why when I write even the word 'G-d,' I do it with the vowel removed."

I asked him to drop me a note about G-d's name so I could have his exact thoughts. Here is what he wrote:

The Lord's Prayer

Everybody has a name. Without a name, nobody "exists."

So also *G-d:* He has a name!

Already the prayer, from G-d's Son given to us *(gelehrt),* the "Lord's Prayer," begins with "Hallowed *(geheiligt)* be thy name!"

But what is this name? There are different answers, explanations, if you ask others about it, but all the answers are not satisfied about the name of G-d or of the Father, etc.

I know out of a lifelong experience that *nobody,* or nearly none, are interested in finding the name of G-d, or at least I myself haven't found anybody interested in it, although there are hundreds of refer-

---

*In German, the pronunciation of several letters is different from English. J is pronounced like Y, so *ja* is "yah."

ences to G-d's "name" and the importance of His "name" and knowing His "name" in the Bible.

He gives comfort in times of catastrophe during your life, if you know about a "Burg" (fortification) offered in the Bible: "The *name* of G-d is a strong fortification, the just one races to it and is secure!"

Instead of the word "name" in the Bible are often four letters "JHWH."* But now the question: how to pronounce it? There are different versions, but only one of them can be the right one, but which one? I give the answer:

The name of G-d is so endlessly holy that nobody is able and allowed to say it.

You are not punished if you willingly say Jehovah or Jahwe, but certainly none of them is the true one *because* G-d's name is so holy that it cannot be pronounced.

But nevertheless there must, must, must (!!!) be an answer to the question: how to pronounce this important name of G-d.

We must know it, otherwise how shall we use the Name in order to have the "fortification" you can race to if the world is "burning."

It is very simple and easy: ask G-d for enlightenment. He does give light about His name. I know it. And I am endlessly thankful for it.

On February 20, 1996, I received a relevant fax:

Dear Brother Thomas!

A wonderful discovery:

On the cross of Jesus was a plate with the words "Jesus of Nazereth, King of the Jews" in three languages—Hebrew, Greek, and

---

*Often translated into "Jehovah," "The LORD God" (usually with "LORD" in allcapital letters) or "Yahweh" depending on which translation and version of the Bible you're reading. In the original Hebrew there are no vowels in "The Word" or the Name of G-d, which has led to a millennia-old debate over its correct pronunciation that continues to this day among biblical scholars. Moses, Jesus, and others in the Bible refer to or use the "power" of the Name, which implies that being able to correctly pronounce it may confer on a person the ability to perform miracles (and may destroy a person who tries to use that power in "vain" or for ill purposes). This theme runs throughout the Bible (including the injunction to not take the Name in vain), and has been pursued by both Jewish and Christian mystics for thousands of years.

Latin, but in Hebrew: Jeschua Hanozri Wumelech Hajehudim if you take the beginning of each word you have G-d's JHWH

So, dear brother Thomas, if you use these four letters, you praise not only Jesus when he was on Earth, but as Creator of Heaven and Earth, of the Universe!

Pilate did not know why he had to put the four letters on the cross of the Messiah. For you and for me this discovery is wonderful and gives us strength in our prayers, thankful that it is also on our emblem!

Love and blessings,

Gottfried Müller

After the discussion of the name of G-d and the importance of knowing it, and having it on the pin fastened "in front" of me, we drank wine and told stories and Herr Müller made jokes. Then, as the evening was drawing to a close, he became serious again.

"The Earth is in a terrible situation," he said. "Everywhere there is war and famine. They cry 'Peace,' but there is no peace. Yet there are little points of light, little protected places. This is one of them."

I could see, hear, and feel it as he spoke: I'd experienced it when I first arrived, like stepping under a giant dome. Even the air smelled different, the light seemed a different color.

"I had a vision just recently," he said. "I could see a light from the throne of G-d shining down on Europe and America. And then I saw that the light was moving. The light moved from Europe and America, where it had been for 2,000 years, to Africa. It also moved to the Gypsies, and I realized, 'Ah, ha! This is the fulfillment of the words "the first shall be last and the last first." And the light means the Grace of G-d.'"

"So Africa will play an important role in the future?"

"It does already," he said. "These are the signs of this time. Therefore, we must look for a place in Africa to begin a peace work, a Salem work."

"And then that work in Africa will be protected by light?"

"Eventually, yes," he said simply. "As we are here."

He took a napkin and drew two lines which intersected to create a backwards L. "If you look at the speed of transportation for millions of years, it was the same," he said, drawing a straight line just above the bottom line of the backwards L. "Then they started to ride horses," the line went up a bit, "then cars," a bit higher, "then airplanes," higher still, "and then jets and spaceships." At that point, he shot the line straight up to the edge of the vertical line of the backward L. "The same is true of how much energy humans consume. And of the population of the Earth. And of the number of evil acts committed. And of good acts. And of the destructive power of weapons and bombs. And, and, and. Always, at the end, the curve ends with this radical upward sweep, the point it cannot go beyond without collapse, and it is happening now, in our lifetimes."

I nodded in agreement. "Do you believe this is the time referred to in Revelation? The battle of Armageddon?"

"Yes," he said. "Time moves in cycles. This is the dawn of a 'new age.' Most people who use that phrase do not know what it means, however. It will be a time of great tribulation, pain, and suffering, and also of great joy and the arrival of the Messiah on the Earth along with many spiritual souls. It is a necessary cleansing of the Earth, a regeneration."

"Earthquakes, famine, disease? The Four Horsemen of the Apocalypse?"

"*Ja!* And war and changes in the climate. Perhaps a shift of the Earth's poles."

I nodded in agreement: it was a validation of information I'd been accumulating for years. We're facing a planet-wide physical crisis, which has a spiritual and cultural basis.

That conversation took place almost two decades ago, and today there's abundant scientific evidence that the changes in the Earth Herr Müller predicted are in fact happening—*now*. Over a third of America's usable topsoil has been lost, and we continue to lose another five billion tons a year. Much of the remaining soil has been pumped so dry that it's filling with saltwater, so it can't be used for farming. And you probably haven't seen a wild honeybee recently, because over 70 percent of them are now dead.*

With the accelerating loss of the forests that are vital to stabilizing

---

*See my book *The Last Hours of Ancient Sunlight* for much more information on these and related topics.

our climate and producing new topsoil, with the looming crises in water and energy, I knew (even back then) that Herr Müller's words were not just the type of "the world ends tomorrow" talk that's been with us for thousands of years. The world is now facing a crisis, and it's one that is largely caused by our thinking that we're separate from—disconnected from—the rest of life and the environment in which we live.

He continued: "This is why you and I and many, many others are here, on this Earth at this time. We volunteered to be here, to prepare and shepherd the Earth and its people through this time, and then we forgot that we volunteered because we had to be born in human bodies in order to do the work."

I was touched: it could have been Master Stanley speaking, and also things I'd taught others for years. "I understand and agree," I said.

He looked straight into my eyes and said: "I have been waiting for your arrival for many years."

I knew then that I had been waiting for him, too, and wondered if he might be the man Master Stanley had once referred to as my "next teacher."

At that time, I referred to Gottfried Müller as "Herr Müller" instead of "Gottfried" because we had just met and, particularly in German culture, one never calls a person by their first name until a close relationship is established. (German even has different words for "you"—*du* and *Sie*—depending on whether or not you're close friends with someone.) Most of the people I know around him do the same, although he is not bothered by people (particularly Americans, who don't understand European protocols) calling him by his first name. I've continued to call him Herr Müller in the years since then, however, as a sign of respect. As you'll see and hear in the next chapter and beyond, I feel that respect was well-earned.

The Lapis Ring

And this our life, exempt from public haunt,
Finds tongues in trees, books in the running brooks,
Sermons in stones. . . .

—SHAKESPEARE, *AS YOU LIKE IT*

It wasn't any one particular story in this book or other event that revealed to me the true nature of Herr Müller; rather it was a number of events that I may not have believed had I not lived them myself.

The first came a month or so after my first meeting him in March 1978 in Stadtsteinach.

Herr Müller scheduled a two-day trip to the U.S. to visit the halls we had succeeded in booking, and for a meeting with Andrew Young, who was the United States' Ambassador to the United Nations. He was also invited to meet with Ambassador Young's wife, Jean Young, who was then the UN's Director of the International Year of the Child. I flew to New York to meet Herr Müller's flight at Kennedy airport, and drove into town with him in a taxi.

On the way into town, I remarked to him what a beautiful ring he had on the ring finger of his left hand (his wedding ring was on his right hand in German tradition): it was a simple gold ring with a deep blue stone in it.

"The stone is lapis lazuli," he said. "You should get one yourself."

"Because it's the color of the Salem logo?" I asked.

"Maybe your wife would think it looks good on you," he said, and laughed. I could tell he was evading my question.

I'd met people over the years who believed that certain minerals or crystals had particular healing or spiritual properties, and was wondering if he thought so, too. So I persisted: "Does the stone have some particular significance?"

He shrugged. "You have not read that angels have eyes the color of lapis lazuli?"

"No," I said. He was still avoiding my question. "Why should I get one?"

This time he turned and looked me directly in the eyes, lowered his voice slightly as if he didn't want the cab driver to hear, and said, "The stone has a particular resonance. Like a tuning fork. A vibration. It would be good for you."

"What's the vibration?"

"Spiritual purity."

I was interested to hear the answer, because I had several friends who put great stock in the ability of crystals and stones to resonate with certain of the Earth's more subtle frequencies, affecting people's mental, physical, and spiritual being. Being an old amateur radio operator, I'd used germanium crystals connected to wires to extract from the air the invisible waves of distant radio stations; it seemed possible there might be something to the ancient Vedic science of using crystals for healing and fine-tuning the body. On the other hand, it may all be just fantasy: this is an area in which I was and am not an expert.

But beyond my interest in his answer, I was also irritated that he'd made me drag it out of him. If was nearly a year later that he told me that the mention in the Bible of not casting your pearls before swine meant that on important spiritual matters one should never indulge people who were merely curiosity seekers.

His spiritual mentor, Abram Poljak, had taught him that in most cases he should avoid directly answering a spiritual question of importance until it had been asked three times. Fortunately, during that first year, I was tenaciously persistent with my questions; this man, I knew, had answers to questions that were at the core of my sense of life's mysteries, and I was going to get his thoughts on these things no matter how many times I had to ask.

"So where should I get this ring, and how will I know the stone has the right vibration?" I said, deciding in that moment to find a lapis ring.

He reached across the seat and put his hand on mine gently, then said, "It will be the only one for you, it shall be your first, and it will take everything you have." He then squeezed my hand, as if to assure me he wasn't making a joke or evading my question, and let go of my hand.

"You're being evasive," I said.

But he shook his head, a serious look on his face, and said, "All your life your most difficult challenge has been to have faith."

"Yes," I agreed, catching my breath, "but what does that have to do with your answer?"

"You'll understand before the day is finished." He leaned forward in his seat. "Driver, where are the jewelry stores here in New York? Isn't there a special place?"

"There's an area on 47th Street," the driver, a Chinese man with a thick accent, said. "Many diamonds, especially. And much gold."

"Drop my friend there," Herr Müller said. I started to protest, but he raised his hand. "I must buy a small gift for my wife," he said, then pulled a pocket watch out and popped it open. "It is now 3:17. Pick me up in front of Macy's at 3:53." His voice was soft, but clear. "By then you will have your ring."

The driver swung around onto 47th street in front of a row of jewelry shops and stopped to let me out.

"Three fifty-three," he repeated, as I nodded agreement and closed the door.

The first jewelry shop I walked into had thousands of rings in row after row of felt cases under glass counters.

"What do you have in a lapis men's ring?" I asked the man behind the counter.

He pulled out a tray from the far end of a nearby counter and placed it on the glass in front of me.

"Unfortunately," he said, "at this moment I only have one in the store. Of course I'm sure you'll find dozens of others up and down the street, but this is a particularly nice one." He lifted a simple gold ring with a lapis stone in it about half the size of a dime. "Try it on and see what you think."

I put on the ring, and it fit perfectly. "How much is it?" I asked.

He flipped over the tag on the tray. "One hundred twelve dollars. Plus tax, of course. That's a very good price, because the setting is eighteen karat gold."

I fished into my pocket and pulled out a wad of bills and a few coins. I'd absent-mindedly forgotten to get extra cash to take with me on the trip, and had planned to cash a check sometime later in the day.

"Do you take credit cards or checks?" I said.

He shook his head. "Only cash." He picked up a small calculator and began pushing buttons as I counted out the cash in my pocket.

As I got to the end of the crumpled bills, I'd counted $120.

"With the tax," he said, "it's one hundred twenty dollars and ninety six cents."

My hands began to tremble as I counted out three quarters, a dime, a nickel, and, six pennies. It was every cent I had.

It was all too weird: I had to do a reality check. "Hang on to the ring," I said, "and I'll be back in a few minutes."

Without protest, and not offering a discount or any alternatives, he put the ring back into the case.

I spent the next 20 minutes walking from one jewelry store to another, trying on dozens of rings. Only one other one fit, and it was both garishly ornate with diamonds around the lapis stone, and was over a thousand dollars.

At 3:45, I returned to the first store and exchanged all of my cash for that first ring.

Out front I flagged a cab, hoping that Herr Müller would be waiting for me at Macy's and that he'd have money for cab fare.

As we swung around the corner of 34th Street and 7th Avenue, I looked at my watch. It was 3:56. Herr Müller was standing on the corner with a small Macy's bag in one hand, looking very old-world European in his long dark-green wool overcoat, gray slacks, and hat.

The taxi pulled up and he hopped in beside me, pulling the door closed with a snap.

"You're three minutes late," he said, as if it were something quite important. He didn't sound irritated, but it was important, it seemed, for him to make that point.

"I'm sorry," I said, then told the cabby to take us to Lincoln Center.

"It's not three minutes," Herr Müller said. "it's that if you are to succeed in the work ahead of you, you must both learn to pay attention to even the smallest details, and to know that your word is your word."

"But three minutes?" I said, wondering for a moment if he was one of those types who wash their hands thirty times a day.

"The three minutes is meaningless," he said. "It is the power of your words you must come to understand. Did you say 'yes' or 'no' to fifty-three minutes after the hour?"

"Well, here in America we'd round the time off to the half- or quarter-hour, or at least to five minutes, and a few minutes one way or another. . . ."

"Did you say 'yes' or 'no'?"

"I said 'yes,' but. . . ."

"Yes is yes and no is no. Words represent thoughts, and all the reality you see around you, all these buildings and cars and clothes and lights, they all began as thoughts. Thoughts are things, they have substance, and words are their first manifestation. Look at that building," he said as he pointed at an ornate brick building.

"Ok," I said.

"It began as a thought in somebody's mind. One person's mind. Then came words. Then drawings and on and on. But first as a thought. You must learn the power of your words as you intuitively know the power of your thoughts."

"I thought you were talking about my agreement, my commitment to be here at that time."

"Of course," he said. "And that has to do with your honor and credibility. But even more important is that you learn that your words have power." He leaned back in the seat, "When you learn Hebrew and study the story of Jehoshaphat, you will clearly understand. But that will be later. Now, show me your ring."

I held up my hand.

He reached over and pulled the new ring from my finger, then, without even giving it a careful examination, gripped it in his fist and held it at the height of his shoulder. He closed his eyes for a moment.

"This is not a ring," he said. "It is *your* ring."

"Yes, it. . . ."

He handed the ring back to me. "I give this ring, and you, my blessing. It will carry you through the first stage of your work."

"The first stage?"

"Moses destroyed the first set of stone tablets. Always it is."

"What do you mean?"

"Trust me. One day you will remember that I said this." He smiled, the mischievous look of a little boy. "I am your second teacher, is it not so?"

I sat back in the seat heavily. I'd never said a word to him about

Master Stanley and, for that matter, didn't even really consider Herr Müller, at that moment, my teacher.

He leaned back in the seat, closed his eyes, and appeared to fall asleep, then suddenly stirred. "Don't worry about the cab fare," he said. "I have enough cash." And he laughed, then went back to appearing to be asleep.

I was stunned, but there was also still that skeptical voice inside me that's been there since I was a child, and which became very strong and loud when, at the age of six, I learned the crushing news that Santa Claus was a lie. I looked at him, eyes closed and apparently comfortable with himself and the world. I listened to the sounds of the city outside the cab, the traffic, the horns, people shouting, the wind. I felt the cold air and the smooth vinyl of the seat against my trenchcoat. The world was real, this moment was real, and yet there was still a part of me that didn't want to believe what had just happened could have happened. It had to be a coincidence.

Ten blocks up 8th Avenue we entered the Times Square area, where I was to receive a shock nearly as strong as my first meeting with Master Stanley.

The Trap

I know my soul hath power to know all things. . . .
—SIR JOHN DAVIES, *NOSCE TEIPSUM*

In 1978, Times Square was the sex capital of New York City. The streets around 42nd and 8th Avenue were covered with X-rated book stores, peep shows, and movie houses as if some ancient hand had deposited the seeds of Sodom. In the heat of the city they had sprouted and grown until they filled the streets, competing for gawkers and customers the way overgrown weeds compete for sunlight.

One particular place caught my eye as we drove up 8th Avenue: it was an old movie theater, now shabby and gray with litter swirling across the stained cement sidewalk in the sharp April wind. The marquee that had once advertised vaudeville shows and feature movies now proclaimed, in huge letters, "LIVE SEX ACTS ON STAGE."

I'd never seen another couple having sex live and in front of me, and it seemed exotic and exciting, stirring my male-animal curiosity. And that part of me that had had a lifelong fascination with psychology wondered what type of person would want to get up on stage and do such a thing for an audience.

The door to the theater was a rounded arch, and a thick, black blanket was hung behind it to keep the wind out. The dark, curved opening into the building reminded me of the cartoon mouse holes from the Tom & Jerry cartoons I'd grown up watching on television. Free associating, my mind wandered from mouse holes to mouse traps, and, looking again at the sign as we drove by it, I thought to myself how many people, from King David to myself, had been caught at one time or another in their lives by the trap of sex.

Just as that thought ran through my mind, Herr Müller roused himself and leaned over against me. He grabbed my upper arm with his hand, an urgent and hard grip, chuckled softly as I turned to look at him, and said, "It is a trap."

I gasped, blinking rapidly, and he let go of my arm, settled back into his seat, closed his eyes and pretended to go back to sleep. A faint smile tickled the corners of his mouth.

My first rational thought, as I seized my composure, was to wonder how he did that trick. I looked around the taxi, up and down the street, half expecting to see a theater with the word "trap" prominently displayed. There were none.

Then I thought, well, it was just another good guess on his part. He probably does this all the time, just popping these things out of his mouth, and if he does it often enough he's bound to amaze people. But that didn't ring true: he appeared to know exactly what he was saying, and exactly what it meant, and exactly why and when to say it to me.

He'd read my mind.

That's pretty damn amazing, I thought. What a great trick.

But then I realized the obvious and truly frightening thing that I had at first overlooked: if he knew that thought, then maybe he knew my other thoughts. Thoughts that I would never want another person to know, thoughts that, while I'm sure all humans have, represent our darkest and most embarrassing secrets.

My heart started to race. If he knew those thoughts, if he knew my doubts and weaknesses, if he knew even the sarcastic or judgmental things I'd thought about him in the past few minutes, he would realize what an utterly unworthy person I was. He would hate me, or, even worse, refuse to see me again, which would cut me off from the spiritual insights and knowledge that I was becoming certain he had and I wanted.

As this series of rapid-fire visions raced through my mind, he coughed and opened his eyes. "Something important you should know," he said in a soft voice, his eyes following the people on the street.

I said nothing, fearing the worst.

He turned his body at an angle toward me, and his green-brown eyes looked into mine with a compassion which swept away my fear.

"I am not a magician," he said, "and I do not know other people's thoughts. Sometimes, however, I receive a direct order to say or do something."

I nodded my head, wondering if he was just trying to calm my concerns. If so, he wasn't doing a very good job of it: I hadn't told him that he'd read my mind, yet here he was referring to my next thought, my mental question about what he'd done and how he'd done it.

"The lesson for you, Thomas," he said, putting his hand on my leg for a moment as if to reassure a child, "is that whether another person can know your thoughts is not important. What is important is that you know, every moment of every day, that G-d knows all your thoughts. And, despite that, He will always, always love you, and He will never abandon you." He interlaced his fingers and stretched them out in front of him, looking out at the New York City street scene. "You can only be free when you know that G-d knows your every thought, that He knows you better than even you know yourself. And that He loves you without condition or judgment, even knowing you that well."

I fell back into the seat and closed my eyes hard, fighting back tears. He had so easily and elegantly touched a place deep within me, gone right to the core of my skepticism and fear and hope: an inner barrier broke down and I felt naked and free, frightened and liberated. I looked again at him, sitting on the seat next to me, and decided in that moment that I had to know this man better.

A Visit by Angels

One must not always think so
much about what one should do,
but rather what one should be.
Our works do not ennoble us;
but we must ennoble our works.

—MEISTER ECKHART

After visiting Lincoln Center, we went to the United Nations building, where we were received at the office of Mrs. Jean Young.

She was a beautiful and gracious woman, charming and poised, and she seemed fascinated with the story of Salem and the works that Herr Müller had initiated around the world. Although I was there in the role of, essentially, flunky and escort, she treated me with the same deference, respect, and genuine interest I imagined she would have shown a visiting ambassador or head of state.

At one point she left the room to fetch some papers about the international Year of the Child.

Herr Müller turned to me and said, "Did you see the angels?"

I assumed he was referring to what a beautiful and kind woman Mrs. Young was, and said, "Yes, she truly is an extraordinary person."

"No, no," he said. "I mean the angels. There are two with her. You did not see them?"

"Angels?" I said, wondering if he were joking or testing me.

But he nodded solemnly and said, "Yes, angels. There is one that stays right beside her at all times, and another who is in that far corner of the room." He pointed at the area behind her desk near a window. "When she left, they left, although the one in the corner was here when we first came in."

"You're serious," I said, astonished. I'd seen auras and had all sorts of extraordinary experiences in the years I'd known Master Stanley, but

I'd never seen, or known anybody I took seriously who said they'd seen an angel. On the other hand, seeing angels was a relatively common experience in the literature of Christian (and other religions') mystics, and I was willing to believe either that they were real and I simply hadn't yet tuned the "receiver" of my brain to their frequency, or that Herr Müller was experiencing the hallucinatory state often associated with mystical ecstasy.

"Yes, of course," he said, a hint of impatience in his voice. "We are in the presence of a holy woman. Look when she returns."

Mrs. Young came back into the room with a large white envelope with a United Nations logo on it and handed it to me. As she was telling me about its contents, I was looking all around her head and around the ceiling, trying to see her angels. I must have been somewhat conspicuous, because she stopped in mid-sentence, looked at the wall behind her, and asked if anything was wrong. I apologized and made an excuse about my eyes hurting from lack of sleep the night before. She smiled, friendly but not at all patronizing, and finished her story about her UN program.

I never did see her angels, but I could agree without hesitation with Herr Müller that she made an extraordinary first impression. When she died in 1995, I was not surprised to read in the paper many comments to that same effect from normally taciturn or hardboiled politicians who'd known her, most through her husband Andrew, who had also been the mayor of the city of Atlanta. I was in Germany a few weeks later and mentioned to Herr Müller that she had died, and he replied simply, "A bright and important light has left the Earth."

Changing the World
by Changing Ourselves

All creatures desire to speak G-d in their works: they all
of them speak him as well as they can but they cannot
really pronounce him. Willy-nilly, in weal or in woe they
are all trying to utter G-d who yet remains unspoken.

—MEISTER ECKHART

The summer I lived in the tipi, I thought a great deal about the monastic experience. I'd read *Dark Night of the Soul* by St. John of the Cross, and several books by Thomas Merton, and throughout my life had been drawn to the idea of solitude as a way of speeding up spiritual experience and growth. And that had certainly been my experience in my semi-monastic summer: I received knowledge and insights that I doubt I could have gotten any other way.

Before I went into the forest, into the tipi, I'd always considered the monastic experience to be both intensely personal and intensely selfish. A monk, I thought, was a person working on himself, and only affecting him or herself.

But that summer I realized that my spiritual practice was having an effect on the world. I could feel it: it was as if the world itself had a particular vibration, made up of the buzz and fire of all the life upon and within it, and when I was peaceful it made the world a bit more peaceful. When I was agitated, the world became more agitated.

My conclusion from this admittedly subjective experience was that I really was affecting the world. That monks are spiritual warriors, and monasteries are places from which powerful beams of positive spiritual energy fan out from the men and women in them to transform and help the world. While not so common among the writings of contemporary monks, this view was clearly held by those people who chose a monastic life in the centuries and millennia preceding the last hundred years or so. And so I worked at making myself more pure, so I could add purity to the world.

But throughout this there was also part of me that thought this was a subjective experience, perhaps with no objective reality. It seemed, on that level, that it wasn't possible that I could be so closely connected to the world that I could have any significant impact on it just by my state of being at any given moment (or throughout my life).

Because it was "me" experiencing the world, then of course the world would change as I changed: my point of view was shifting, or being contaminated by my own mental state at the moment.

This assumption was the result of my training in science.

SCIENCE: MAKING DISTINCTIONS AND SEPARATING THINGS

Science is something unique to those cultures who were influenced by the Greeks. In Indian, Chinese, and Native American cultures, there is no equivalent. They have philosophy and spirituality, which integrate what we call science with what we call mysticism, but not what we would refer to as a pure science.

Two of the primary tenets of science are that things are ultimately divisible into tiny, definable building-blocks, and that for there to be a "true" reality, the observer must be separate from the observed. In our dreams, we're both the observer and the observed: it's "unreal." In daily life, we're the observer and the things around us, separate from us, are the observed: they're "real."

In this world-view, the entire universe can be separated into pieces, the first and primary division being that of observer and observed, subjective and objective. Science believed (and Aristotle, Descartes and others taught) that if the subjective observer could rid himself of his personal and instrumentational subjectivity and identify all the relevant factors, then a truly objective "truth" about the world and reality could be seen, measured, or determined.

This belief, accepted as an absolute truth and the underpinning of our modern culture, led to viewing humankind as separate from the natural world.

The classic question "If a tree falls in the forest and there's nobody there to hear it, is a sound made?" assumes that the "nobody there to hear it" would be human. Only humans, so the story went, were capable of classifying and separating things, breaking them into pieces as Aristotle taught us, and understanding their separate meanings. Only humans would recognize sound as "sound." (Some people would say, "Well, if there were animals, they could certainly recognize a sound and you could see this by their reaction to it." So then the question becomes "What if there were only vegetables? Would there be a sound then? Or what if everything was 'dead' and there were only minerals? What then?")

But as science divided matter into smaller and smaller pieces, a disturbing trend began to emerge. It was found that supposedly inanimate matter seemed to be affected by the act of observing.

The first response to this was Heisenberg's Uncertainty Principle, which stated that things were constantly in a state of flux and so if anything were observed at any moment, by the time the observation itself was made, things had already changed. Therefore it was impossible to ever "truly and absolutely" observe anything, because by the time we'd registered the observation, by the time the photons of light had hit the retina of our eye, the thing we were observing had already changed.

It was also noted that the act of observing was not purely passive: with an electron microscope, for example, electrons are bounced off of, or passed through, things, to produce an image for viewing. Similarly, a conventional microscope only works when photons of light bounce off the specimen and into your eye. Light and electrons are bits of matter or energy that could have a demonstrable effect on the things being observed, further increasing the uncertainty of the accuracy of the observation. Heisenberg went so far as to say that the exact location of anything in time and space could never be known, regardless of method or instrumentation.

So, it seemed, we really couldn't "know" anything as an absolute and "real" state. All we can do is engineering: working with things because they work (such as electricity), even though we don't know *why* or *how* they work (as is, in fact, the case with electricity). This allows us to manipulate the world around us, to build machines and make things work, but it also leads us to the dangerous assumption that to be able to use something is to "know" it.

This is mirrored in human nature, too. We're constantly affected by our experience of life, and our experiences change our personality, our world-view, and our behaviors. I'm not now the person I was before I met Herr Müller , nor am I now the same person I was just a week ago or even one minute ago. We grow, change, and are constantly in a state of flux. And this provides us with an opportunity to develop the spiritual sides of ourselves, and—by doing this—to make the entire planet more spiritual.

So, this aspect of the scientific approach turned out to be wrong: it is in fact not possible to separate the observer from the observed.

SOME INSTITUTIONS GROW IN INFLUENCE BY SEPARATING THEMSELVES FROM US

Recently I was waiting for a flight to depart in an airport lounge, and a situation comedy was on the TV. As I walked by, I heard the lead character ("Drew") say that he wanted to be a minister. It caught my interest and, not having watched prime-time TV in a few years, I sat down, curious.

The star of the show wanted to become a pastor in an unidentified Christian denomination. He went to the local church's priest with a test he'd taken (he was ultimately rejected because he hadn't answered the questions correctly). While the pastor was out of the room, the show's hero practiced from the pulpit: "All stand, all sit, all stand, all sit. . . ." He—and the studio audience—seemed to derive great delight from his vicarious exercise of power over the imagined congregation.

The dramatic high point came while he was in the church alone pretending to be the minister and a woman came in from the street and presented him with a moral dilemma: should she take a drug dealer's money to feed her hungry child?

While this was interesting (and, at times, funny in the way it was presented), what struck me were the assumptions the show presumably shared with its viewing audience: that the "hard work" of the pastor in a church was to interpret the legal issues of morality, and the "fun work" was to lord over people, exercising personal power over them.

Master Stanley, Herr Müller, and John Davis all provided me with a totally opposite role model in this regard. None was or is interested in legalisms or personal power. And all were touched by the importance of *sharing the experience of spiritual insight.*

I believe this illustrates the difference between spirituality and religion. From my experience, religion is about the rules and regulations, systems and hierarchies, the order of succession and the perpetuation of the religious *institution*. Ultimately, it's about power.

Spirituality, on the other hand, is about personal, individual, intense, and often even secret experiences of the presence of G-d.

After a few minutes of initial laughter, I watched that TV show with a growing sadness. Clearly, this is how many Americans view their religious experiences or opportunities—as being under the power of another, or having to worry about legalisms from a book written thousands of years ago. They are what Herr Müller calls the "TV People," the lost souls of the world who have disconnected from the possibility of spiritual experience, who have bought in totally to modern culture.

I am not a perfect person: far from it, I am regularly afflicted by lust, anger, greed, sloth, and any other of the "deadly sins." But simply by believing that miracles were possible, and then searching for them, I have touched spiritual insights and experiences which some would call miraculous.

I don't consider these miracles, not by the definition of their being something normally unavailable except by divine intervention. In my opinion, such states, experiences, and insights are available to all humans, and it is only our acculturation that causes people to think such experiences are odd, abnormal, or unavailable to them.

The true basis of religion is spirituality. I believe that everybody, regardless of their behaviors, is really seeking love. We want to be accepted, loved, and to touch bliss.

Often our methods have been twisted by upbringing and environment. Nonetheless, I believe that all humans—even the most depraved—are engaging in their particular behaviors because they're ultimately seeking profound and transcendental spiritual experience. That experience is available to ordinary people; I've seen it happen with hundreds of individuals.

But most of our contemporary religious and economic institutions keep this possibility hidden. I long found this puzzling, but then I think back to how the Roman Empire subsumed early Christianity (a grass roots movement) and built an organization with centralized control. I saw why our institutions today would still benefit from it: spiritually empowered individuals in a society means disempowered "spiritual leaders."

I saw that it's in the nature of power-seekers to tell others they're incapable, that they're basically bad, that they need guidance—guidance that ought to come, of course, from whichever power-seeker happens to be speaking.

In a word, that relationship, however well-intentioned each individual may be, is about dominance. And dominance requires that one party be separated from the other.

That stands in stark contrast to the non-dominant, empowering, inclusive example I'd experienced with Master Stanley and my other mentors.

In fact, I believe that the capability of experiencing transcendental states is built into all of us, and have found that a surprising number of otherwise "normal" people have known such states but are reluctant to discuss them in "polite company." The ability and desire to achieve altered states is part and parcel of our humanness.

But another level deeper than this is the issue of holiness and holy people. While I don't believe that graduation from a seminary or ordination confers on one spiritual insights, I do know from my own personal experience that there are many people in the world who have had extraordinarily spiritual insights, and even a few who are capable of helping evoke those types of experiences in others.

But just like those who have a very elegant grasp of mathematics or literature, or eloquent speaking abilities, having these insights and abilities doesn't necessarily ensure a state of enlightenment. The assumption that they do is one that has led many people into spiritual and real-world dead-ends.

EACH OF US IS CONNECTED TO SPIRITUAL TRUTH

I'm convinced that spiritual insights and experiences are available to everybody, all the time. The capability of experiencing the divine is hard-wired into the brains and nervous systems of all humans, and virtually everybody touches the lowest level of these ecstatic states when they fall in love. *We're designed to be able to know G-d.*

Similarly, Jesus quite bluntly said, "These things that I have done (referring to His 'miracles'), you shall do also. And even greater things than these, because I must now go back to be with my Father." So even the ability to manipulate the stuff of "reality" is within us, He said.

Often, however, what happens is that somebody works at gaining spiritual insights until they have some rather powerful experiences and the certainty of spiritual realities that comes along with them. Through the strength of their passion (derived from their experience), or because they've gone the next step and actually learned how to confer "spiritual experiences" on others, they draw people like a magnet. Everybody, I'm convinced, is hungry for the experience of G-d, deep down in the inner-most reaches of their souls. So if a person can do "magic tricks" (to use Master Hamid Bey's term), then people will be attracted to her/him and may even begin to deify her/him.

I know this is so because I've experienced it myself. The main reason why I quit teaching about spiritual matters in Michigan, and then again a decade later in Atlanta, was because people were beginning to "guru-ize" me. While I'm perfectly willing to teach and share, and even to move energy around to the extent that I can, I am not a guru, not a savior, nor even a particularly holy human being. I've broken many of the laws of human and societal conduct, I'm regularly afflicted by the temptations of living in these human bodies, and I'm far from perfect.

But while the truly spiritual back away when people try to build a pedestal for them to climb onto, I've observed that there are many people in the world who not only embrace the idea of being a guru, but will even build and bring to the party their own pedestal.

Herr Müller, Master Stanley, and Master Hamid Bey are not in that group, and would not take on such people as students. All of these men, while having what are to me extraordinary spiritual knowledge, insights, and powers, are very clear and up-front about not wanting to exercise power over any other individual. They do what they do out of love and commitment and obligation to G-d, not out of a desire to seek power or gather followers for their own self-aggrandizement.

As such, they put into practice the truth that the most important spiritual work we can do is internal.

So often we demand changes in others, but it's our state that has the greatest impact on the world. Each of us as individuals, walking along our own personal paths to enlightenment, enlightens the entire universe. Our small acts of mercy, our filling our rituals with an awareness of spirit, our striving to live with ever-increasing integrity and purity: they all raise all of humanity and all of creation.

This is true spiritual power, as I was to vividly feel when I began my own full-time work with Salem.

Starting Salem in New Hampshire

He who helps in the saving of others, saves himself as well.
—HARTMANN VON AUE

In July and August of 1978, Herr Müller's children's orchestra came for four weeks to the U.S. and toured the halls which he had requested and which Louise Sutermeister and I had set up and publicized, as well as taking a trip to Florida. I traveled with him and the kids, and in each city, Herr Müller gave speeches to groups of invited guests.

In one city, only two people showed up to hear him. He knocked himself out, giving a powerful and enthusiastic speech about Salem, the coming times, the work he was doing. He was dramatic, dynamic, and moving.

Afterward, I asked him why he'd gone to so much trouble for just two people: he could have just sat with them and talked.

"When only a few people show up, then you know it is the most important speech you must give," he said. "Just as when a person donates only one dollar to Salem, that is the most important donation." It reminded me of the story Jesus told in the Bible about the widow who could only afford to give a few mites (pennies) and how her contribution was more important and spiritually powerful than those of the wealthy elite. Similarly, one person has often been at the pivot point of world changes. If that one person happened to be in an audience which only had a few people—or even only that one person—then giving that speech may be the event which could eventually lead to the transformation of the world.

The last week of July, I flew home to help my wife, Louise, give birth to our second child. After the horrific experience we had with our first in a suburban Detroit hospital where the doctor showed up late and drunk (it was Christmas Eve) and the nurses tied Louise down to the bed and forced her knees together until he arrived, we decided to deliver our second at home.* A friend was a midwife and she joined us, and another friend who was an M.D. and lived nearby was "on call" for us. In preparation, Louise had attended several births with our midwife friend, and I'd joined in helping our neighbors deliver their baby at home. After two hours of labor, about three in the morning, Justin slid out into my hands. It was a miracle! We gave him the middle name of Noah because Herr Müller so often referred to Salem villages as "arks" in a sea of chaos and turbulence and his birth seemed to signal a turning point in our lives in that direction.

A week later, Louise, Justin, and I flew to Washington to see the Salem orchestra perform at Kennedy Center and attend a dinner for Herr Müller that Louise Sutermeister had arranged at the Watergate Hotel. It was a gala event, with some of the biggest names in Washington society as sponsors, including Maestro Rostipovich and Celeste Holme.

It was the end of the tour, and the logical end of my association with Herr Müller. I'd done the job he'd hired me to do (although I never ended up sending him a bill because of the events which followed shortly), and the reasonable thing to do now would be to return to Michigan and continue with my radio program, the advertising agency, and the herbal company; back to my old, crumbling mansion built by R. E. Olds (founder of Oldsmobile) and our new Volvos. Back to making money and being spiritually unfulfilled. But I wasn't prepared to do that, and had been wondering if and how I could reorganize things to work more closely with Herr Müller.

As we ate delicious vegetarian meals prepared by the hotel's staff, Herr Müller turned to me and said, bluntly, "Why don't you sell your business and join us in this work?"

I felt like he had put a knife into my heart. It was everything I wanted, and yet also so many things that I feared. So much change; so much to leave behind.

---

*For a wonderful discussion of the differences between midwives and American obstetrics, see John Robbins's book *Reclaiming Our Health* (1996).

I looked at my wife. Louise, breast-feeding Justin, smiled and nodded in affirmation.

"Ok," I said. "'What should we do?"

He shrugged. "Start out by helping Louise Sutermeister raise money for Salem here in America."

And so we went back to Michigan, arranged to sell and transfer our businesses, quit my part-time job at WITL radio station, and in October of 1978 moved to New Hampshire. For the first half-year, I tried to raise money for the Maryland program, but it was not to be. I gave speeches and visited donors, but nobody wanted to give money to somebody who wasn't "doing the work" themselves. So, Louise (Hartmann) and I decided we should start our own Salem program in New Hampshire.

We began by taking three foster children into our home. Louise did most of the child care, while I did fundraising, gave speeches, and wrote grant applications. I created a nonprofit corporation, and jumped through the hoops the state provided in order to get a license as a group home and, eventually, a residential treatment facility.

Over the next few years, as word spread, we drew some wonderful people to help us, and donations came as a result of our PR and fundraising efforts. We moved up north to a rental property on Stinson Lake in Rumney, and in 1979 opened several houses for kids.

The first of our first two houses was an old, white building that once was a summer camp and at another time a school. It had started out as a farmhouse, overlooking the lake, but several additions followed in the hundred years or so since it was first built. Children and houseparents lived in the old house part, and staff and a school we started filled the other quarters. It was located several miles up a long, winding mountain road to nearly the top of Stinson Mountain, where Stinson Lake settled like a filled-in volcanic caldera.

Next door to "the white house" was "the brown house," an old four-bedroom vacation house that we re-insulated and that became home to a second "family" of six children.

The edges of the road were the beginnings of the White Mountain National Forest, about 20 miles west of Plymouth, and, local lore said, the woods extended without a stop all the way up through the state, into Canadian forest land, and all the way on up to the Arctic Circle. Bears, moose, foxes, deer, and wild turkeys would occasionally show up in our yards or forage through our trash.

The children we took in were, in Herr Müller's paraphrasing of the Bible, the least of the least. They were the children who had been rejected by one after another foster family, often rejected by other institutions, and some even came to us from the state mental hospital or the state-run prisons for children. As one of our houseparents told J. Tevere MacFadyen, who wrote a marvelous article about us for *Country Journal* magazine, "These kids here are those who by definition couldn't make it in a family. That's why they're in a group home. We've had one girl, thirteen years old, who'd been through twenty-nine foster homes before she got here. At the last one she broke her foster mother's leg with an iron. These kids eat foster parents for breakfast. They just run right through them, burn them out, and when it becomes evident to the social worker that they're not going to make it in a foster home, they go into an institution."

On the other hand, the reason these kids are so tough is because they've been given nothing but hell all their lives. They arrive with dossiers an inch thick, often with broken bones, cigarette burns, or the psychic scars of emotional or sexual abuse. One boy came into the program after having been drugged in another institution to the point of drooling with Thorazine, a powerful antipsychotic, and was often tied to his bed for days at a time. After a few years with us, without drugs or restraint, he graduated from high school with honors.

The "magic" part of our formula, in my opinion, was Herr Müller's revelation about the need for family. Those of us who grew up in a "normal" home tend to take family for granted. As Robert Frost said in "The Death of the Hired Man," "Home is the place where, when you have to go there, they have to take you in." I've always known that if worse came to worst I could turn to my parents, siblings, and extended family for help and support. That knowledge has enabled me to take chances and step out into areas that others may consider adventurous, and provided me with a lifelong sense of security.

But these children usually have no place to call home, no safe place where they can return and be accepted. Such a reality is unthinkably frightening to most of us, even as adults: imagine how terrifying it must be for a child.

So instead of throwing kids out of the program when they reach 17 or 18 and the funding stops, they're told that they're always welcome. They can stay if they need (although, as in a normal family, we work to help them become self-reliant out in the real world and make the transition to adult independence). If they hit a rough time in their lives in the future, they're always welcome to come back.

In 1981 I went into Uganda for Salem with comedian and social activist Dick Gregory. On our way to Africa we stopped at the Salem Children's Village in Stadtsteinach. It was a week or two before Christmas, as I recall, and we had dinner with one of the families. In addition to the six or seven children in the home with their houseparents and helpers, there were two young men in their early twenties at the table.

"Who are they?" Dick asked the houseparents.

"They grew up here," the housemother answered, "and one is now in the army and the other has a job in Frankfurt. But they came home for Christmas."

Home was the core, the central and most effective therapy.

Our treatment plans drew heavily on the work of Alfred Adler, Rudolph Drykers, and others who advocate "logical consequences" instead of punishment. Children must learn that there are consequences to their actions, and that they have choices in life. When they grow up, there won't be people to follow them around and dose them with drugs or restrain them if they get out of control: life's lessons began at Salem with learning to put away the bicycle, clean up one's own messes, and interact rationally with other children and adults.

Within a year of the time we moved up to Rumney, we had three sets of houseparents, twelve children, a teacher, a cook, a carpenter, a child care assistant, a secretary, a therapeutic Program Director, and I was the Executive Director. We hired part-time therapists, psychologists, and psychiatrists to work with the children individually and to train and consult with our staff on a regular basis.

We were blessed with some truly brilliant individuals: Ken, our cook, ended up writing numerous hot-selling cookbooks in later years; Barbara stayed in child care and teaching; one of our houseparents earned his Ph.D. in divinity school, while others moved into other related social-work fields. A man in his late sixties, "Grandpa Irving," stayed with us nearly a year and lent a multi-generational flavor to the program as well as teaching us all about how to most efficiently gather firewood from the forest and plant vegetables. At that time, everybody was earning between $25 and $112 per week, plus room and board. We became a community as much as an institution, and there was an intense sense of camaraderie.

As word about us spread and we were written up in *Country Journal, East-West Journal, New Age Journal, Mother Earth News, Prevention,* and other similar publications, we drew an advisory board of famous vegetarians. I spent several evenings in New York at the apartment of Gloria Swanson, who lent her name to our work and loved to cook vegetarian meals with me. Dennis Weaver and his family did two fundraising concerts for us, as did Dick Gregory. National Public Radio sent Sanford Unger and Nina Ellis up to do a report on us, and that 18-minute segment—the longest they'd ever run up to that time on the *All Things Considered* show—drew what Unger later described to me as "one of the biggest responses we've ever had to that type of piece on the show."

As time went on, we learned that 137 acres on the other side of the lake was for sale, and, through a series of events I can only call miraculous (described later in this book), we were able to buy the land and begin building houses.

A half-dozen or so young men and women, most in their early twenties, volunteered for the brutal job of building a passive solar house from scratch throughout the course of the harsh New Hampshire winter. These courageous volunteers, particularly Daniel, Sam, Anita, and Michael, referred to themselves as "the Siberians," and lent an even stronger sense of mission to our work as they labored in the freezing temperatures, often for ten or more hours a day, until the first house was completed and we were ready to move the program from one side of the lake to the other.

A SECOND VISIT BY ANGELS

Soon after we'd purchased the land on Stinson Lake for the children's village, Herr Müller mentioned angels to me a second time in more than an abstract sense.

In the past, he'd often said that each child who came to live at Salem, because of their circumstances of severe abuse or abandonment, brought with him or her an angel, and that such a collection of children represented a powerful collection of spiritual forces . . . as well as a lot of noise and kinetic energy.

But in 1980 he again saw angels in my presence, this time with a startling ferocity.

We went down to the lake, to an area that wouldn't normally be frequented by people, and he told me a story his mentor, Abram Poljak, had told him forty years earlier. It seems that when Abraham wandered through the desert for years, wherever he found an important "power point" on the Earth, he'd build an altar. Generations later, when Moses was again wandering through the same desert, he'd invariably come upon these old altars, even though they were now the victims of time, usually hidden by the sands. The altars aligned the powers of the Earth, Herr Müller said, and, like a dowsing rod, allowed the planet's spiritual energies to flow through the people who prayed at them (as Master Hamid Bey believed was the purpose of the pyramids).

So, Herr Müller said, we should build an altar on the new Salem property to have a place to pray for the success of Salem and for the lives of our children. It would be, as were most of the spiritual things he taught me, something we wouldn't tell the staff and others about unless they had a genuine interest. But it must be done.

So we wandered around the area for a few minutes, gathering up twelve stones ranging in size from that of an orange to that of a grapefruit. He said that Abraham probably used larger stones, but that it didn't really matter.

We piled the stones together in a spot that Herr Müller said felt right to him, and he pulled from his pocket a small bottle with a medicinal label on it.

"Are you familiar with the Rock of Moriah?" he asked.

I said I was not, although I remembered the song that referred to the wind by that name.

"In Israel," he said, "there is an area where once Solomon had his temple. It was destroyed and rebuilt so many times over the years that the area where his temple was is now located thirty meters underground. This temple also housed the Holy of Holies and the Ark of the Covenant, and so there are signs all around the area signed by the head Rabbi of Jerusalem warning Jews not to walk on that area because they may accidentally stray over the top of the area of the Holy of Holies, and therefore accidentally defile all of Israel and bring a curse upon the country. This is the area that is behind the Western Wall, also called the Wailing Wall, which you must visit one day. When you pray at the Wailing Wall you are standing in front of the area where Solomon once had his temple: it is now buried in the earth behind the wall.

"This area behind the Wall was not entirely flat in ancient times, and in one area there was a steep hill. At the top of this hill is a huge boulder, and it was on this rock, sometimes called the Rock of Moriah, that it is said Abraham brought Isaac to sacrifice him. The Arabs, however, also hold it holy because they believe that it was from this rock that Mohammed leaped up to heaven at the end of his earthly life. So when the Arabs controlled Jerusalem, they built a mosque around this rock, and this mosque is called the Dome of the Rock. It's the golden dome you see in tourism pictures of Jerusalem.

"This rock, then, is one of the most powerful and holy places on Earth. It was on the hill next to the temple Solomon built, where Jesus first revealed himself: probably He prayed there, also. So I went in there one day with a little bit of oil in a small bottle and, when nobody was looking, poured it on the rock. I then collected as much of it as I could back into the bottle, and that is this oil." He waved the bottle in my direction. "We shall use it to anoint this altar."

He poured a few drops of the oil onto the pile of stones and we stood on opposite sides of it. Replacing the bottle in his pocket, he told me to hold out my hands so my palms were facing the altar, and to close my eyes. I did so, and he chanted a prayer in Hebrew, which I later learned was the Aaronic blessing. Here is how it sounded to me (I later asked him to repeat it and I wrote it down phonetically):

Yev aracchecha Ya (silently the HWH or say Adonai), *vi-yesh merecha, yo er Ya* (silently) (or Adonai), *panaf elecho vicho necho. Yeso Adonai* (or Ya) *panaf elecho vi yosem lich-ha shalom.*"

After this, he asked me to say a prayer in English. Remembering the Sermon on the Mount, Herr Müller's favorite set of instructions from the Bible, I recited the Lord's Prayer from that chapter of Matthew.

After I finished, I stood with my hands out and eyes closed, expecting him to say "amen" or some such thing, but instead there was a strange silence. I could hear the wind in the trees and nearby birds and the soft lap of water at the edge of the lake, but could no longer hear

Herr Müller's breathing. I wondered if he'd walked away while I was praying, and so cracked open my eyelids to sneak a look in his direction.

He was as motionless as a statue. His face was turned up toward the sky, his eyes open but unmoving, his arms at his sides. His mouth was open in a small o, as if he'd been surprised and then frozen in that position. He was not breathing.

My first thought was that he'd had a heart attack or a stroke. He was, after all, pushing seventy.

Then he shuddered, and turned his face toward me. His eyes moved frantically from side to side, glancing around my face, at the air around me, into the treetops and across the lake.

"Do you hear them?" he said in a loud whisper, as if he were afraid his words would disturb something.

He grabbed my arm and gripped me so hard it hurt; his hand was trembling, and tears appeared in his eyes, then rolled down his cheeks into his beard and mustache. "Don't you hear them? You must hear them! They're singing!!" He was now no longer whispering; his voice was half-cry and half-scream. "They're singing to us!!"

He fell on his knees, bringing me down to the ground with him.

"Listen!" he screamed at me, shaking my arm. "Listen to them!!"

I closed my eyes, feeling the pain of his hand gripping my arm, his body trembling, hearing his sniffling as the tears filled his sinuses, but I couldn't hear anybody singing. After a few minutes, I said, "Who's singing?"

His voice was again a whisper. "The angels." He shook me and I opened my eyes to look into his. The earth was cold and damp on my knees and the wind rustled the leaves in the trees. "They're finished now," he said. "They gave us and this place their blessing."

There is no doubt in my mind that the experience of the angels in both these situations was absolutely real for Herr Müller , as real as I experienced seeing the office buildings or the trees. Had it been merely a story I'd read, or a second-hand tale, I may have been skeptical, but he was really seeing angels. Whether they were "there" or "hallucinated" is really beside the point: it was, for him, an utter and undeniable reality.

Watching him go through those experiences strengthened my belief both in the possibility of seeing angels and in the inner reality of the world of spirit to him. It gave me hope, strengthened my belief, and put another crack into my rationalist skepticism. Whether the place was blessed by the angels themselves or by the power of Herr Müller's faith, I know that today when I go down to that lake in New Hampshire to pray, I feel a lightness and purity and presence that I rarely experience in other places on this planet.*

As we walked back up the steep hill, it occurred to me that he'd always used his right hand when giving blessings, and on the rare occasions I'd seen him bless others. I'd also seen him hold up his right hand as if he were pointing his palm at somebody when I knew that he was silently blessing them, often from across the room, often when they didn't even know he was doing it, didn't even know who he was. I'd seen him do that with some of the sick people who'd come to the clinic in Stadtsteinach.

"Why do you always use your right hand when you're giving a blessing?" I asked him as we walked along the trail, wondering if he was familiar with the ancient doctrines of Vedic medicine that the right hand could convey healing power, or Master Stanley's teaching of a technique to move spiritual energy with the right hand.

He shrugged as if the answer was commonsense. "The right hand is the one from which light can be sent to others. The left hand is the receptive hand. If you want to send some of G-d's light to somebody, just point your right palm at them and visualize and feel and hear the light coming from it and going into them. Sometimes you can actually see them stand a little straighter, walk with a better spring in their step."

An idea occurred to me. "In the Bible, Jesus said that when somebody asks for help we shouldn't turn away from them. Yet in some

---

*When Dave deBronkart, who'd helped edit one of my first books and did major editing on this one, read this chapter in early draft, he dropped me a note saying: "At some point you might want to inject the story of when I first set foot at Salem in New Hampshire. Do you remember what I said, having never heard a word of anything in this book? Out of nowhere, I had the unprecedented clear sense that there are forces of good and evil in the world, and that this place is a defiant outpost, doing good no matter what the odds. And that was before I'd ever heard anything of the spiritual story behind Salem."

places there are so many beggars, or, like in New York, there are people who are begging as a way of life, a way of earning their income."

"*Ja,*" he said.

"So how about instead of giving them money, I give them a blessing?"

He laughed. "Of course. Even if you give them money, it is more important to give them the blessing."

"Point my palm at them and send them light?"

"Of course," he said. "But do not be like the priests about it. You must do your works in secret."

"Discreetly give them a blessing?"

"Of course. If you make a great show of it, then it is not a blessing but just a show. Do not do it for yourself, or even for them. Do it for G-d."

"But you've given me overt blessings, telling me that you were giving me a blessing. Are those of less importance?"

"No. I do that because you understand what we are doing, and you take it seriously." He smiled. "And sometimes a show is useful for somebody's spiritual progress, as Jesus said in his last prayer in the garden. But do not mistake the show for the real blessing, which still must be done in secret."

Since I've started sending light like this, and shared the technique with a few others, I've found it both an inner inspiration and a powerful spiritual exercise. It builds empathy, and connects me to others in a new way. And, I believe, it adds more light—and, therefore, more peace—to the world.

Once Herr Müller commented to me: "I live like a king. I have the best food, the best friends, horses to ride, a forest to walk in, and a work that I would pay to do if I had to. What could be better?" This from a man who owns only his clothes and books, and a bit of furniture.

But the fact is that Salem work (or any type of service work) should only be done for the fire in the work, the joy of doing it that's derived *right then and there.*

People who do things because they expect to be rewarded in heaven are often not alive: they're living in a future that has not yet come. (Those who avoid things because of a fear of hell are not living in the moment, either.)

While heaven may be a useful side-effect of the work, it's only a small part of why one should do the work.

The clearest, most real motivation comes from the knowledge that the quality of the work we do, the spiritual vibration it spreads around, is based on the reasons for our doing it. If we do things as martyrs, we are merely spreading around martyrdom. The value of that is pretty minimal, and, as in the case of the suicide bombers we've seen so much of lately, can even be profoundly destructive.

But if we do our work out of joy, love, and an enthusiasm borne of the work itself—be it meditation and prayer, feeding the hungry, caring for the sick, building community, or whatever—then we're pumping into the world joy, love, and a general lightening of the vibratory universe we all live in.

For example, when Herr Müller decided he wanted to reduce the number of animals who were unnecessarily suffering because of medical and cosmetic experimentation (vivisection), he didn't go out and bomb research laboratories or try to portray scientists as evil people. He didn't go out into the world with hatred or anger.

Instead, he created The Salem Research Institute, hired a biochemist and a few other scientists, and compiled a two-inch-thick hardcover book published in English which chronicled tens of thousands of experiments where working with human tissue in culture (in a petri dish) was a more effective—*and cheaper*—way of doing research than using animals. (One of the best examples: human tissue sample tests showed that Thalidomide had the potential to cause mutations, but the studies on rabbits required by the British equivalent of America's FDA didn't show such activity. So the product went to market as a "proven safe cure" for morning sickness even as some scientists working with human tissues were worrying out loud that it might cause birth defects.)

After compiling all this research, and other books with information about how and where to obtain human tissue cultures and how to do research on it, he sent his scientists out to all the big drug and cosmetics companies to talk with their directors of research about ways they could both save money and produce more valid research results. The result was that many companies changed their policies, and millions of animals were spared from vivisection.

They were campaigning against vivisection, but not in a way that spread the vibration or energy of war and opposition. He reframed the idea of research, and thus changed the world for the better. And he did it from a place of cooperation and help, not saintliness or martyrdom or a crusader's zeal.

Salem's efforts to reform the child care systems in Europe and the United States were similar: when we'd speak at conferences about the advantage of family-based residential treatment models we didn't talk much about how it was "right" or "good" or anything like that. Instead, we talked about how it would reduce the number of children in care who would grow up to become "institution-created criminals" and thus add to the financial and social burdens of the government organizations funding child care.

Similarly, when I talk about teaching meditation or doing the Salem work, even the painful things such as working in the slums of Bogota or ducking bullets in war-torn Uganda, please don't think of me (or think that *I* think of me) as a saint or a martyr. I do these things because they're more self-actualizing than anything else I've ever known, and because I love to be fully alive in the moment. Hopefully that was the vibration I was spreading through both the work and the world as I was doing those things, and am now helping to create in talking about and showing them to people.

The years at Salem in New Hampshire taught Louise and me more about ourselves and our capabilities than any other time of our lives. They gave us a vivid insight, a powerful feeling, of our purpose for incarnating into this Earth.

The people we worked with, both at that time and in conversations in later years, have shared with me similar comments about their own experience of working at Salem.

From this, I've come to firmly believe that when we help others, even in small ways such as by sharing smiles or unnoticed acts of kindness, we come closer to our own enlightenment, our own salvation. As so many before us have found, serving others is one of the most useful routes to spiritual transformation.

Herr Müller
Meets a Priest

A handful of sand is an anthology of the universe.
—DAVID MCCORD, *ONCE AND FOR ALL*

When we took the first three children into our new home in New Hampshire, our first challenge was finding a competent therapist who could help them work through many of the issues which had led to their being in the child welfare system. Judy, a social worker we'd grown close to, recommended a woman she knew who was working in a program with kids in Nashua, and we spoke to her about our search for somebody with solid psychotherapeutic credentials and experience. Her name was Shelley, and she recommended we meet and talk with her fiancée, Hal Cohen.

Hal was (and is) one of those Truly Good Human Beings. Tall, bearded, and good looking, he was known to one of our kids as "a friendly bear." We met, hit it off, and he agreed to do weekly therapy with the kids on a freelance basis.

Over the next year, we found the land on Stinson Lake and moved up there along with John and Nancy Roy, our first houseparents. Now, more than a therapist, we needed a program director. I asked Hal if he'd consider the job, and he agreed to come work with Louise, me, John, Nancy, and the others then at Salem in New Hampshire.

Hal was Jewish, and intensely so. He'd studied Kabbalah and other mystical traditions, and had a rich and deep insight into the Old Testament. Discussing spirituality quickly became our mutually favorite spare-time activity. He introduced me to Kabbalah and gave me copies of The Ten Luminous Emanations, walking me through many of the concepts one at a time. We studied Isaiah and the Psalms together, and good-naturedly discussed Messianic prophecy.

He taught me Hebrew and I shared with him what I knew of Christianity. Neither of us was out to "convert" the other: it was as if we were long-lost brothers of the same Father who just happened to have grown up in different towns.

A few weeks after Hal started working full-time as Program Director of Salem, I called Herr Müller in Germany and mentioned the addition to our staff.

"He's a Cohen?" Herr Müller said. It was a curious question, not implying anything negative.

'Yes," I said.

"A Cohen? Do you know what that means?" he said.

"No. I thought it was a pretty common name."

"The name Cohen means he's a priest," Herr Müller said. His voice became thoughtful. "It must be why he came to you."

'You'll like him," I said.

"I know him already," Herr Müller said. "I've been waiting for him to come to Salem."

I wondered if his reference had to do with Abram Poljak, his Jewish mentor, but didn't want to get into it during our phone conversation. "When can you next come over here?" I asked.

"In a few weeks," he said. "This is important, you know? Spiritually, before G-d, this is important."

A few weeks later, I picked Herr Müller up from the Boston airport and brought him up to Salem. He met Hal and went for several long walks with him. They clearly liked each other.

On the last day of his two-day visit, the three of us met in my office and had a very long and interesting discussion about the nature of the soul and the possibility of reincarnation, as presented in Kabbalistic teachings. It seemed to me that Herr Müller was "getting the flavor" of Hal and learning from him, both at the same time. And apparently that was the case, because at the end of our discussion, Herr Müller did an extraordinary thing.

He was sitting on the couch in my office, Hal sitting next to him. I was in my office chair, facing them. Herr Müller said, "Hal, would you please give me your blessing?"

"My blessing?" Hal said, somewhat taken aback.

"Yes," Herr Müller said. "You are not only a Cohen in name, you are truly a priest. And so you have a duty: you must give a blessing. And here I am, asking you for a blessing."

"How?" Hal said.

'Put your hands on my head and say the Aaronic blessing. Do you know it?"

Hal knew the first few sentences in English, and about half of it in Hebrew, but Herr Müller wanted it done entirely in Hebrew, so he walked Hal through the entire prayer. It took about ten minutes. And then Hal put his hands on Herr Müller 's head and said the prayer. (In my memory, Herr Müller was on his knees: Hal told me in 1996 that he was pretty sure Herr Müller had just sat on the couch and he stood over him.) As I stood watching, I fought back a lump in my throat. Herr Müller became so child-like, so innocent, and Hal assumed a presence and strength I'd not seen before in him. The experience changed both of them, and it changed me as well.

Afterward, Herr Müller's eyes were shining and his face had taken on a pink glow. "Thank you," he said, his voice now soft as if he had been given a great gift.

Hal, realizing the importance of this to Herr Müller, said, "You're welcome."

Over the next year Hal and Shelley visited Herr Müller in Germany, where Herr Müller gave Hal a blessing back. Herr Müller often talked to me about what a gift from G-d it was that Hal was with us at Salem, and encouraged me to learn as much from him as I could.

One day Herr Müller came back to visit us in New Hampshire and, while he and Hal and I were sitting in my office having one of our perennial discussions about spirituality and the coming times, Herr Müller said to Hal, "Have you ever thought of going to Israel?"

"All the time," Hal said. "I've always wanted to live in Israel."

"You should go there, take your spiritual power there," Herr Müller said. "There is an important work for you there."

"Doing what?" Hal said.

"Start a Salem program there!" Herr Müller said.

"But Salem is based in Germany and you guys are Christians. I don't think that would fly so well in Israel."

Herr Müller waved his hand. "You are Jewish, Israel is Jewish, start a Jewish program. You don't need to name it 'Salem,' but don't you think that there are parts of the Salem child care and educational model that you've learned here, that you work with here, that would be good in Israel?"

"No doubt about it," Hal said. "And I'd love to get something started over there."

"Then go with my blessing," Herr Müller said. "I know some people who would like to donate money to a Jewish charity; and I'm sure Thomas does." I nodded: several of our donors were Jewish. "We can help you in the beginning."

It was both a painful and a joyous transition for me. Hal and Shelley moved to Jerusalem and started Orr Shalom, a Jewish program for children that's entirely independent of Salem but applied much of the Salem model of family homes and (Kosher) vegetarian diet to child care in Israel. Louise and I went over to Israel many times during the following years to visit and keep up with Hal and Shelley. Hal, an entrepreneurial powerhouse, built the program up and then, after a half-decade, turned it over to a competent detail-lover to administer. It's still there today, one of the better-run and larger child care charities in Israel, with children's homes nationwide.

Pictures, Images, TV, and the Face of G-d

Thou shalt not make unto thee any graven image.

—EXODUS 20:4

I didn't notice it the first few times I was at Salem in Germany, but slowly it dawned on me: nowhere were there pictures of living things. Nowhere. Not in Herr Müller 's residence, not in his office, not in the Salem children's houses, not in the guest house or clinic—nowhere.

When I first "went to work" for Herr Müller, in 1978, producing the flyer for the children's orchestra tour of the United States, he'd told me he didn't want any pictures of him or the children—or anything else, for that matter—in the brochure. "It'll be more interesting to people if it is just words," he said.

Being in the advertising business, I didn't accept that for a moment. "Pictures always draw the eye faster than words," I said. "They're powerful tools to get people to look at something."

He nodded. "Too powerful."

"What do you mean?"

"There are no pictures of living things at Salem. None in our newsletters, none in our literature, none in our homes. None."

"Why?" I asked, now puzzled.

"Think of somebody you know very well but who you have not seen in several years," he said.

I thought for a moment, and my maternal grandmother came to mind. "Ok,"I said,

"Did you ever see a picture of that person?" he said.

I remembered a picture of my "GaGa" that had sat on my mother's bureau for years after her death. And another image from a home movie my father had made when I was about three, that we'd

93

seen several times, usually when the family was together for Christmas. "Yes," I said. "I've seen pictures of her."

He leaned closer to me. "Can you remember her face, or just the picture of her face?"

I felt disoriented, as if the world had just turned sideways, as my mind raced through the dim recesses of memory looking for memories of my grandmother's face. I remembered her house, the black-and-white kitchen tile, the hardwood floors, the mahogany dining-room table, a green-felt desk blotter. I remembered the house in Charlevoix right down to its smell, the brick building where she worked and the sound of the noon siren, the swing-sets in the playground where we played. But I couldn't remember her face, except from those photos.

He could see my difficulty. "Try somebody more recent," he said. "See if you can remember them from a real moment."

I thought of my father, who I'd seen just a few months earlier. But the image that came to mind was from a picture of him and my mother that my brothers and I had commissioned ten years earlier. I'd spent two weeks with him just a few months earlier, but the picture from my dresser was the dearest image I could recall. I told Herr Müller about this.

"Often that is how it is," he said. "Pictures are frozen in time, while reality flows in time. When you look at something living for a few minutes, it makes millions of little time-moment pictures. But when you see a frozen picture, all those time-moments become filled with the same image. And so it will destroy the other, more fragile, but real images you have in your memory."

"That's why you don't have pictures at Salem?" I said.

"No, that is why G-d gave Moses the commandment."

"That we shouldn't worship idols?"

"It is much more specific than that. And you must know that there are many levels on which one must understand the Bible, not just the literal words."

"So it's against one of the Ten Commandments to have pictures of living things?"

"Yes. And again you see it explained in Deuteronomy."

"And the reason is because pictures are so powerful and unnatural."

"That could be one reason. I do not know G-d's intention."

"And why you have no TV."

"*Ja!* TV is the worst of the 'picture forces.'"

Over the next dozen years or so, I discovered many different religions, from the Jains to the Moslems to many sects of Judaism to the early Lutherans, who agreed with Herr Müller and eschewed pictures of all sorts.

When researching my book *Beyond ADD*, I came across a startling amount of information about how destructive TV can be, and what an insidious and pervasive force it's become in Western civilization. While most people think that the *content* of TV is what's so destructive about it, it turns out that that is really the least important or destructive element of the medium. What I learned in my research is that the coupling of sounds and pictures together in one package is the main way the brain-weakening effect of TV comes about.

For example, brain development in children follows several specific stages, starting just around the time of birth and concluding just after puberty. During these stages* there are small explosions of brain growth, followed by three major periods of brain-cell die-offs. The growth phases prepare the brain to learn and be molded, like giving a sculptor an extra-large chunk of clay to work with. The die-off phases of the brain are when the "extra" connections—those that were not used during the learning phase—are stripped out of the brain in a process called demylenation. If they're not used, these brain connections are cut away the same as a sculptor cuts away and disposes of unwanted clay or stone, leaving behind the finished product.

A vivid example of this is the inability of most people to learn to flawlessly speak a foreign language or to develop perfect pitch after the age of seven or eight. About that time, the second massive demylenation of the brain occurs, and those parts of the brain that would have been able to learn how to perfectly pronounce foreign language sounds are lost forever. So, while people can still learn foreign vocabularies, they'll never speak a new language with the fluency of a native speaker, as they would be able to if they'd learned it before the age of seven.

---

*These stages are outlined in considerable detail in my book *The Edison Gene*, where you can also find the scientific references and additional footnotes.

This is an example of the old cliché "use it or lose it" actually having some truth. If the brain isn't exercised in particular areas before the big demylenations occur a few years after birth, around the age of seven, and around adolescence, then abilities which could have been formed are lost forever.

One of the most important abilities that the brain needs to develop is learning how to instantly and automatically convert language into internal pictures or visual images. Another is the ability to look at one's environment and "see" it in detail, and to be able to translate that seeing into words.

These two skills are at the root of competent memory and abstract thought, and form the core of imagination.

Convening words to pictures is most powerfully learned by hearing stories. Listening to somebody tell stories, or reading stories yourself (although by the time most children learn to read, the first great demylenation has already occurred), have been part of human tradition since the dawn of time when people sat around caves or campfires and shared their experiences on the hunt, or passed down the oral traditions of the tribe from one generation to another.

This process of telling stories to children, particularly ones that require high degrees of visual imagination and empathy, is critical to the development of empathy and imagination. It fires up the parts of the brain that convert words to pictures ensuring that those parts of the brain will not be cut away when the brain releases the demylenating chemicals to strip away unused connections.

Children who do not hear stories when they're young experience a developmental stunting, and permanently lose the ability to visualize, imagine, and, to a large extent, empathize.*

Before television, children were told or read stories, which activated the imagination processes and centers in the brain, converting the heard words into internally seen pictures. Humans have been doing this for two hundred thousand years.

But with TV in a home, parents rarely tell stories to their children, and even when they do it's usually only perfunctory, such as a short

---

*A wealth of information about this can be found in Joseph Chilton Pearce's book *Evolution's End.*

bedtime story. Storytelling and imaginative play don't constitute most of the day as they once did: that's replaced by television viewing and elaborate TV-marketed toys.

Because television stimulates both the auditory and visual centers of the brain simultaneously and, unlike the natural environment, does so in a way that's rich in drama and entertainment, the brain never needs to fully develop its ability to process auditory input into internal visual images. Around age seven, and again around age twelve, substantial chunks of the brain are chemically stripped away and the ability to accomplish these important human functions is lost forever.

It is true that seeing over a dozen violent images an hour on television can cause children to grow up tolerant of (and maybe even enthusiastic about) violence. But a profoundly more destructive consequence of using TV as a baby-sitter and entertainment center is that we have now produced a generation of children lacking in critical thinking skills (so they readily march to the tune of corporate or political agendas that are presented in one-sentence slogans) and lacking in imagination (so they don't question the "wisdom" of being a good little drone in a corporate world). While this is advantageous for corporate advertisers and political demagogues, some, like Joseph Chilton Pearce, see it as an actual reversal in the evolutionary processes of the human race; a "dumbing down" that we see the results of in our crime statistics, and that's so insidious and destructive we will one day see the ultimate result of it in the disintegration of human society.

If you doubt that this is happening in America, please note that our "one-sentence slogans" are becoming even briefer, even dumber: we now have ads whose entire verbal content is "Just do it" or frogs breaking a beer's name into three one-syllable words.

Why are advertisers making this change? Having once been in the advertising business, I can assure you: they do it because it works. They test, test, test, on live audiences, and they do it thoroughly, because they're spending millions of dollars to broadcast those ads. Dumber, simpler slogans are now the most successful way of reaching today's young American mind.

But back to pictures.

On another occasion, Herr Müller asked me if I had yet seen the face of G-d. I told him "no" and asked him how I should go about doing so, and a later letter he sent me best summarizes his words on the subject. He wrote (in German, and then himself translated to English):

Wie seit Gott aus?

In the Lord's prayer we pray to G-d as to our FATHER. Does with us on Earth a father HIDE himself in front of his children? Certainly not. In contrary: a father wants to be with his children, wants to embrace them, wants to make himself visible to them that they may feel his love.

And the children? Are they satisfied if they know that their father is somewhere, but is invisible, so they cannot FEEL him? No, never! The children want to SEE and FEEL the presence of their father!

Exactly the same situation exists between us and G-d our father in front of us, but nearly nobody on Earth—I do not know a single person—has the desire to see the heavenly Father!

But listen! In the Bible you can read: **"You shall search for MY face!"** Therefore people **must** search for G-d's face because of that **commandment**. I myself understood it many years ago and did not stop searching for G-d's face until I saw—as in a cloud, in a fog—something of G-d's figure.

Moses and his brother Aaron spoke with G-d, "face to face," as did Noah and many others. It is a **contempt** to G-d, our Father, that we are not at all interested in searching for Him, to be with Him, to delight in Him.

My search for G-d's face was successful. It is not difficult at all. If you **want** to see Him, if it is your **will!**

"Blessed are the pure in heart, for **they** will see G-d!" (Sermon on the Mount)

Why so late: **after** our life on Earth? Where is it written in the Bible that we have to wait to be "on the other side"? Why not here, just now, and without delay!? The question is, whether we love the heavenly Father so much, that we cannot do anything other but to see, to feel Him, that we are able to tell HIM of our endless LOVE. . .

After receiving this, I asked him what it would take to see G-d's face. He replied (in his own English):

"Blessed are the pure in heart, for they will see G-d!"

To the "pure heart" not only is belonging to the pure heart as spiritually seen.

A wise man, a Christian, once said to me: "If you want to understand something out of the Bible that you cannot understand, **ask a child!**"

If I ask a child, what is a heart and where the heart is to find, without delay he will show with his hand to his or your heart. Therefore is the "pure heart" of the Sermon on the Mount **also meant earthly material.**

I am sure that it is so!

Therefore is pure or muddy blood in your heart?

Muddy is it through the smoker, but also through everybody who takes other poisons into his body, for example poison from eating dead animals. As soon as meat from dead animals comes into the stomach-intestine channel, it begins to decay (faulen) and produces (Laichengift) poison of carrion, carcass. The blood is poisoned and remains year by year, lifelong . . . if one does not stop that poisoning, that poisoning of the blood, of **the blood of the heart!**

This was a new turning point for me in my meditation. I began to think about seeing G-d's face, looking for His face, and to imagine what it may look like.

On one of my visits to Germany, I said to Herr Müller, "I see G-d's face, or at least what of it I can see, as being Caucasian. Do Africans see Him as Black? And Asians as Asian?"

"Of course," he said. "But you must realize that the face you see is only an aspect of G-d. His true face is light, and light has no specific race or color. It is all colors."

"How do you see G-d's face of light?" I said.

He tapped the center of his forehead. "Use the spiritual eyes, not the physical eyes. For me, I think this is the point of vision, and that is probably where G-d's spiritual eye is."

"When I was with the Coptics, Master Stanley taught us that if we looked at the point between our eyebrows with our eyes closed, eventually we'd see a light, and that light would be the pathway to G-d."

Herr Müller nodded. "That is right," he said. "But most people will never understand that. Only those who have chosen to pursue G-d."*

"Is that what Jesus was referring to when he said, 'If therefore thine eye be single, thy whole body shall be full of light'?"

Herr Müller lifted his hand, palm up. "I do not know, but it probably is so. There are many mysteries."

I could certainly agree with that—those mysteries are at the core of my own lifetime spiritual search.

---

*On several occasions I've seen Herr Müller interacting with "new age" teachers who were a bit full of themselves, confident that they had a lock on what "truth" is. With such people, Herr Müller sometimes plays the role of an old man who is overly fond of red wine, or some other role that he "has been told" that person needs, His goal is to evoke things they must confront within themselves (particularly pomposity!). One such "guru" sadly told me how sorry he was to inform me that Herr Müller was just an old drunk; he left the next morning, and Herr Müller then told me this man was stuck on a path that did not allow expansion or growth. "He's a teacher," Herr Müller said, "but he'll never be a pupil. This is a tragedy, because to know G-d you must first be willing to become like a little child."

The Hundredth Monkey

If you seek the kernel, you must break the shell. And like-
wise, if you would know the reality of nature, you must
destroy the appearance, and the farther you go beyond the
appearance, the nearer you will be to the essence.

—MEISTER ECKHART

Master Stanley used to tell me that *what* I was doing was nowhere near as important as the place within myself from where I was doing it. For example, a person could be teaching others out of a selfless motive, or out of a desire for power or glory: the former had a positive impact on the world, whereas the latter had a negative impact, even though the same identical teaching may have been imparted.

"It's the spirit that's important," he would say. "It's even more important than the act. Going to work in a gas station and providing for your family out of love is more important than creating a mighty religious work out of a desire for glory or power."

I always thought this was pretty solid stuff, and at first put it into the model of psychology I'd learned in school. For example, people can unconsciously sense your true motivations and goals, and that taints the type of learning they experience. If you are pure in your desire to serve or to teach, then they'll sense that and the teaching will be more meaningful or important to them.

But Herr Müller took my understanding of the concept to a whole new level.

In the first months that I knew him, he'd often invite me to go with him for long walks through the mountains behind Salem headquarters in Stadtsteinach. While he walked so fast as to be marching, he'd discuss philosophy and religion and the teachings that had been given to him by his teacher, Abram Poljak.

In that part of Germany, the Frankenwald of north Bavaria, it often rained. So, very often when we walked, there would be earthworms on the street or in the path, wriggling helplessly on the pavement or the sidewalk or the trail.

Herr Müller always made a point of picking each one up, giving it a few reassuring words, and placing it in the grass where it could safely burrow back into the earth. I assumed that he was doing this for my benefit, as teaching and show, as much as out of an inner appreciation of earthworms, who aerate our soil.

Then one morning after a return flight from China, experiencing jet-lag I woke up around 5:00 A.M., and looked out the window onto the street in front of the guest-house in Stadtsteinach. It had rained the night before and the sidewalk glistened, reflecting the pre-dawn pink of the sky.

Herr Müller was walking alone on the street this time, unaware that anybody was watching him at 5:30 in the morning. He was hunched over, zigzagging across the street, picking up worms and carrying them to the grass with a speed and fervor that I'd never seen in our walks.

It was then that I realized that all along he'd been downplaying his concern for the worms when we walked!

I threw on some clothes and went outside and found him halfway up the block, getting as many worms as he could.

"What're you doing?" I asked.

"In an hour or so the cars will come," he said softly.

"Why are worms so important?"

"Because they are the least of the least, the least powerful, the helpless victims of our cars and society."

"So?"

"Jesus told us that in the least of the least we would find Him."

"Jesus in a worm?"

"Jesus in compassion," he replied simply.

A year or so later, we were planning to fly to Switzerland together from Germany.

"Be sure to order vegetarian meals," he said.

I explained that on these short flights the vegetarian meals, in my experience, were awful: more often than not an apple and some carrots. If we got a regular meal and just ate around the meat, we'd at least get a good salad and some good bread. Maybe even some hot vegetables.

"But you must still order us vegetarian meals," he said. "The momentum is more important than our taste buds."

Again, I misunderstood his meaning. I thought what he was saying was that if the airlines got enough requests for vegetarian meals, then perhaps they'd begin to pay more attention to them, and maybe even improve them. Or maybe he meant that the ordering of a vegetarian meal was a statement of nonviolence: even if we didn't eat the meat, it had been killed for our plate if we took the regular meal.

While he certainly agreed with these two rationales, his real reason was even more subtle than that. He wasn't as interested in converting the airlines to vegetarianism as he was in changing the entire human race. And that didn't just mean starting with the airlines.

I'd taught this years earlier when I was with the Coptics, but always used spiritual metaphors to describe it: our every act echoes out throughout space and throughout humanity, and affects it all. In 1994, I began reading the books and work of scientist Rupert Sheldrake, who'd put the name Morphic Resonance to this concept that Master Stanley had taught. Realizing that my previously-"mystical" belief—the same that Herr Müller was operating from—was now "validated" by science, I wrote about it in a book published in 1996 titled *Beyond ADD*.

It may sound absurd at first, that learning can be transmitted from one member of a species to another without any direct communication or even any contact. Even Pavlov, when confronted with it, assumed it was a sort of genetic transmission of learned behavior. He trained a group of rats to run to a particular feeding place whenever he rang a bell. The first generation of rats he trained took an average of 300 tries before they learned to always run to the feeding place when Pavlov rang the bell. Their offspring, however, leaned how to find the food when the bell was rung after only 100 ties. The children of this second generation got it after 30 tries, and their children learned how to find the food after only 10 tries. None were given an opportunity to learn this behavior from their parents, however, and that fact boggled Pavlov. He died, however, before he was able to follow it up.

But it was followed up, with startling results. From 1920 to 1950, one of the longest studies in the history of behavioral science was conducted at Harvard (and, later, other institutions) by Dr. William McDougal. He put together a test for rats where they were dropped into a darkened tank of cold water, from which there were two exit ramps. One ramp was lighted, but gave the rats an electric shock when they tried to use it. The other exit was dark and hard to find, but provided safe escape from the cold water.

Using standard white laboratory rats, McDougal found that the first generation of rats he tested took over 165 tries to master this test. By the time he got to the thirtieth generation, however, the rats easily mastered the test in fewer than 20 tries. When he first published the results of this experiment, it of course raised skepticism. The idea that behavior might be inherited was odd, to say the least, and might have enlightening or chilling implications if it were applied to humans.

So biologist F. A. E. Crew tried to replicate McDougal's Harvard experiment in faraway Edinburgh, Scotland. Using genetically similar standard laboratory rats, but ones which had no relation to McDougal's (which were still in Boston), he found that on the first try, his rats could learn the water test with only 25 tries.

The results of this stimulated biologist W. E. Agar in Melbourne, Australia, to try the test out with his rats. He found that his first generation also learned the test with about 25 tries, and as he continued training rats through subsequent generations, he was able to get this down considerably by the fiftieth generation, over twenty years.

What Agar did that was different from Crew or McDougal, however, was that he kept another group of rats breeding in a separate room, unrelated to the test rats, for the same fifty generations without ever giving them any tests or training. When he finally tested his control group, he discovered, to his and everybody else's shock and amazement, that they learned the maze with a speed identical to offspring of the tested and trained group.

One of the most famous examples of this "remote shared learning" occurred in Britain where for nearly 100 years milkmen have left bottles of milk at homeowners' doors during the dark hours of early morning. In 1921, the first incidence of a small bird opening the top of one of these milk bottles was recorded. It happened in the small town of Southampton, the bird was the blue tit. By 1937, 11 species of birds had begun this activity, and it had spread to 89 different cities in England.

Then the jump occurred. A certain critical mass appears to have been achieved in Britain, because suddenly blue tits in Sweden, Denmark, and Holland began to attack milk bottles. It was impossible that this could have been a learned behavior or something that these birds observed.

To further compound the mystery, milk bottles were not used in Holland during the years of World War II, and were only reintroduced in 1947. None of the blue tits alive then could have ever seen a milk bottle: the last ones placed on doorsteps were during the era of their grand- or great-grandparents. Yet as soon as the bottles reappeared, the tits began to attack them.

Another well-known story of this occurred off the coast of Japan in 1952, on the island of Koshima. Scientists studying the behavior of a local band of monkeys (Macaca fuscata) began feeding them by droping sweet potatoes on the sand on the beach. The sand made the potatoes difficult to eat, and one young female, Imo, learned to wash the potatoes in the ocean before eating them. She taught this behavior to her friends and relatives, and pretty soon many of the members of this band of monkeys were imitating Imo's food-washing behavior, The scientists observed this with interest, watching how the behavior slowly spread through the tribe, until one day something startling happened: every monkey in the tribe began washing their food.

Amazed by this, the scientists reported their observation—at the same time that another group of scientists at Takasakiyama on the distant mainland had noticed an odd and eerie phenomenon: suddenly all the Macaca fuscata monkeys they were observing had begun to wash their food in the ocean!

Dr. Rupert Sheldrake calls this phenomenon "morphic resonance," and points out several human examples in his book, *The Presence of the Past.**

Before 1953, in all of recorded human history, no person had ever run a mile in less than four minutes. This was widely regarded as an unbreakable barrier, having to do with basic laws of physics and human anatomy. Then, in 1954, Roger Bannister ran a mile in under four minutes and shocked the world. The widely held assumption at

---

*Park Street Press, 1988

the time was that Bannister must have been some sort of a freak, a super-human runner, to have accomplished a feat that everybody knew was patently impossible.

But even more amazing than Bannister having broken the four-minute-mile was the fact that within a year over a dozen people had matched his feat, and within a decade over a thousand had. By 1985, the "barrier" was redefined by Steve Cram, who ran the mile in 3 minutes 46.3 seconds. That this feat was duplicated not just in Bannister's native England but all over the world is testament to the fact that this didn't represent some sudden evolution in the technology of running shoes or human nutrition: it was the newly-shared knowledge that it was possible.

Extending this to learning, it was found that when students in England or the United States were presented with two poems in Japanese, one a classic nursery rhyme known to millions of Japanese and the other a made-up rhyme similar in structure and form, the non-Japanese-speaking students were able to memorize the "real" poem 62 percent more easily and faster than the made-up rhyme.

To test if this effect were merely the result of the real rhyme having survived some sort of natural selection process in Japan because it was somehow structurally or intrinsically easier to learn, Yale professor of psychology Dr. Gary Schwartz put together three sets of seemingly nonsense words, each made of three characters. One set was 24 three-character words in Hebrew which were common in the Old Testament. The second set was 24 three-character Hebrew words which were rare in the Bible. And the third set weren't Hebrew words at all, but scrambled anagrams of the first two sets, comprising 48 nonsense words that were structurally similar to the two sets of real words.

These 96 words were then randomly projected on a screen, and students were asked to guess at their meaning, and also to rank how confident they felt that they'd guessed right. None of the students had any knowledge of or background in Hebrew:

Dr. Schwartz was impressed to discover a "highly statistically significant" result: the students felt far more confident about their guesses when they were looking at real words, and they were more than twice as likely to feel that way when looking at the common real words than the uncommon ones.

A similar test but using Persian words in Arabic script was performed in England by psychologist Alan Pickering, with similar results.

The concept of people having shared memories or knowledge isn't new, although the scientific validation of it is. Gestalt psychology has long held that there is a psychological field that people are immersed in, and Carl Jung saw this in his concept of the psychological archetype. Prior to the many scientific experiments recently and currently being carried out to test the hypothesis of morphic resonance, this was largely kept in the realm of metaphysics, with proponents such as Edgar Cayce, or as a core concept in the religions of Hinduism and Buddhism.

But now it's widely becoming accepted that what author Ken Keyes called the "Hundredth Monkey Phenomenon" is real.

So in May of 1995, I ran across Ken Keyes' book about the hundredth monkey phenomenon in a used bookstore and re-read it (I'd first read it nearly 20 years earlier, but then lost it in one of our moves), and, at the same time, was reading Sheldrake's *The Presence of the Past*. Here was scientific evidence that we're all connected, that we share a sort of collective, racial (as in Human Race) consciousness. This could explain how entire nations would go insane and engage in wars, how religions could sweep the world, why jokes seem to appear instantaneously all over the country, or even fads like Nintendo's latest game, Nike's newest shoes, or the Hula Hoop. It could even explain epidemics, such as influenza, if you accept the Christian Science or metaphysical view that illness can start in the mind.

We're all connected: we have shared knowledge, and that knowledge—for better or worse—is constantly evolving and changing.

So in July of 1995, after visiting Bogota, Colombia and discovering that the Salem program there was in trouble, I booked a flight to Germany to discuss the Bogota program and these issues with Herr Müller. When I got to Germany, he suggested we go for a walk.

It's an odd experience climbing a mountain with an 81-year-old man and having to work to keep up, but it's even odder to bring something that you think is a major revelation, a truth you've held in a variety of ways over your life, to your teacher, only to discover that he's not only known it all along, but has been trying to tell you about it in his own way for years.

As we were climbing the mountain, heading for the rock where Herr Müller had inscribed the secret name of G-d in the stone and we always went to pray, I told him the story of the hundredth monkey and the rats. Part of me figured he'd just confirm the idea, having known it all along, and part of me expected him to either argue with it or treat it as a revelation.

He said, "Of course. This makes sense."

"You knew about this?" I said.

"No, I never heard of these studies," he said, "but they are very interesting."

We were walking along a narrow trail: to our left was a mountain covered with pine trees that went nearly straight up, to our right, nearly straight down, was a valley 500 feet below us with a small river bubbling and leaping through it. The path we walked was less than two-feet wide in most places. One misstep and we could fall all the way to the river—a rather severe mistake.

He pointed to the river. "I have been talking about the river for years." He waved his hand to the left. "But most people only see the mountain."

"But don't you think it's interesting that science is validating what mystics have been saying for centuries?"

"Scientists are always the last to know," he said, and laughed. "Why would we order those terrible vegetarian meals on airline flights? Why would I try to find as many helpless worms as possible? Why have I always told you that the greatest tool for good, the most powerful way to change the world, is to secretly commit little acts of compassion?

"It does not matter that people know what you are doing, *but rather that you do it.* When a large enough number of people finally *do* something, or something is done enough times, be it prayer or vegetarianism or whatever, it will then happen everywhere, to everyone. It will suddenly seem to be just normal.

"That's why our Salem work is so important. Even if we only save a few children or a few thousand, what we have done is to put into the air the saving of children. Or being a vegetarian: because we do not eat meat, there is that much less pain and anguish in the world."

He stopped and turned and looked directly into my eyes. I could hear the river and the wind, feel the sharp air ruffling my hair, and see the flecks of brown and green in his eyes. "Thomas," he said gently, "You must behave as if your every act, even the smallest, impacted a thousand people for a hundred generations. Because it does."

Cosmic Consciousness
in a Prison Cell

The swiftest steed to bear you to your goal is suffering . . .
Nothing is more gall-bitter than suffering, nothing so honey
sweet as to have suffered. The most sure foundation for this
perfection is humility, for he whose nature here creeps in
deepest depths shall soar in spirit to highest height of deity;
for joy brings sorrow and sorrow brings joy.

—MEISTER ECKHART

Sister Lotte was one of Herr Müller's spiritual warriors: a woman who'd been with him, helping him, since he started Salem. When I met her she was well into her seventies and infirm, living in her own apartment in a place of honor at Salem in Stadtsteinach.

Before she died in 1994, every Friday night Herr Müller and Frau Bethge (his secretary, a former nun) would make a pilgrimage to Sister Lotte's apartment, on the far edge of the Stadtsteinach Salem property. They'd climb the two floors to her flat, and there she would, with her failing eyesight and trembling hand, light the nine candles in the candleholder and say a prayer. Herr Müller would give a small collection of quotes from the Bible about G-d being light, and that Jesus Christ was the light of the world, and that we individuals must be certain that we didn't hide our lights under baskets. And then he'd select a page or so to read from the Bible. After this, Herr Müller would go home to his family, his wife and his two young children, and there they would perform his version of the traditional Jewish and early Christian Shabat ceremony, lighting the candles, saying the prayers in Hebrew, and blessing, eating, and drinking the bread and wine.

One of the absolute highlights of my visits to Salem, and of the year I lived there, was when Herr Müller invited me to share in these

Sabbath events. Afterward, we'd often finish off the ceremonial bottle of wine and talk late into the night about the work of Salem or philosophy or religion.

One of the most interesting parts of these Sabbaths was the way Herr Müller would select the Bible passage to read. Sometimes, if he had a particular issue in mind or had been teaching me about something, he'd find that passage that was most directly relevant. Sometimes he'd just open the book and drop his finger, the technique he had used in despair in the 1950s when he was a successful businessman with an empty spirit, remembering a promise he'd made to G-d in a faraway prison camp. At that time, his finger had fallen on the passage where Jesus told the rich man to sell everything he owned and give it to the poor before he could follow Him: the next day Herr Müller sold his business, his home, and all his possessions except one suit, and gave all the money to two elderly Jewish widows he knew who had survived the Holocaust. His wife was furious and left him. And that week he started Salem.

"When I started Salem," Herr Müller told me back in 1978, "I said to G-d, 'I would like to have an agreement with you!' And, to my surprise, He said, 'Ok, what agreement?' I said, 'I will do your work on three conditions: that I am not crucified, that I may remain vegetarian, and that when I leave this world I may sit at the wedding feast with Jesus Christ.' There was a long pause as He thought, and then I heard clearly the word, *'Ja!'* And so, I began."

But back to the Friday nights. Often he'd select the Ninety-first Psalm to read, and when I was there, he always asked me to read it out loud in English while he'd recite it in German.

One day I asked him about his affection for that Psalm, and he told me the following story:

During World War II, Herr Müller was in the intelligence service of the Third Reich (the regular army, not the SS—he'd responded to the draft call). He spoke seven languages fluently, and had spent time as a teenager bicycling through the Middle East. Oil was a precious commodity for Hitler's war machine, and Herr Müller volunteered to put together a small squad of men to parachute behind the enemy lines into British-occupied Kurdistan (now the northern parts of Iraq and Iran) and help the Kurds overthrow the British. The theory was that the

Kurds would then be so grateful for their independence that they'd sell their oil to the Germans.

Herr Müller tells this story in his book *In The Burning Orient,* but because he wrote the book immediately after the war "as a catharsis, to just get it out so I wouldn't ever again have to think of it," he didn't include in that book the spiritual dimensions of his experience.

After a year's training in the Kurdish language, the terrain, and local politics, Herr Müller along with two Germans and a Kurd named Ramses were parachuted into the area.

The plane, however, instead of dropping them in a safe spot out in the countryside, parachuted them directly into a large British military installation. (Herr Müller later learned that he'd been betrayed because of his support of his brother's outspoken pacifistic views; his brother later died during his first days on the Russian front while Herr Müller was in prison.)

They were immediately captured. And, since they were out of uniform and carrying false papers, they were correctly identified as spies. During time of war, the penalty for spying is death, and after months of torture which left two of Herr Müller's compatriots dead and one insane, he, the commander and sole survivor, was sentenced to death.

However, the British preferred hanging, whereas the Iranian authorities who then controlled the area thought their prisoners should be shot. Since both together sentenced Herr Müller, both wanted to execute him . . . each in their own way.

So he was put in a steel cage at the foot of the gallows and allowed to sit in the hot desert sun while the two governments argued over who'd have the right to execute him, and how.

Every morning the guard would play a cruel joke by banging on the bars and telling Herr Müller that a decision had been reached as to his execution method, and then he would say either hanging or shooting, whichever struck his fancy that day.

"Sitting in that death cell, I had a lot of time to think," Herr Müller told me. "I thought about the meaning of life and death, and decided that I would never participate in the taking of a life. I was fortunate that I had not been in battle and never had to kill another person, but I decided to take my commitment to peace a step further. 'Peace must begin with your mouth,' I remembered from the Bible, and so I decided

I would not speak words of violence and I would not take into my mouth the fruits of violence. In the death cell, I became a vegetarian."

Having grown up a normal German in a heavily meat-dependent society, Herr Müller assumed this decision would cost him his life by malnutrition, if they didn't shoot or hang him first. Everybody knew that meat protein was essential to life, he thought, and by making this decision, he was also deciding that even if it meant his death he'd stick to his principle of peace. (It may be easy to say that they were going to kill him anyway, which he fully expected, but the measure of his commitment to this can be seen from the fact that he still hasn't eaten meat, and it's now been over 50 years since he made that decision.).

"Along with my commitment to nonviolence, I decided I should learn to know my maker," Herr Müller told me. As a child, his very religious parents had taught him several Bible verses and psalms, including the Ninety-first Psalm. He decided to use that as a vehicle to petition his Creator.

So he sat in his cell, day after day for months, silently reciting the Ninety-first Psalm, over and over again. When he joined Frederick (another German prisoner in the camp who was assigned as his cellmate), he continued this practice whenever they weren't working on dismantling their cell.

"A strange thing happened from this," he told me. "At first I wanted to die. I'd failed my mission and was in this cell, sentenced to death. And then I wanted to live. These swings of emotion were very intense. And then, as I recited the Psalm for hour after hour, I reached a point where living and dying seemed trivial concerns: it was the presence of G-d that I craved, whether alive or dead."

In his book *In The Burning Orient,* in which he omitted most of the spiritual things that he thought might cause people to think him or Salem odd, he wrote: "But soon, in spite of everything, I recovered my equanimity and was able to smile to myself, comforted by the certain knowledge that I was not alone and that G-d was with me, helping me and protecting me.

"Previous Christmases that I had passed in prison had always been a terrible time. One knew that somewhere dear ones were looking out sadly into the night thinking of one, as one was of them, with eyes fixed on the stars as if they formed a bridge with home. I had always been so utterly depressed and inconsolable that I had been able to do little more than weep quietly to myself and address silent words to Him who had once lain as a child in a cradle.

"This time it was different. My celebration of Christmas was private and personal, within my own soul. I regarded everything around me as if it were the action of a film. It passed me by without disturbing me."

Within hours of his reaching this realization, part of his new wish was fulfilled.

He was sitting in the cell on his hard wooden bed, the bottoms of his feet mending from having been split open by the interrogator's batons, reciting the psalm silently in this mind. Then a strange and sudden stillness seized him. It seemed that he stopped breathing and his heart stopped beating. His eyes were closed, but he could see all around him, and not just in front of him: his vision filled the cell. And then it extended out beyond the cell, into the area around it, throughout the camp, the bodies of the guards and soldiers shimmering like ghosts. His vision continued to expand until it took in the entire valley they were in, and then stretched beyond that, slowly growing to take in the entire world and then the stars and the universe. He was filled with ecstasy, love pouring over him, and it seemed as if the entire creation were his own body and mind. Then, as his body took a breath, it all dissolved and he was back in his cell. But now he was filled with a new knowledge, a new love, and a new power.

A few days later he was moved to a concrete cell, along with another German prisoner named Frederick. Together, they planned to break out of the prison, carefully and slowly taking out pieces of the wall and replacing them with bits of bread from their meals so the guards wouldn't see the damage. It was a desperate effort that they thought had virtually no chance of succeeding: even if they did burrow through the wall, they'd still have to cross the prison compound, then the prison perimeter with its perpetual guards, dogs, guard towers, and high barbed-wire fence. Beyond that it was twenty kilometers of desert between them and the safety of the road to Cairo.

But they persisted, until one day Frederick proclaimed the hole in their wall adequate for them to slip out through. The next day, he said, they would escape. Herr Müller was filled with trepidation and excitement.

That night Herr Müller was awakened from his sleep by a bright light in his cell. He sat up and saw before him a man dressed in the white robes of the local nomads, the garb that the men who followed Jesus wore. The man shimmered and glowed with an otherworldly light, yet also looked quite normal. Herr Müller recognized the man as the Archangel Michael, who he'd met before his birth into this Earth.

"Tomorrow night," Michael said, "walk out of here. You have an important destiny to fulfill."

"What about the guards, the dogs?" Herr Müller said.

"Do not worry about that," Michael said.

Herr Müller bowed his head in acknowledgment, and Michael was gone; the cell returned to normal.

The next evening they tried their escape. In his book, Herr Müller wrote:

Frederick was thinner than I, so he went first leading with one arm, his head following. I pushed him until he was finally through, standing erect in the pale moonlight. Then it was my turn and he had to pull for all he was worth. Soon I was outside. As soon as we took one step away from the barracks all the prisoners could see us. They were not all German and it would have been to anybody's advantage to have reported us. But there was nothing we could do about it. We just pulled on our shirts, walked boldly across the exercise areas as if it was the most natural thing in the world and disappeared behind the wall of sacking.

So far no dog had made the slightest sound. We jumped the ditch to face the first wire fence, the mesh of which had been prepared with special care; one only had to touch it for it to make a loud rustling sound. Fifteen meters to the right of us was a recreation room. I could see a number of our guards through the wide open doors. On the other side of the fence, which was brightly lit, was a road and beyond that, a canteen with soldiers continually coming and going. There was no possibility of turning back. We simply had to press boldly on.

I had already worked my way half through the wire when Frederick tugged at me.

"Look out, there are two men coming this way!" he whispered.

The fence rattled dangerously as I made frantic attempts to get loose. Just as I managed with Frederick's help to free myself, I saw two soldiers coming toward us from a distance of about fifteen to twenty paces.

It's just not possible that they didn't see us or hear us, I thought. I was in my prison clothes, the top half of my body had been exposed in the brightly lit and otherwise empty road. They must have been struck blind and deaf, there was no other way to explain it.

From there, they went on successfully to Cairo where Herr Müller stayed for some time before being recaptured. This time, though, while he was put in a much more horrible prison, he at least survived to the end of the war. The orders for his execution mysteriously vanished when the documents about him were transferred to the new prison.

And so he is alive today, working every day to save the world. "Always with the Ninety-first Psalm," he said.

Psalm 91

He who dwells in the secret place of the most High shall abide under the shadow of the Almighty.

I will say of JHWH, He is my refuge and my fortress: my G-d; in whom I trust.

Surely He shall deliver you from the fowler's snare, and from the deadly pestilence.

He shall cover you with his feathers, and under His wings will you rest: His truth shall be your shield and buckler.

You shall not fear the terror by night; nor for the arrow that flies by day;

Nor for the pestilence that walks in darkness; nor for the destruction that wastes at noonday.

A thousand shall fall at your side, and ten thousand at your right hand; but it shall not come near you.

Only with your eyes shall you see the punishment of the wicked.

Because you have made JHWH, which is my refuge, even the most High, your habitation;

Therefore no evil will befall you, neither shall any plague come to your dwelling.

For He shall give his angels charge over you, to keep you in all your ways.

They shall bear you up in their hands, lest you dash your foot against a stone.

You shalt tread upon the lion and snake: the young lion and the dragon you will trample under foot.

"Because he loves me," says the Lord, "therefore will I deliver him: I will set him on high, because he knows my Name.

"He shall call upon me, and I will answer him: I will be with him in trouble; I will deliver him, and honor him.

"With long life will I satisfy him, and show him my salvation."

I deeply admire Herr Müller's force of faith, and his power of will. His experiences make the struggles in my life pale by comparison. Yet the apocalyptic, Biblical side of him is balanced by a compassion and hard-earned empathy which he never forgets.

The Sack of Gold

Knowledge without love is cold light,
a false light which leads into the abyss.

—ABRAM POLJAK

In 1978 we'd started the New England Salem Children's Village in a rental property on Stinson Lake, New Hampshire. We'd brought on board as houseparents a marvelous couple, John and Nancy Roy, and were taking in children and beginning fundraising. We were in two old houses on Stinson Lake, one a vacation property and the other a former part of a boarding school, which had been, prior to that, an old farm house. It had about ten individual rooms that could be used as bedrooms, and several bathrooms and a few, large public areas; we'd added a sauna and an industrial-sized kitchen.

But this property, while it was nice, wasn't at all our dream of our own, unique, Salem property. So, even though funds were tight and a good week's fundraising meant $50, we kept looking for something more consistent with the Salem model as created in Europe by Herr Müller.

In the early summer of 1980, we found it. It was an abandoned summer camp previously run for Jewish kids, on 134 acres of mountainside land. The land went clear up over the top of the mountain, was wooded, had streams and a beaver pond (which was virtually inaccessible), and a few hundred feet of frontage on Stinson Lake, a mile-across lake which filled the top of Stinson mountain as if it were a volcano's caldera.

The land was owned by the uncle of a friend of mine, and the uncle was in a crisis. For some time the land had been tied up in some sort of legal issue, and now it was free. But along with that freedom, the uncle had to raise a large chunk of cash to pay the taxes by August 31, or he would lose the land. That deadline was less than two months off, so the

118

uncle was willing to sell the property, which today is worth almost a quarter million dollars, for a tiny fraction of that . . . but only if the buyer could come up with $10,000 of nonrefundable earnest money to hold the deal, and an additional $30,000 cash to close the sale on August 31. If those terms were met, he would finance the rest of the sale himself, which, from our point of view was absolutely necessary as we were a new charity with no assets and no cash-flow; my personal income was only $25 per week, and no bank would even consider granting us a mortgage to buy the land without a huge down payment to provide repossessable equity.

In fact, the total assets of our fledgling organization were just over $10,000, money we still had from a friend's rather substantial donation and my and Louise's savings.

I visited the land, on the other side of the lake from our rental property, several times, alone and with others from Salem, and the certainty grew in me that it was the perfect property for us. I prayed over it and got what I felt were clear answers: we should buy it. We would have to build houses, of course, because the property was largely just raw land, and all the old camp buildings had deteriorated to the point of uselessness. But, still, there was something about it, about the view that extended across the lake and to the mountains around us, about the strange inner tingle I'd get when I walked on the land, that made me certain that this property was here to further the Salem work.

So I called Herr Müller and asked him his advice. He flew over a few days later to see the land, and was very enthusiastic. "This is perfect!" he said. "You must buy it!"

"But where will I get $40,000?" I said. "If I put down the deposit now, and can't come up with another $30,000 within about six weeks, I'll lose both the land and my $10,000."

"Don't be afraid," he said. "Trust in G-d and He will provide the $30,000."

At this time, of course, Herr Müller was the director of one of the largest child care organizations in Europe, with three children's villages in Germany that were very well-known, and he had substantial cash-flow from his donations and money from the government. So, in the back of my mind, I assumed that his enthusiastic push of me to put up my own $10,000 was in part supported by his willingness to loan or give us some or all of the remaining $30,000 if I failed to find it else-where.

So we went to town, visited with my friend's uncle, gave him a check (which virtually cleaned out our account), and signed an agreement to purchase which included a clause making our $10,000 fully nonrefundable.

Herr Müller went back to Germany, and I began to raise funds as hard as I could. First, I called all of my old business acquaintances. That brought about $300: for some reason (probably because this wasn't my first call to them with my hand out) they were less than enthusiastic about giving us money at this time.

I prepared a fundraising mailing and sent it out first-class to our list of about 90 friends, relatives, and donors: that brought another few hundred dollars back.

I gave hastily-arranged speeches at nearby Rotary clubs, Lions clubs, women's garden clubs, and anyplace else we could wrangle an invitation. A few of them were quite generous, and a week before our August 31 deadline, I'd managed to raise almost $2000.

During the preceding 45 days, I'd called Herr Müller at least weekly to give him progress reports.

"I've raised $300," I'd say, and he'd say, "That's wonderful! Keep up the good work and that land will be a Salem children's village!" Again, I interpreted his enthusiasm and certainty as an indication that, at the last minute, he'd send me a check for the balance I was unable to raise. And when I expressed concerns or doubts about my ability to come up with the full amount, he'd always say, "Trust in G-d!" Trusting in G-d was a good enough idea, but deep down inside, in a place I wasn't even consciously confronting, I thought that trusting in Herr Müller's bank account was probably more reliable.

Another event was happening during these weeks, now on an almost daily basis: the people with whom I worked were jokingly questioning my sanity. "You've just given away our entire cash reserves!" one would say, and dire predictions of what would happen on August 31 dogged me, it seemed, everywhere I went on the Salem property. Even the kids got into the act, giving me sad or amazed-he'd-be-so-stupid looks. Finally, to get them off my back. I told them all at a staff meeting that Herr Müller had encouraged me to do this, and so therefore he must feel some responsibility for our success, and would almost certainly come through with whatever money we were short. Although this did not fully calm the skeptics, at least it reduced the level of doomsday talk and gossip around the place.

Now it was D-day, one week before the deadline, just long enough for a check to arrive from Germany by air express and clear our bank. I'd spent some of the money I'd raised to cover the fundraising expenses of travel, postage, and long distance calls, and had a total of about $1800. There was no more in the pipeline, and I'd exhausted every resource I knew of except for Herr Müller himself. So I called him.

"Hello, Thomas!" he said, sounding jubilant to hear my voice. "How are you?"

"Not so good," I said. "I'm almost $29,000 short of the amount of money I need by next week."

"Just by coincidence," he said, his voice still jovial, "I have a similar problem. Our mailing house mislabeled a quarter-million newsletters and then mailed them. I had paid for the postage and the printing before the mistake was discovered, and now there are no contributions coming back in from the mailing. I may even have to ask my staff to wait a week or two for their paychecks. But don't worry," he added, "it's all G-d's will. It will all work out."

"You have no money?" I said, my heart dropping.

"None!" he said emphatically. "In fact, if you could arrange a loan to me it would be a big help. I need two hundred thousand dollars."

"This is a joke, fight? You're teasing me."

"No joke. But, as I said, it's no problem. G-d will provide for those who do his work."

"And what about us?" I said. "What about the ten thousand dollars we're going to lose?"

His voice became serious for the first time. "If you have no faith, then you shall lose the money,"

"I had faith in you!"

"That was a mistake: I am a man, and you must learn to trust in G-d. And, Thomas, I never said I would give you any of that money."

"But you were so encouraging! You suggested we should sign the papers, and you even put your hand on the contract and said, 'In G-d's Name!'"

"Of course! That land has its own destiny as a Salem village. Only your lack of faith can prevent it."

I hung up the phone stunned. We were doomed. We could hardly meet our operating expenses, I had staff people working 80-hour weeks for $50 a week, and I'd just given away virtually all of our operating capital in the nonrefundable deposit.

I sat for a long time in my office, staring at the phone. Then I prayed, with sincerity and fervor, that if it was G-d's will that we have the land, that He would open the door to the money. And that, if not, I could handle the consequences.

Herr Müller's turning me down was a blessing and a reminder. Both he and Master Stanley had often told me that I shouldn't turn them into gurus or messiah-figures. "There are men out there who will steal your freedom," Master Stanley once said. "Beware of them." Herr Müller similarly has a visceral distaste for spiritual leaders—from yogis to traditional pastors and priests—who demand obedience, obeisance, and unthinking devotion of their followers. "Such men are not of G-d," he often said. "They can even pull people away from G-d, much to their own and their followers' detriment."

So here I was, slipping into the very easy groove of trying to give over to him decision-making power for my life. And he kicked it right back at me. If I was to depend on any greater power, it had to be *the* Greater Power.

The next morning I drove into town to talk with the bank. The loan officer was very polite, but made it quite clear that we weren't even close to qualifying for a loan of those proportions. We had no assets, were in debt, and agencies that depended on the weird method of financing child care in New Hampshire were such a poor bet that our ability to repay such a loan was totally in doubt. There was no possibility of a loan, even with the land as security.

When I returned from the bank and pulled into the driveway, Barbara, our teacher, was standing there with her arms folded over her chest and a scowl on her face. There was an old car I didn't recognize just behind her: it was rusted out, the tailpipe held in place by a bent coat hanger, and the back seat was covered with a blanket as if the plastic seat-covering had disintegrated with age.

As I climbed out of my station wagon, Barbara said, "You've got to get him out of here!"

"Who?"

"The man who's waiting to see you in the sauna. The man who owns that car!" She waved a hand at the dubious piece of machinery, and I noticed that one fender didn't match the color of the rest of the car.

"Somebody I know?"

"I don't think so," she said. "He asked John if he was you. But he'll only talk with you. Says he called you a week ago because he saw that little article about us in *Vegetarian Times,* and you invited him up to look around."

"I invite everybody up," I said, laughing at how indignant Barbara was.

"But 'everybody' doesn't make themselves at home in the sauna while they're waiting for you!"

I told Barbara I'd take care of the situation, and went into the building, up to the second floor, and down the hall to the sauna. Inside was a rather scruffy looking man, clad only in swimming trunks, sweating like a pig. He had long black hair to his shoulders, a goatee, piercing brown eyes, and an apparent speech impediment or sinus problem, as his words came out with a thick New England accent smothered in a nasal sound.

He introduced himself and I'll refer to him as William, and he mentioned the call. It was one of a half-dozen or so a week that I was then getting as a result of publicity about us in a few magazines and the 18-minute segment National Public Radio's *All Things Considered* show had done on us, and the only reason I remembered his particular call was because of his odd voice and accent.

My immediate measure of him was that he was wasting my time. I had money to raise, people to call, or, at worst, my friend's uncle to call to beg for some part of our ten thousand dollars back although I'd heard from my friend a few days earlier when I first brought up the possibility, that his uncle had already used the money to pay back-taxes on the land, necessary to clear the title so he could sell the land to us when we came up with the final down payment of $30,000.

So there I sat in the sauna with this guy, thinking of all the things I had to do, trying to come up with a way to get him to leave quickly. He was making small talk, and I was about to offer to hand him off to one of our staffers for a quick tour on the way out, when I remembered Herr Müller, a year earlier, telling me the biblical story of how Abraham had fought with three men until he realized that they were actually angels. "Never judge another man," he'd said. "You can never truly know his motives or power, and he may even be an angel."

So instead of giving William the bum's rush, I took an hour and showed him around the program, introduced him to the staff and a few of the children, and then spent an hour in my office with him talking about one of my favorite topics: Herr Müller. William was particularly interested in the spiritual aspects of Herr Müller's work, and I was careful to point out to him that the children's villages weren't any sort of personal evangelism for Herr Müller or me or our points of view, but, rather, an expression in the real world of our beliefs.

Frankly, it was a welcome respite from the troubles of the day, and I'd come to truly like this eccentric fellow. It gave me an opportunity to forget about our looming crisis, and so I never even brought it up with him. Finally, I walked him out to his car to say good-bye.

As he was climbing into his car, he pressed a $20 bill into my hand and said, "This is for the children. Thanks for taking all that time with me."

Three more days passed, and I was only able to extract another $500 from old friends and a former business partner; the situation was hopeless, and there were only two days left before our seed money, so hard-earned and kindly given, and so carefully hoarded over the past year, would be gone forever. (My friend's uncle had corroborated his story of the taxes; the money was already gone, having vanished forever into the bowels of some tax agency.) I'd called Herr Müller one more time and he'd reiterated that he had no money for our program, and practically shouted at me that I must trust in G-d.

Over dinner that night William called. "I was wondering if you could drop by my place tomorrow," he said. "I'd like to hear some more about this Herr Müller, if you don't mind,"

I didn't tell him how much I'd welcome the opportunity to be anywhere except at Salem the next day, but instead simply said, "Sure, I'd be pleased to come visit for an hour or so." He gave me directions and I wrote them on a piece of paper towel by the phone.

The next morning, August 31, was a Friday, and I was grateful that by evening it would be Shabat and I could have a glass of wine and forget the previous six weeks. I got up early and skipped breakfast (and the staff) to drive the hundred-plus miles to William's apartment.

He lived in an unremarkable part of town, in an unremarkable apartment. Welcoming me in, he apologized for the mess. The place looked like a typical bachelor's apartment: cold pizza and empty beer cans on the coffee table, well-worn and mismatched furniture, and piles of books and magazines everywhere in various stages of being read. There was a conspicuous purple Chivas Regal velvet bag with gold stitching on the coffee table, and I assumed it had a bottle of booze in it.

William and I had coffee and talked for about three hours. I was coming to like him very much: he had a sincere and genuine interest in both life and things spiritual. He'd been raised Catholic, and was fascinated by the mystical side to that religion's traditions.

Finally, it was time to leave: I had to go face the staff and call my friend's uncle to tell him the money wouldn't be in the bank today. I stood to shake William's hand and to thank him for his time. He shook his head. "May I tell you a short story before you leave?" he said.

I sat back down. "Sure."

He waved at the room. "I'm living here because my wife and I are separated. We went through a stressful time. We had three children. Our oldest daughter is now just hitting her teenage years, and her younger sister is six. And I had always wanted a son. Not that I don't love my daughters: I'd also always wanted a daughter, and two is just fine, but I'd also wanted a son. Somebody to teach baseball to, and to help grow up. You know what I mean?"

I nodded, thinking of how much I loved and appreciated my own son.

"And we had a son, just two years ago," William continued. "Named him Aaron, after the priest of Moses, the guy in the Bible, because I'd always had this feeling that my son would do something important and spiritual." He paused for a moment and pulled out a handkerchief and blew his nose.

"Aaron was just short of a year old when, one night I woke up out of a sound sleep with a totally panicked feeling. I didn't know what it was—some premonition or something—but I knew it had to do with Aaron. Something bad was going to happen to him. So I decided to go into his room and say a prayer over him. I got up quietly, so as not to wake up my wife, and put on a bathrobe, and walked softly and barefooted down the hall to his room. I didn't want to wake him up, either."

Tears were now welling up in William's eyes, and I had a terrible feeling I knew where this story was going to end. I sat quietly, willing myself to say nothing but to be totally and completely present for him, right there in that here-and-now moment.

"He was dead," William said, and then he put his face in his hands, bent over his knees, and started sobbing. "He was already dead. There was nothing I could do. I tried to resuscitate him, but he was dead." He sobbed for two or three minutes, keeping his face covered, occasionally apologizing for the outburst. I reached over and rubbed his shoulder, and he just sobbed even harder.

"What caused it?" I said, wanting to give him as much of a chance as possible to complete his catharsis.

He took a deep breath and wiped his eyes on his sleeve and looked up at me. "The doctors said it was SIDS. Sudden Infant Death Syndrome. I'd never even heard of it, and it killed my son."

"SIDS has taken a lot of children," I said. "It wasn't your fault. There was nothing you could have done."

He continued on as if he hadn't heard me. His eyes were wide and red from tears, and he looked at me with a pain that, thinking of my own infant son, I prayed I'd never know. "I always knew that Aaron had a spiritual destiny. And so when I found his body, after I'd tried to get him breathing again and I'd dialed 911 for an ambulance, but before I went to wake up my wife, I picked up his little body and said to him, 'Aaron, wherever you are I know you can hear me. And I promise you, before G-d, that I shall do something worthy of you in your name.'"

His voice was breaking up, and he took a moment to recover his composure, blowing his nose again. "So that was almost a year ago. My marriage may not survive the shock of our losing Aaron, and my wife and I divided up our savings and separated. I decided to use my half for something in Aaron's name. But I didn't know what that would or could be.

"I'm not a vegetarian," he said, "but last week I was walking down the street in Boston, past this newsstand, on my way to a meeting with my former business partner. I'd sold out when we broke up, my wife and I, left the business world and even let my hair grow out like when I was a teenager, and the money from that was much of what we split up. And I was walking past this newsstand and I saw this magazine, *Vegetarian Times,* in the window, and I just walked in and bought it. I tell you, I have no idea why I did that. I like meat! I took it to my office and it sat on my desk for three days before I picked it up and read it while I was waiting for a meeting. And there was this little article, only a few paragraphs, mentioning that there was this vegetarian children's home in New Hampshire. The magazine just fell open to it when I went to read it, and there it was, looking at me. And again I don't know why, it was like I was acting in a dream, watching myself as I was doing it, and even a little bit amused, I guess, as I called information to get your number, and then called Salem and you answered and invited me up. And so I went."

"I'm glad you did." I said. "I've enjoyed getting to know you."

"Me, too," he said, nodding, smiling for the first time since he'd started his story. "And when I came back home here from visiting you, I had the strangest dream. Aaron visited me. He was grown up and a little baby at the same time. I don't know how to explain it. But he talked to me, and he said that he remembered my promise, and that I should keep it now. And then I woke up."

William glanced over at the Chivas bag. "I fought it for a couple of days. Maybe it was just a dream. Maybe I just made it up. Maybe I didn't understand." He shook his head and tears welled up in his eyes again. "And then, day before yesterday, that night while I was asleep, he came to me again. 'If you wait even one more day, Daddy, it will be too late,' be said. And I woke up and couldn't get back to sleep at all that night."

He glanced at the Chivas bag again. I had a lump in my throat that made it difficult for me to talk, and I wondered if he was going to pull out a bottle of liquor to try to soften his pain. I would have shared a drink with him just then; this was raw in its intensity.

Instead, he resumed his story. "So I went to the bank and took out some money. It wasn't really very much, but I grew up Catholic and was always told to give ten percent. So I took ten percent of what I figured was the value of everything I owned. And I had them give it to me in cash. Cash seems more real, you know? And my wife and I had gotten into buying gold as an investment years ago we thought there was a depression coming, subscribed to one of those newsletters, you know?"

I nodded. I'd done the same five years earlier.

"And so there was some gold, too, and I decided to just toss in part of that, ten percent of my half of our gold." He reached over and picked up the Chivas bag and handed it to me. "And that's it. For your children. I don't know if you need it or not. I appreciate that you spent two hours with me and never asked me for money, but that's not why. Aaron told me that I have to do this, and my heart told me, too. So that's yours. Salem's. Don't open it until you leave, and I'll come up in a week or so for a receipt, after you've had a chance to sell the gold and know what it's all worth, because I suppose we can use the tax deduction. The price of gold is going up, so you may want to keep whatever you don't need right away as coins."

I took the bag, which was surprisingly heavy. "Thank you," I said. "We really are in need right now, and I appreciate your thinking of us."

He nodded. "People doing good works are always in need. I knew this would help. Please say a prayer for Aaron when you use this money, okay?"

"I promise," I said.

When I left William's house, Chivas bag in hand, I drove for a few miles before I could gather myself together enough to pull over to the side of the road and open the bag. When I finally did, I discovered $10,000 in hundred-dollar bills, all neatly bundled in bank bands, and a large double-handful of Mexican gold coins. I drove to downtown Nashua, and found a coin shop.

The proprietor was an old man, gray hair thinning and thick glasses, and the store was filled with coins in little plastic display cases, ranging from Kennedy half-dollars to Roman denarii from the year 10 B.C.E.

"What are these coins worth?" I asked him, pouring the gold coins out on his counter.

He scooped them up, examining each one carefully. He wrote something on a piece of paper, then pulled down a book, then a magazine of some sort, then *The Wall Street Journal,* making more notes. Finally, he said, "I'll give you twenty-four-thousand three-hundred dollars for these coins right now. And," he added with a smile, "that's really what they're worth. You can double check it with anybody if you wish.

However, the price of gold changes daily, so tomorrow it will be slightly different."

I made an instant decision. "'Write a check for twenty thousand of it," I said, "and make it out to the Salem Children's Trust. And may I use your phone?"

I made it home just after lunch, and showed Louise the stacks of hundred-dollar bills, the check, and a few of the gold coins that I hadn't had to sell to cover the money I had to pay by the 5:00 P.M. deadline. She was astounded. I called Herr Müller and, breathless with excitement and fighting back tears, told him the story.

I expected him to be enthusiastic, even joyful, that we could now buy the land. Instead, he said in a very matter-of-fact tone of voice, "Of course, Thomas. Now, tell me something new."

"Aren't you amazed?" I shouted into the phone. "This is a miracle!"

He laughed and said, "Thomas, all of life is a miracle. This is nothing special."

I understood his message. And so, knowing that it was now important for me to convey this message to my compatriots at Salem, I arranged the kitchen table with stacks of hundred-dollar bills and gold coins . . . and a deck of cards.

I called John at the children's house next door. "How about a game of poker?" I said. "I have everything all set up."

His slow answer and tone of voice told me that he thought I'd snapped under the strain of the gone-awry land deal: "Okay," he said. "Nancy and I will be right over."

"Bring the others!" I shouted into the phone.

"Okay, Thom," he said, his tone now even more cautious and patronizing.

John and Nancy walked in with one of the other staff people, and stopped at the doorway into the kitchen, looking bug-eyed at the table covered with hundred-dollar bills and gold coins.

"Good grief," John said. "What happened?"

I started to laugh although my eyes were filling with tears. "A miracle happened," I said. "That's all."

Visiting Jerusalem

The mystic's words appear in a hundred different forms, but if G-d is one and the Way is one, how their words be other than one? They do appear in different guises, but in substance they are one. Variety occurs in form; in substance all is unified.

—JALALUDDIN RUMI

As I recall, 1981 was the first year I visited Jerusalem with Herr Müller. Since that time, I've been back many, many times, but that first visit carried several extraordinary lessons for me.

I flew to Germany and spent a few days at Salem in Stadtsteinach, and then flew from Munich to Tel Aviv with Herr Müller on El Al airlines. We chose a taxi from the dozens at the curb and had the driver take us halfway across this tiny country to Jerusalem, across miles of desert and scrub-land that was home to Bedouins and the echoing footsteps of ancient prophets and warriors.

Approaching Jerusalem I saw the city for the first time: it was a startling sight, as the sun was just approaching the horizon. Virtually every building in the entire city is faced with or built of "Jerusalem stone," which is a straw-yellow rock of some sort (it looks like sandstone but feels like granite), and the red-tinted light from the setting sun painted it a deep gold. I could see the wall going around the ancient city, now within but still rising above the larger metropolitan area, and the steep hillsides and valleys that interlaced the city and surrounding areas. The air was warm and dry, smelling of dust and desert brush, and the street signs were printed in Hebrew and English.

We checked into a hotel, and Herr Müller suggested we go for a walk. He led me through the streets of the city with the geographic confidence of a native, explaining that the first time he'd been here was in the 1920s when he was a teenager and had, literally, ridden his bicycle from Germany to then-Palestine one summer. When we encountered people who spoke little English, he'd use Hebrew, Arabic, French, or German (he also speaks Kurdish, and passable Spanish and Italian).

He led me deep into the center of the Old City, to the Western Wall, where about twenty men were standing praying. We put on paper yarmulkes provided by the guard, entered the area, and stood at the wall as the sun set, praying, for about a half hour. The cracks between the huge stones that made the wall were filled with tiny pieces of paper, prayers from petitioners who preceded us. As I prayed, breathing the air exhaled by prophets, saints, the patriarchs, and Jesus, I felt a thick spiritual power fill me. It was a rumbling resonance, as if I were surrounded by millions of ancient voices all chanting "Amen" in such a deep bass that it was just beyond the range of my hearing, but vibrated my body and my heart.

As we left, he said, "You must learn the prayer of Jehoshaphat," and told me the story of how when Jehoshaphat was the King of Israel he had to face several mighty armies who were coming to attack him. When he asked G-d what he should do, he was told through a prophet that he should put himself and his priests in front of the army and march off into battle singing: 'Praise G-d, for His mercy endures forever." And when they came to the place where they were going to confront the armies, they discovered that the different armies had met each other during the evening and fought until nearly everybody among them was dead. Like my experience with the gold that paid for the land, it was a final "proving' that helped determine the future course of Jehoshaphat's life.

So Herr Müller taught me the prayer in Hebrew, and I recited it as we walked until I had it memorized.

We walked down a series of narrow streets until we came to a gate into the Mount Zion area of the old City.

Entering Mount Zion was an odd experience: it was as if the air changed, had become thicker and more still. We walked to King David's tomb, and, just a half-block away, he led me up a narrow side-stairway to the rooftop of an ancient building. The roof was covered with a stone-like material, and all the way around it was a brick wall that came to my waist, about a foot thick.

"The room below us is where Jesus held the Last Supper," Herr Müller said. (Later I returned during the day, and there was a tour group in there hearing the same thing from a local tour guide.) "We are above a holy room, and this is also one of the highest points you can get to on Mount Zion."

In one direction I could see across the valley to the Mount of Olives: just below us, behind the building we stood on, was an old and over-grown cemetery dating back to the Crusader days with above- and below-ground tombs. A mile or so to my left, I could see the Dome of the Rock above the Wailing Wall. To my right in the distance, I could see the entrance to the road to the nearby small town that was known for its bakeries in ancient times: the "house of bread" or, in Hebrew, "Bet Lechem," pronounced in English as Bethlehem. Behind me, rising above the buildings, was the millennia-old wall around the Old City.

Herr Müller pulled a carefully folded sheet of paper out of his pocket. "Did you bring your list?" he said.

"I forgot." He had mentioned to me before I left the United States that I should bring along a prayer list, and I'd made one, but in the con-fusion of my departure, I'd left it behind.

"Tonight carefully make up another one and then come here again," he said, his voice stern. "It is very rare that a person can have prayers said for them from the top of Mount Zion, and we must take this responsibility very seriously."

"Yes, sir."

We stood for a long few minutes in a contemplative meditation, then he said a prayer in German, Hebrew, and English. Then he went down his list of people, asking for special blessings or specific things for each one as noted on his list, occasionally waving at the sky and shouting. At last we were done, and we went off to visit our friends, Hal and Shelley Cohen, at the Orr Shalom Children's Village they'd started in Jerusalem.

The next day I came back to the Mount Zion rooftop alone, fol-lowing Herr Müller's instructions. I brought the list I'd written the night before, and climbed the stairs. It was about 1:00 in the afternoon, and the sun was strong. There was a light breeze blowing from the direction of Bethlehem.

I said my prayers, going carefully through the list. Then I sat on the brick wall and faced the Wailing Wall, the place where Solomon had built his temple and where legend had it that the Messiah would reestablish the new temple when He returned.

I began to softly chant the prayer of Jehoshaphat just under my breath. It was relaxing: it took a single breath to complete each recitation of the prayer. The cemetery below was quiet, and nobody could see or hear me. After a few minutes, I began to chant louder, just above a conversational volume.

The air began to shimmer.

At first, I thought maybe I was hyperventilating, but then realized this was different from anything I'd ever experienced before. Parts of the city glowed in a soft, golden light, and I could see within them the movement of luminous shapes. I wondered if I was hallucinating.

The sky was populated with beings, and they were humming or singing along with my chant. I picked up the tune, and increased my volume a bit more. And then the buildings began to shift and change. Entire blocks of buildings became transparent, and I could see the soil beneath them. At first, I thought I was seeing through the buildings, but then I realized that in most cases there were trees or plants growing "within" the buildings: I was seeing the city as it had been at some ancient time, and the modern reality of the city was shimmering like a mirage of distant water on a long, hot road.

A sudden sensation rippled through me that felt like fear. But it wasn't my fear. I was sensing it from people who populated that moment in the past I was seeing. And sadness: a deep, profound sadness. I looked in the direction of Golgotha, about a mile away, and could make out some sort of activity through the shimmering light. The thought of it, what it might be, hit me in the stomach and tears filled my eyes. I continued chanting.

Parts of the city continued to fall away until everything was light. My heart was light, my body was light, the world around me was light, the sky was light. It was an ecstatic light: it had a presence, a reality, and a consciousness, as close as that word can come to expressing it. I began to cry softly, tears of joy, and the world returned to normal.

I walked back to the hotel and met Herr Müller, and we went for a walk to Mount Moriah, where the Dome of the Rock is built, behind and above the Wailing Wall, where Solomon had built the first temple. It was at this place, on this rock, where Herr Müller had secretly "blessed" his oil.

It was Friday afternoon, and as we walked around he mentioned to me that we should begin to prepare for the Sabbath, which would begin at sundown. I said something about the inconvenience or difficulty that Sabbath presented, interrupting our travels and all, and he shook his head.

"Shabat isn't just a weekend off," he said. "Shabat is the holiest of all the holidays. The *most* holy. And it happens every week!"

I knew that keeping the Sabbath was the fourth of the Ten Commandments, but didn't understand why it was so important that in the Old Testament it said people who violated it should be put to death. It seemed to me like a *healthy* thing to do, both physically and psychologically, but not something worth such draconian punishments if broken. I asked Herr Müller if the mental-health aspect of it might be why it was so important.

"No," he said. "Some people think that Shabat is the day of rest from the workdays of the week. But that is backwards." I don't remember his exact words beyond that, but this is my recollection of what he said:

> Before the beginning of creation, G-d was. That was JHWH, the infinite. From that came forth the creation, including the 'face of G-d' that David sought (and Herr Müller teaches about seeing). Everything sprang forth from that, in six stages, as is told in Genesis. All of creation is imbued with the presence, the fire, of this creative force, of G-d (as Herr Müller often points out to me as we walk through the forest and he talks to the plants and trees around him). And then, on the seventh clay, G-d "rested" or flowed back into His own consciousness. (This consciousness, this fire of life that fills all matter, is what he said I'd touched on top of Mount Zion, and before in my meditation chair, and on many smaller, less profound occasions during the years.)
>
> The purpose of human incarnations is to realize G-d. To know Him, to see His face, to feel His presence, and to do His will and work on the Earth during our lifetimes. Ultimately, this is "resting" in His consciousness, and that is the goal of Shabat, to "rest" in the presence and consciousness of G-d.
>
> Experiencing G-d's presence is the meaning and goal of life. It's what we should, ideally, be doing all the time, and what we all crave (although most people experience that craving in distorted ways, such as craving love, affection, sex, approval, recognition, etc.).

But if we spent all of our time "resting" in G-d's presence, then we wouldn't work: food wouldn't be gathered or grown, the world would become overgrown and wild, and our ability to "rest" in G-d's presence would be diminished.

So, just as G-d lifted Himself out of his "resting" consciousness and "descended" to create the heavens and the Earth—to do that work—we are allowed to work for six days each week in order to keep the explicate world and our bodies in it alive. But that seventh day is set aside as an opportunity for us to "rest" back into the presence of G-d.

This is why Jesus said, "The Sabbath was made for man, and not man for the Sabbath," and why he went out of his way to "violate" the Sabbath in front of the priests of his time. But he only broke the Sabbath with works of compassion or to fulfill his mission as Messiah: it was always as part of his "resting in the presence of G-d." He was trying to show them the true and intrinsic meaning of the law.

When we understand the meaning and purpose of Sabbath, it ceases to be an obligation or law, and instead becomes a joyous opportunity— something to be looked forward to and to savor fully.

I've always seen this in Herr Müller—as the end of the week approaches he gets excited about it, as I had as a child waiting for Christmas morning. He quits work early Friday afternoon, takes a walk, talks, becomes philosophical, and smiles and laughs. He loves to tell jokes and stories on the Sabbath, and Friday afternoons always herald the beginning of them. And he absolutely will not allow the "worries of the week" to intrude: discussion of business is *verboten*.

For years I assumed he was just following the commandment, and that he had decided to have a good time in doing it. But that day in Jerusalem I realized that, for him, the week was just what you have to go through to get to the Sabbath: Shabat is the highest goal of the week, the year, and represents the highest goals of life. This is why it's the most holy of the holidays, the only one that is mentioned in the Ten Commandments, and mentioned over and over again by Jesus, who also kept the Sabbath.

When I was in Germany in January of 1996, I spent a Sabbath with Herr Müller and we talked at length about this book. There were a few ideas I wanted to write down, but said I was reluctant to because it was

Sabbath and that would be "work." He told me to go ahead and write them down, that that was part of the purpose of Sabbath, and pointed to Jesus's parable about the man saving his animal on the Sabbath, and Jesus's saying, finally, "Wherefore it is lawful to do well on the Sabbath days."

When I asked if we were legalistically splitting hairs, he pointed out that the real indicator is in the heart: "If it is in your heart to do something on the Sabbath for G-d's honor and glory, then do it."

And so now I do.

The Miracle Baby

*Every man takes the limits of his own
field of vision for the limits of the world.*

—SCHOPENHAUER,

FURTHER PSYCHOLOGICAL OBSERVATIONS

John and Nancy Roy are two of the finest people I've ever known. As houseparents at Salem in New Hampshire, they were loving, considerate, hard-working, dedicated, loyal, and, above all else, wonderful parents to the foster children the state had put into our care and for whom they were Mom and Dad. They also both possess a powerful intellect that made conversation with them both a joy and a challenge.

But there was a hole in their lives. They'd been married several years, and had tried everything they could think of, but they couldn't produce a baby. They never confided in me the exact reason, but Louise and I both knew that for years they'd wanted a child of their own, and had repeatedly been frustrated in their attempts.

So one day Herr Müller visited Salem in New Hampshire. As I recall, his visit was because we'd already bought the new land, and he'd accompanied a dowser to tell us both where we should drill a water well, and also where we should consider and avoid locating the new houses we were intending to build.*

Herr Müller was staying in our guest house, and had brought along Horst Von Heyer (with whom I've visited Uganda, Russia, Bogota, and other places) and a professional German dowser whose name I forget.

---

*He views the Earth as having "lines of power" that cross it, places where the "energy" of the planet is better or worse for human habitation, and showed me how to "set" them. This is an understanding I later learned is shared by many Native American mystics. Dowsing is an ancient practice in Europe and the United Kingdom, and was used historically to set the locations and corners of Europe's ancient cathedrals. It is similar in many ways to the Chinese discipline called Feng Shui.

Within a few days they'd determined that:

1. The new land was a confluence of particularly good "power lines," and,
2. There were specific locations that were particularly good and bad for building children's homes because of the vibrations of the Earth under them.

It was particularly interesting to follow the dowser around. He was quite definite about his results. Most often he used a locally cut twig in the shape of a Y, but he'd always double-check his work with a metal dowsing rod of more modern design and construction that he'd brought with him from Europe.

While Herr Müller, Von Heyer, and this man were visiting, one morning we all had breakfast with John and Nancy. The conversation roamed over many topics, and eventually came to the issue that they were childless and unhappy about that situation. And, as they were both credentialed, degreed health-care professionals, this was particularly troubling: they knew the options, and had tried all but the most radical.

We sat over a breakfast John had made of whole-wheat pancakes, local maple syrup, and strong coffee. Herr Müller listened to their concerns and fears with a mischievous smile. When they were finished, he stood up from the table and walked around to stand behind Nancy. He placed both hands on her head.

"In the Name of G-d," he said, "I tell you that one year from this date you shall have the child you want."

That he was so emphatic about something so hopeless caused me to assume that he was going to bring his spiritual energy to bear on the matter, or that he'd been "told" to say what he did, as often happens with him. John and Nancy, however, while exercising the finest of manners to their guest, clearly thought that he was just trying to make them feel better. They thanked him, but in the way that one thanks an elderly person in a rest home.

That evening, John confided that he thought the whole thing had upset Nancy, and that it may have been "out of line" for Herr Müller to have done such a thing. I just nodded, thinking that I'd wait a few months before passing judgment.

Four months later, Nancy came over to our house quite flushed with excitement. She and John had just come back from the doctor: she was pregnant. The news was both a pleasant shock and an almost spooky validation of Herr Müller's pronouncement.

One year from the very day Herr Müller had given Nancy his blessing, she gave birth to Erica, their daughter and, to this day, their only child.

When we checked the date, I wondered if Herr Müller had seen the future, had created the future, or if the power of his own belief had simply been so great that it caused some subtle change in Nancy's mental state, leading her mind to alter her body. Or had he brought down some sort of divine power with the ability to heal Nancy's damaged reproductive system?

I'll never know for sure, of course, but this is only one of dozens of extraordinary things I've witnessed around Herr Müller and his belief in blessings: I'm inclined to suspend my doubts and set aside attempts at "scientific" explanation.

This summer (1996) Louise and I spent a week on the South Carolina seacoast with our youngest daughter, Kerith, and John, Nancy, and Erica. Every time I look at Erica, now a teenager about the same age as Kerith, I remember that day and marvel at Herr Müller's certainty in his blessings.

The Blessing of Elijah

And it came to pass, as they still went on, and talked, that, behold, there appeared a chariot of fire, and horses of fire, and parted them both asunder; and Elijah went up by a whirlwind into heaven. And Elisha saw it, and he cried, 'My father, my father, the chariot of Israel, and the horsemen thereof.' And he saw him no more: and he took hold of his own clothes, and tore them in two pieces. He took up also the mantle of Elijah that fell from him, and went back and stood by the bank Jordan. . . ."

—1 KINGS, SECOND CHAPTER

One of Herr Müller 's first instructions to me was that I must read the Bible. Not just a bit here and there, but the entire book.

I did this three times during the first years that I was executive director of Salem in New Hampshire. It was a fascinating and difficult task: discovering the horrible orders that G-d was said to have given to Joshua, for example, and reading the lists of names and seemingly trivial instructions in Numbers and Leviticus.

One of the stories that I discovered, however, had a sudden personal resonance for me. It was the story in 1 Kings about Elijah and his assistant, Elisha. Before Elijah was taken up to heaven in a chariot of fire (the way he "died"—according to some interpretations of the New Testament he later reincarnated as John the Baptist), Elisha was successful in extracting from Elijah a promise that a double measure of Elijah's power and blessing would fill him upon Elijah's death.

Upon reading this, I immediately booked a flight to Germany, and went to visit Herr Müller. It was sometime in the summer of 1980, and we walked along his special path through the forest and mountains surrounding Stadtsteinach.

"Do you remember the story of Elijah and Elisha?" I said, knowing that it was like asking a physics student if he'd ever heard of an atom.

Herr Müller nodded as we walked along the narrow trail on the side of the mountain.

"You know how Elijah promised his student Elisha that, when he died, a double measure of his spiritual power would be conferred to Elisha?"

"*Ja,*" he said. "This is a well-known story."

"Would you make that promise to me?" I asked.

He stopped and looked at me for a long and uncomfortable moment. I felt as if he was searching my soul. We resumed walking, wordlessly, and I followed him for another half-mile or so, higher and higher up the side of the mountain. At 68 years old, he kept moving up the trail with no apparent effort, although he'd been hospitalized with a rather severe heart attack a year earlier. To our left the pine forest rose starkly. Light, filtered by the dense trees into a dark green, was sprinkled with sharp, white rays of sunbeam the diameter of needles or pencils that made the ground sparkle. To our right, the mountain fell off sharply, a 500-foot drop through the trees straight down to the rushing Steinach river.

Finally we came to the spot along the trail where a bit of granite cropped out from the side of the hill. I knew that on this rock Herr Müller had scratched the four Hebrew letters for the most secret name of G-d: we had often come here to pray together, placing our hands one atop the other on the rock. He referred to this place and the trail leading to it as his "prophet's way."

He turned to me and said, "Kneel."

I did.

He pulled from his pocket the little bottle of oil he'd used to anoint the altar in New Hampshire, the holy oil he'd brought from Jerusalem.

"Do you know what it means to be anointed?" he said.

"I know that in my Bible, the word 'Messiah' is footnoted as meaning 'The Anointed One,'" I said.

He laughed. "Do not think this will make you a messiah. But it will change you forever. If you want this blessing, this shield, then you must be willing to take the burden that goes with it. It is not just as in the Twenty-third Psalm, 'He anoints my head with oil': it also means that you will take on a great responsibility, that a table will be prepared in the midst of your enemies. *You must help to save the world.* Do you understand?"

"Yes," I said.

"No, you do not," he said softly, his voice filled with compassion, "but you are willing and, for now, that is enough. After you are anointed, you will notice changes in your way of viewing the world, things will be forever altered, and then you will understand fully."

He looked up to the sky and rested one hand on the stone and said a long prayer in German. Then he said a prayer in Hebrew. Then he poured a few drops of the oil into my hair and on my forehead, put the bottle back into his pocket, placed his hands on top of my head, and said the Aaronic blessing in Hebrew.

I was kneeling and now had my eyes closed: fireworks were going off in my head. Between bright sparks of multi-colored light, I saw a kaleidoscopic series of little bits of scenes, like clips from a movie. Some were pedestrian and I didn't then understand their significance: a young man on a bicycle riding across the desert, a group of white-robed people walking across the same landscape, a young Herr Müller preaching in a huge European cathedral. Others were startling: myself in great pain; a hill with three crosses on it, the sky behind it black and swirling as the air was split with huge yellow and purple cracks of lightning; scenes of men dying on battlefields and children dying of starvation. None lasted more than a few seconds, yet each hit me with an emotional punch in the stomach.

Finally he said, "A double portion of my power and blessing shall fall upon you when I am no longer on this Earth, and until that time you have my full blessing."

I opened my eyes to look up: a roaring sound filled my ears and the air shimmered. The trees around us seemed semitransparent and I could see the sap flowing up in and through them. I could see across hundreds of miles of countryside, all shimmering with a gossamer light as if made of the most delicate fabric and floating in water.

He grabbed me by the arm and I gasped: I realized I had not been breathing. The world returned to normal as he pulled me to a standing position, and I felt a sadness at "coming back" so deep that tears filled my eyes.

He put his hand on the rock, over the sacred letters, and told me to put my hand over his. "Pray," he said, and so I said the Lord's prayer. When I came to the last part, the "for Thine art the kingdom . . ." he stopped me. "That part was added by some church people," he said. "It's better to end there with, 'but deliver us from evil,' or 'deliver us from the evil one.'"

I repeated the prayer as he'd instructed me, and when I finished he waved his hand toward the sky and shouted, "Amen!"

I said amen, too, but there must have been a quizzical look on my face because he said, "There is an old story that when a person prays, his petition goes to the gate of heaven, but it's when he or somebody else says 'Amen!' that it actually gets kicked across the threshold. If you really want it propelled, with great attention personally to G-d, and you want it bound on Earth even as you say it, by both His power and your own, you may even add, 'Selah!' after the 'Amen.'"

This was an important lesson for me, as I was just about to enter the most desolate place I'd ever seen—Uganda, during the war with Idi Amin—where I prayed often and silently always said, "Amen."

Uganda

*You can't say, "Civilization don't advance," however, for
in every war they kill you a new way.*

—WILL ROGERS, *AUTOBIOGRAPHY*

I first traveled to Uganda in 1980 with Herr Müller, and then went back
a year later with Horst Von Heyer to locate and negotiate the acquisi-
tion of land for a Salem village and hospital. My first trip there was
both spiritually devastating and enlightening, and I carried along a
small notebook and a pen; every night before I went to sleep I wrote
down the day's events. A few months after my return to the United
States, I published my notes in our newsletter, and one of the readers
who was the editor of *East/West Journal* asked me if he could publish
it in an edited form. I consented, and the publicity from that article
appearing led to several appearances on NPR and gave a big boost to
our efforts to raise money for Uganda.

From this experience, I saw firsthand the impact of Herr Müller's
prediction of the "curve of time," and how world events are accelerating. I also learned how the older tribal cultures of that part of the world
view the future. And I saw Herr Müller putting into action, with no
pomposity or high-sounding words, his philosophy of practicing acts of
mercy as a spiritual work.

Here's a copy of my original notes, along with some of *EWJ*'s
editing.

UGANDA SOJOURN:
LIGHT IN THE HEART OF DARKNESS
by *Thom Hartmann*
First published in edited form in East/West Journal, July 1981

Kampala, covering several square miles, is built on seven hilltops.
Before its destruction, it must have been one of the world's most beau-

tiful cities. Now everywhere are burned-out buildings, broken glass, and tens of thousands of hungry, haunting faces.

Young boys urgently cry out "cigarettes" among the thick crowd. Burlap bags lay empty upon the ground with small piles of tobacco and salt upon them. They are part of sales in the vast, teeming black market. Corrugated metal and cardboard shacks house thousands of people in endless rows of fetid squalor. Urine and rotted waste clog the dirt-paths of the market, as we gingerly navigate through the crowd, avoiding mud and pools of overwhelming stench. There has been no running water in this city for over two years. Young children everywhere stagger about in dazed desperation, their parents brought to death by famine, disease, war, and the insane, random murders by soldiers and associates of the former president Idi Amin.

Night is approaching. We must flee the market before the 8:00 P.M. curfew falls and an army of young Tanzanian soldiers, their rifles puncturing the night sky with staccato bursts of machine-gun fire, fans through the city. Two years ago, when Amin was overthrown and his brutal dictatorship ended, Ugandans welcomed the Tanzanian liberators from the south. But the combination of an unprecedented drought in this area as in other parts of East Africa, and an escalating civil war by factions still loyal to Amin and other dissidents have plunged this once peaceful and fertile land into another round of fear and chaos.

In the morning we find the bodies of those who could not find shelter before the night descended. During a short walk, Mr. Müller counts nine corpses, huddled in death next to buildings or sprawling naked in the streets.

Everywhere we come upon razed buildings, bullet holes, and the devastated ruins of a once-beautiful country. The first night we stay in a church dormitory with no water or electricity. The only food is white rice and stale white bread. Boiled rainwater is served on request, caught from the gutters, runoff from the roofs. We sleep on small steel cots in cement block rooms. There are half-inch steel bars on the windows, and the massive gray door in our cell has only a small glass-with-embedded-wire window. We are locked in for the night.

In the morning we rise early and leave by 8:00 A.M. for Mbale, a small town on the fringe of the famine district and the site of a large refugee camp. Our route will take us through miles of jungle and over the waterfall which is the source of the Nile.

We arrive at the Mbale camp just as the sun begins to set, a heavy grayness covering the jungle. Approaching the first cluster of mud huts, we are surrounded by perhaps a hundred people: children, adults, enfeebled elders at the end of their lives. Sweat, urine, and the smoke of hundreds of small twig fires make the air bite and cut into my nose and lungs. The earth is hard as stone, a red clay, and all about us are littered small bodies—crying, moaning, yelling for food or water, staggering about or sitting, staring emptily. Hunger haunts us as we walk about, incessantly tapping us on the shoulder as everywhere we are brought face to face, hand to hand, skin to skin with the hollow pain of empty bodies and frightened souls.

A toothless, graying old woman makes her way slowly through the crowd toward us. Her shuffle is slow, and she seems to wince with every step. Her breasts lie flat and dry, hanging down to a wrinkled and shriveled stomach. She cries out softly to us in Swahili. Rev. James Mbonga, a government official who is accompanying us, interprets: "I am a widow with eight young children. As my husband is dead, no one will help or care for me and my children. We shall die. Will you please help us?" A lump fills my throat.

"Soon," says Mr. Müller gently. "Soon, I promise, we shall return with some food for you."

As we walk back to our car through the makeshift "village," night descends. The air becomes cold, and people retreat into their huts. Outside one deserted hut we find three young children lying on a mat, naked to the approaching evening chill. Two of them are nearly dead. Their bodies look like skeletons, swollen heads on shrunken skin, too weak to even lift up or to make a sound. The third, a bit older, lifts himself up with obvious pain and tells his story. Their father is dead, their mother has never returned from a trip looking for food. Tears choke my eyes as we turn and walk away from these dying children. Forcing down the trembling in my throat, I whisper a silent prayer. I recall that back home in the United States today is Thanksgiving.

Tonight Sanford Unger of National Public Radio's "All Things Considered" show has arranged a satellite call to us, routed to our hotel. He interviews me about the situation in the camps and the bush, and I later learned that the interview ran that night in the United States as ATC's Thanksgiving special. Twice while we're talking to NPR we're cut off by the military when Unger asks me questions about troops and the dangers of being shot.

The next morning we leave for the northern region of Karamoja where starvation and disease are reportedly at their worst. We load into an aging Mercedes and pull out of town. The sky is a vast expanse of blue, the sun burning down, scorching both earth and people alike. As we travel north on the dusty, broken road, the terrain gradually becomes more and more desert-like. We pass through expanses of scattered grass-covered plains dotted with occasional mesquite-like trees. A game preserve, this area was once home to herds of lion, buffalo, zebra, elephant, and other African mammals. Now all are gone, the victims of poachers and hungry, fleeing troops and refugees.

As noon approaches, the air becomes painfully hot and dry, the plains pregnant with death. Rev. Mbonga points out some skeletons by the side of the road, those who couldn't make the eighty-one-mile march to Mbale. Their bones were picked clean by buzzards and ants. Empty eye sockets stare at us as we pass.

About 1:00 P.M., we come to a huge, barbed-wire-enclosed compound with cement and corrugated iron buildings: the Namalu prison Farm, scene of countless atrocities under the reign of Idi Amin, now a hospital and feeding station for the Karamoja refugees. As we pull into the compound, I see several hundred naked children huddled around one large building. From inside I can hear shouting and crying—this is the feeding center. The United Nations has been trucking in food recently, and each child is allotted one bowl of ground corn and powdered milk per day.

We stiffly climb out of the car and walk up to the building. Hundreds of sparkling, expectant eyes and outstretched hands greet us. My hands are grabbed and shaken over and over as we walk in. All around us, pressing against me, are huge bellies, festering sores, malaria, tuberculosis, yellow fever, worms, lice, cases of leprosy. At first I recoil, trying not to touch these sick and dying children. Then I remember Jesus's words, "I was hungry and you fed me, I was naked and you clothed me, I was sick. . . ." Looking into these innocent, helpless faces, I lean forward and meet their handshakes and hugs. Is Jesus here? Truly these children are the least of the least. "As you did to the least of these, my brothers, you have done to me. . . ."

Inside the feeding room we meet Ann, a thin Irish woman with brown hair, green eyes, and freckles who supervises the feeding. The floor of the large building is covered with tattered little bodies, some obviously near death. Ann directs us to the medical station next door. There we are met by hundreds of disfigured and nearly dead people. Dr. Jacques from the French Red Cross shows us around the TB wards, the malaria area, the "emergency" area. All are large, empty, cement rooms—no furniture, smashed out windows, with sleeping, unconscious, and moaning people lying on the hard dirt floors. The human suffering is more than I could have ever imagined.

We spend a few hours walking about and talking with the medical staff, all French nationals. We learn they are out of medicine, that nearly everyone has malaria, and that TB is rampant. Mr. Müller promises to send emergency medicine from Europe.

A mother carrying a baby approaches me. There are tears in her eyes, and her tone is pleading as she lifts her child to show me two large holes in the skin of his buttocks, areas about the size of quarters, where the skin and flesh have been eaten away revealing the muscle beneath. The child makes no sound or movement as the mother continues to stare hopefully into my eyes and cries to me in Swahili. He is the same age as my young son back in New Hampshire, and I wonder what I would be saying if I were her, what I would be thinking, if I would be able to endure the agony of watching my son die as I hold him in my arms.

"She is asking for food," Rev. Mbonga says. "And she wants you to heal her child."

My eyes fill with tears and I have to turn away. Herr Müller says, a crack in his voice, "Tell her we will send food and medication as soon as we can."

Rev. Mbonga translates, as I look back at the woman. When she hears his words, she looks at me for a long moment, as if trying to decide if we are telling the truth, and then silently turns and shuffles away.

On the way back to town and our "hotel," we stop at another refugee camp in Sirocco. A native ceremony is going on, and I take out my pocket recorder to tape it. Children start clustering around, and I play back a bit of their own voices. Shrieking with delight, hundreds of them crowd about me. Meanwhile Rev. Mbonga and Herr Müller sneak back to the car to get out several hundred loaves of organic whole wheat and sesame flat-bread which we have brought from the bakery of the Salem Children's Village in West Germany. The ruse works only for a moment. We had hoped to give the small amount of food we were able to "smuggle" into the country in our suitcases only to the most needy, those unable to come out and beg for it. But as soon as the food is out of the car, Rev. Mbonga and Mr. Müller are attacked by the mob of children and teenagers. A sea of screaming, hungry bodies descends on my friends, threatening to trample them. Within seconds all the food is devoured: we frantically pile into the car and drive off.

In a town between Sirocco and our hotel, we visit another refugee camp. They have some food, although there are hundreds of people on the edge of town who are starving. The village elders invite us to an evening ritual.

Twelve old African men sit around a fire, with Herr Müller, Rev. Mbonga, and me spaced at every fourth man. Near the fire is a brown clay pot about two feet in diameter: it's filled with a frothy brown liquid, and the men each have a long straw made from a reed of some sort that goes from the pot to their mouths.

The man to my right, toothless and shriveled, clad only in a wrap-around that was once half a bed-sheet, says something to me in Swahili and offers me his straw.

"What is it?" I ask Rev. Mbonga.

"It's the local brew," he says with a faint smile. "The women chew up a few different roots and herbs, then spit it into the pot. Water is added, and it ferments for about a week. The herbs are supposed to connect you to their gods: they're probably mild hallucinogens. It's probably alcoholic enough that you won't get sick from it, but you can refuse without hurting his feelings."

"Are you going to drink any?" I say.

He shakes his head. "I don't drink alcohol."

The old man says something to me.

"He said that it will open a door to the future for you," Rev. Mbonga says.

I look at Herr Müller with a question in my eyes. The man next to him offers him his reed, and Herr Müller, without a moment's hesitation, takes a long draw on the straw.

I turn to the man next to me and do the same. It tastes bitter and thick, like a milkshake with wormwood, and the bite of alcohol is unmistakable. The other men around the fire all murmur and drink from their straws.

The men begin to talk to us. Rev. Mbonga translates.

The oldest man of the group, long white hair, probably about 60 pounds, all skin and bones, wearing a cloth around his waist and sitting on the hard dirt cross-legged, says: "The world is fragile. Your American companies, sugar and coffee, they have raped our land. Now the Earth will no longer give us food because it is angry with what we have allowed you to do here."

He is starting to shimmer. His face looks younger, and his features are changing, becoming more clear. I can see the details of the wrinkles in the skin of his face although he is sitting six feet from me, and now the wrinkles are starting to go away. His skin is getting slightly lighter in color, and tightening.

"What can be done?" I say.

He shakes his head. There is a little visual echo left in the air by the motion. "It has gone too far," he says and now I can understand his Swahili even as Rev. Mbonga continues to translate. The men around the fire murmur their agreement. "The Earth cannot be saved by man: this is stupidity. The Earth will save itself, by killing off the men. Perhaps some of mankind can be saved, but the Earth will protect itself." It made me think of the vision I'd seen a decade earlier in my rented room in East Lansing.

Another man interjects. He is younger, perhaps in his sixties, and I can see through his skin. A moment earlier it was black and solid: now it's transparent, and I can see his veins and arteries, red and blue, and his muscles, as if looking through a thin film of dark gauze. His face looks compassionate. "This is the future you are seeing," he says, waving his hand around him at the refugee camp, the bare ground, the dead trees, the big-bellied children squatting and watching us from a respectful distance. "One day it will be the white man's future, too."

I shiver, believing his words.

We sit and talk for another hour about the spirit of the Earth, the future, and the role Americans and Europeans have played in the rape of the Third World. The drug wears off, and I'm left with a dull headache. We leave, and each man shakes my hand in a grave gesture, as if he knows we will never again meet.

Back at the hotel it's a dark night, and sounds of the African wilds fill the air through the open window. We discuss ways to help and decide to begin a Salem "baby home" nearby and to try and start with the three starving children we saw the night before in Mbale.

The following morning, our fourth day in the country, we leave the hotel at 7:00 A.M. to visit the camp just about a mile outside of Mbale. The sun is just rising, the ground and grass are wet with dew, and the air has a penetrating chill. This is the camp where we found the starving widows and the three babies lying on the hard ground. We take with us special food as we had promised. Most of the people are still in their huts, although a few are wandering about when we arrive. Rev. Mbonga leads us through the maze of huts and stinking mud to where the two widows live. One has eight children, the other seven. We leave them all our flat-bread, about thirty pieces. The three children are nowhere to be found. It has been two days. They have probably died.

Driving back to Kampala in the afternoon we stop in Jinja to meet with Mother Jane, a remarkable African lady who has started a "baby home" for thirty-five to forty children in her own residence. About five years ago, she rescued the first one, a baby boy, whom she found on a folded up newspaper at the edge of the river. The baby's fate reminded her of the story of the infant Moses in the Bible, and so her home became known as Center Moses. Since then she has rescued countless other babies and children from garbage cans, burned-out buildings, and parched fields. Those we meet this afternoon range in age from a tiny, fragile six-month old (whose twin sister and mother died when she was born) to a young teenager who appears to be about seven because of malnutrition. They have no toilet, no medicine, no water, and only two more days of food.

"Only G-d knows how much longer we shall survive," Mother Jane says. Despite the great anguish around her and in her eyes, she manages to smile and display a refreshing sense of humor. She tells us that her twenty-four-hour-a-day, seven-day-a-week work keeps her physically and spiritually strong. Her main concern, besides the omnipresent risk of disease and starvation, is people stealing her children for forced labor. We leave her six cans of powdered soymilk for the infants, some whole wheat bread and sesame, and a little chamomile for tea to calm upset or ill children.

One little parentless boy, about three years old, his head barely reaching above my knees, runs up and warmly embraces my legs, holding me immobile. He looks up into my face and smiles angelically. "Will you be my daddy?" he seems to say. I reach down and rub his back and head, and we stand together like this for a minute or so. Then our party moves on, and I have to break his grip. I leave him sadly holding his face in his hands, and a lump forms in my throat.

It is about a two-hour drive from Jinja to Kampala, the capital of Uganda. Having stared down the barrels of hundreds of machine guns this past week, the many roadblocks seem almost normal. We arrive in Kampala and are driven to the International Hotel, a modern high-rise in the center of town, where we are invited to a reception in our honor by the Commissioner of the Ministry of Rehabilitation. The building has obviously been the scene of fighting in the recent war.

I haven't had a bath in four days nor changed my clothes which are now rank with body odor and red Karamoja dust. As we sit down to a lunch of white rice and potatoes, I apologize to the Commissioner for my condition. He says not to worry, he hasn't had water, or, presumably, a bath for over two years, and that, in times like these, we needn't stand on formality. I notice that the clothing of his staff is old and tattered and recall that the factories and local importers haven't been open for over two years either.

The commissioner is excited about our plans to help the French medical team and to start a children's village in Uganda. He comments several times about the problems of temporary relief programs and says he hopes we will become a permanent part of Uganda.

That night we leave for Entebbe and after a one-thousand shilling "payment" at gunpoint to a police officer to pass through customs, we depart for Nairobi, the capital of neighboring Kenya. From there we will fly to London. I realize that I've contracted some sort of dysentery as I have awful diarrhea and every muscle in my body aches. Yet my discomfort is minuscule compared to those thousands of sick and dying people with whom we've spent the past week. My thoughts keep wandering back to Mother Jane in Jinja with her thirty or forty babies. With a cloth wrapped around her head and the copper gleam of her face in the hot Ugandan sun, she appears as firm as a rock. Her love and faith are as timeless as the bones of humanity's earliest ancestors which have been found in East Africa not far from here. I am reminded of the words of the psalmist, "I have been young and now am old; yet have I not seen the righteous forsaken."

Editor's Note from *East/West Journal:* In January Thom returned to Uganda with Dick Gregory and Horst Von Heyer and discovered that the situation had briefly improved following new elections. They negotiated with the government for land to begin a Salem refugee center and hospital near Mbale. However, by spring factionalism had broken out again and the situation has steadily deteriorated. Most international relief organizations, including Oxfam, have now left the country since they can no longer guarantee the safety of their staffs, and Ann, the Irish volunteer, was shot and killed by a sniper's bullet as she was feeding children. In April, Mother Jane and Rev. Mbonga visited Salem Children's Villages in Germany and the United States to help set up a supply line of food and emergency medicine to Uganda.

♦

As you can imagine, this experience was powerful evidence to me that Herr Müller was right when he predicted an accelerating confluence of events and influences with disastrous consequences. But what to do in the face of such a situation? Do what's right: acts of mercy, without regard for the seemingly overwhelming odds.

The odds only matter if you're playing the odds.

The magnitude of the problem only matters if you'll only accept a "well-engineered" response. What's right is a different matter.

By that summer Von Heyer and Uli Bierbach had gone back into Uganda from Germany to start construction of the Salem facility on the land for which we'd negotiated with the government. The village that was started there is now run as both a village and a hospital. It's still operating (1996) and one of the larger of the Salem programs around the world.

Mother Jane died of a heart attack in 1984, and Salem Uganda took in her children.

This experience was, for me, both shattering and strengthening. I'd been in the slums of America and much of the Third World, but had never experienced children dying in my arms or people starving to death as I watched. It tested my faith and caused me to remember Herr Müller's comment that "There are many mysteries, and we cannot know them all," and to accept, simply, the reality of the here-and-now and to do the best I could to help solve the problems.

Wake Up and Take Pictures

G-d cannot know himself without me.

—MEISTER ECKHART

One of the recurring themes in my discussions with Herr Müller over the past 18 years has been his notion that the average person is "asleep." He's described it variously in different ways at different times over the years, but the theme has always been the same: most people walk through life in a state of somnambulance, oblivious to the very real "now" all around them.

I wrote about this in my book *Focus Your Energy,** noting that Master Stanley also often brought up the topic. For myself, it was something I'd first noticed vividly that summer I lived in the tipi in Michigan's Upper Peninsula: there were times when I was very aware of being awake—being alive and present—and there were times when I was running on auto-pilot and might go an entire day before I paused for a moment, looked around, and realized when and where I was.

Since that time, particularly during the years when I taught meditation, I've often brought up this topic with people and found that most folks have virtually the same experience. They run on automatic so much of the day, thinking of the past or the future, that they spend little time in the now. Often we're only thinking of a past or future that's minutes away—judging or evaluating something that just happened or thinking about what we're going to say or do next—but whether we're thinking of what happened two minutes ago or twenty years ago, the effect is the same: we're not awake.

---

*Pocket Books, 1994

To be awake, Herr Müller says, is to know that you are alive and to feel the presence of G-d "in this moment."

Doing this brings a powerful spiritual energy into life. After you finish the next paragraph, stop reading for a moment and look around you. Notice that when you normally look at things you judge them: it's dirty, it's disorganized, it's pretty, it's blue or white, it's sunny . . . whatever. That judging pulls you out of the here and now and throws you back into thinking. And when you're thinking about things, you are not awake: you're asleep in your thoughts. You are separate from what you're observing.

Instead, put down this book and look around you and just see it all. Listen to the sounds. Feel your butt on the chair or whatever you're sitting on, and how that's connected to the floor, which is connected to the Earth, which is spinning through space. Smell the air. Spend a moment, lingering with each of your five senses as you move through them. And, for a moment, just be right here with—not separate from—this book and your place and totally in the present.

Some people don't do this for years—they spend virtually their entire lives asleep. Others do it only for little moments of time when they're in unique situations, such as on vacation, or at high points or during very exciting times. Some do it daily during meditation or prayer times, which is a great beginning. And a few "truly awake" individuals are in that state of here-now much or all of the time.

When I look back over my past, I see little jewels of vivid and bright memories, surrounded by a long fog of blurred time. Those bright memories, when I examine them, are invariably times when—at that time—I was "awake" and living in the here and now.

Herr Müller and Master Stanley taught me a number of exercises to be "awake" more often. They seem very simple, but are powerful when practiced.

EXERCISE 1:
SEE THE PRESENCE OF G-D IN EVERYTHING

The first is to look for the presence of G-d in things, people, and events. You can feel His presence when you're open to it—it's not a subtle thing but very intense. The more often and persistently you look for Him, the more often He will reveal Himself to you. The way I do this is to look at things and tell myself, "That is part of the body of G-d. It's been here billions of years and was created in the heart of a star, exploding out into space. This that I am seeing is part of the body of G-d." I then notice each of my senses and, as I'm doing it, say in my mind, "Thank you" to that which created me. And then I notice the presence of the moment, the time, that I am in the now. Sometimes I'll even carry on a dialogue with my Creator, or feel the things around me and remind myself that they are of and from G-d.

The key to it is to be awake in the present.

"The average person cannot walk even ten steps without falling out of this awakeness," Herr Müller once said. "It is so easy to forget G-d and to forget to be awake and alive here and now."

EXERCISE 2:
NOTICE THE WHOLE WORLD IN THE "NOW"

Herr Müller taught me a second technique during one of our walks through the forested mountain behind Salem in Stadtsteinach. We were on a steep hillside following his prophet's way trail, and Herr Müller was walking ahead of me.

"Thomas, have you ever thought that G-d needs you?" he said.

"To be on Earth for the transition that will come near the time of the millennium?" I said.

"More than that. He needs every person. Everybody. Always, for all time."

"Why?"

"To be His eyes and ears, His senses." Herr Müller stopped and turned to face down the hillside to the river 500 feet below us. I followed his gaze: across the valley was a small crumbling castle called Nordek, first built before the year 900 and now abandoned in the forest. The trees were various shades of brown in their winter leaflessness, the ground covered with browns, reds, and oranges from the fallen leaves, the pine trees around Nordek a deep green. The sky was a bright blue, lightening around the horizon, with thin wisps of white crystalline cloud at high altitude. The air smelled of pine resin and coming snow, cold as it moved through my nose and lungs. I could hear the sound of the wind in the trees, and the rushing of the water in the river below us.

"He created the world, but He is not here in a physical body to experience His own creation," Herr Müller said. "Therefore He created man, to walk on the Earth and see, hear, smell, taste, and feel His creation. And so our lives can be a gift to our Creator."

"How?" I said.

He put a hand on my shoulder and gestured at the valley in front of us. "Look in front of you. Do not look at only one thing, and do not look at everything. But notice it all. All the detail. All the color. All the texture and sounds and smells. And then close your eyes."

I did that, then closed my eyes.

"Can you still see it?" he said.

"No, it's gone," I said.

"Then open your eyes, look at it again, and close your eyes again. Keep doing that until you can see the same scene with your eyes closed as with your eyes open. And be as present in the here and now as you possibly can be: don't think about what you are looking at, just take it all in."

I did it a few times, and gradually I could begin to evoke a visual image with my eyes closed. "I'm getting it now," I said.

"That is the beginning of seeing," he said. "You must learn to see with power. To hear with power. To sense with power. And then keep those images in your mind as a gift to G-d." He slapped me on the back, hard. "It makes Him very happy when you take pictures here on the Earth for Him!"

"And it also seems to bring me into the here and now, into His presence."

"That is His gift to you in return. As you do your work, as you walk, as you talk, as you eat: if you do it in an 'awake' state, you make it holy."

"I have taught something similar to this," I said, "based on the work of Gurjieff and Master Stanley. It was a difficult teaching, though, for my students. For the average person, it's so natural to worry about what's going to happen next week. . . ."

"Thomas!" he interrupted me. "Do you remember the Sermon on the Mount?"

"What part?"

"That you cannot serve both G-d and the world. And if you choose to serve G-d, then you cannot think about the past or the future. You must tell people to forgive the past and trust the future."

That evening as we shared a dinner of fresh Salem bread, cheese, yeast spread, vine-ripened tomatoes, and garlic, he handed me an English-language Bible and said, "Turn to Matthew, the sixth chapter, the twenty-fourth verse, and read it to us."

I did so:

No man can serve two masters: for either he will hate the one, and love the other; or else he will hold to the one, and despise the other. Ye cannot serve God and mammon.

"And now verse thirty-three and thirty-four," he said. I read:

But seek ye first the kingdom of God, and his righteousness; and all these things shall be added unto you.

"I have had that memorized for years," I said. "But it says here that I should seek first the kingdom of G-d, not that I should walk around living in the 'now.'"

"Ah, but where is the kingdom of G-d?"

"Within us, as it says in the Bible."

"Correct. Look at Matthew seventeen, verse twenty."

And when he was demanded of the Pharisees, when the kingdom of G-d should come, he answered them and said, "The kingdom of G-d cometh not with observation: Neither shall they say, Lo here! or, lo there! for, behold, the kingdom of G-d is within you."

He added: "Your entrance to it is within you: you cannot find some gate somewhere in some city that says: 'Here is the entrance to the Kingdom of G-d.' So it is within you. But you can not enter it or know it if you are worrying about tomorrow or thinking about the past. Instead, when you are completely here and now, present, and know that you are alive, then you will live within that Kingdom of Heaven inside you, *then you will touch the power of life."* He lifted his glass of beer and winked at me. "This is a very, very difficult lesson, Thomas."

I knew it was true, and somewhere deep inside, you probably do, too. This is one of the most useful and transformational things I've learned over the years from Herr Müller.

Try it for a day or two: notice the world in the now. Whenever you notice that your thoughts have dragged you off into a not-now world, use that as a reminder to look around, listen to the world, and feel the presence of *here and now*. And in that moment, try saying, "Thank you."

It sounds simple, but is not; this is a very difficult teaching. It's also—perhaps because of its difficulty—extraordinarily powerful.

Leaving Salem in New Hampshire

I see too many men delay their exits with
a sickly, slow reluctance to leave the stage.
It's bad theater as well as bad living.

—JOHN STEINBECK, *TRAVELS WITH CHARLIE*

Toward the end of 1982, I was in full-blown burnout with the Salem program in New Hampshire. Louise and I had been working seven days a week, 52 weeks a year, since September of 1978, without any time off and at a salary that started at zero and peaked at $125 per week. We'd wiped out our savings, and we were both exhausted by dealing with the child care bureaucracy: the easily-bored and impatient part of me was being driven nuts by the bureaucrats. And we were becoming increasingly concerned about the habits and behaviors our own children were picking up from living with the severely abused and disturbed youngsters the state had placed in our care.

Our third child had been born the previous year, too. We named her Kerith Jane: Kerith after a river in Israel that Jesus once walked along, and Jane after Mother Jane in Uganda. The birth of Kerith was another milestone in our lives, a turning point.

And, perhaps most frustrating, the children's village had become successful. The struggle had faded, and boredom was setting in for me.

So I began the transition out, back into the world of business which I knew so well. I didn't view it as "leaving Salem" or leaving a spiritual life, so much as simply a new phase. Hal Cohen once told me that every time a person moves or changes jobs, it's as if they've reincarnated, and they have a whole new set of options and directions for life, as well as a whole new set of lessons to learn.

While I'd always have a connection to the children's village in New Hampshire, I knew intuitively that my ultimate work was somewhere

161

else. Not knowing where or what it was, other than that it probably had to do with Salem, I decided to widen my options and prepare for our oldest child's going to college by earning enough money to set aside some savings.

In my spare time, I started a computer parts company with an old friend in New York, and sought out writing assignments. Within six months, it was clear that we could earn enough to pay rent in town and move off the grounds of the children's village.

I remember when I called Herr Müller to tell him. I couldn't say it to his face: it felt to me like a betrayal. So I called him and told him all my stories and rationalizations and reasons. He listened patiently, and then said, "Thomas, I give you my blessing. I wish you well. You are making your decision, and so it must be the right decision."

"You're not angry?" I said.

"Not at all."

"I want to continue to be available to you. This way I can earn enough money so that I can pay my own way to do travels around the world on behalf of Salem."

"Of course."

"I still have your brotherhood and blessing?"

He nearly shouted: "Absolutely and without a second thought!"

In late 1982 we moved from Stinson Lake into Plymouth, New Hampshire, where we lived for a year to be available to Salem if they needed our help, and I started writing full-time for several magazines. At the end of the next year, I was earning enough from my writing and our computer parts business that we could move to warmer climes: Louise and I looked around the country and decided on Atlanta.

From that time until 1986, I built up the computer company, opened a travel agency in Atlanta with Louise and an old friend, and wrote and sold over a hundred articles. I traveled to Africa and Asia for Herr Müller, and set up sponsorships for programs in Taipei, Nairobi, and Bangkok. I made trips to Germany every few months to recharge my spiritual batteries and spend time with Herr Müller. Always having six projects going, now free of the shackles of the bureaucratic turn my position at New England Salem had taken, I was having a great time. And I was seeing Herr Müller more often than before, and was getting many things done for Salem, both in New Hampshire (I was still on the Board of Directors) and all over the world.

And then, in the end of April of 1986, it happened again. I was visited in a dream by Master Stanley, who, in his thick Swiss-German accent, told me that I must go to live in Europe. It was an idea Herr Müller had suggested some months before—that Louise and I and our family move to Stadtsteinach to help him with international Salem work—and I'd been rolling it around in my mind quite a bit. I didn't know if Master Stanley had actually "visited" me or if I'd created the dream, but even if it was the latter, I considered it a message from my unconscious. The next day I called Herr Müller and arranged to visit him.

The plane landed in Frankfurt the week of my birthday, just as the first and largest radioactive cloud from Chernobyl passed over the city. It was raining and the rain was deadly, carrying radioactive cesium and iodine: the streets were eerily deserted. The next morning I took the train to Stadtsteinach.

"When you encounter obstacles, you know what you are doing is important," Herr Müller said, laughing, when I expressed my concerns about moving my family to the then-very-radioactive region of the Frankenwald. "It must be very important that you come to Europe, that there had to be such a big obstacle as Chernobyl!"

The travel agency had hit sales of about five million dollars a year and been written up on the front page of *The Wall Street Journal*. The computer business was still generating an income for me. And I could always go back to writing. So in the first week of June, Louise and I sold the travel agency and moved to Stadtsteinach with our children and our dog. We lived there for the next year, and it was one of the most difficult and the most fulfilling experiences of my life.

Sent into the World
by Michael

Destiny is not a matter of chance, it is a mat-
ter of choice; it is not a thing to be waited for,
it is a thing to be achieved.

—WILLIAM JENNINGS BRYANT

During that year, Herr Müller told me of one of his most vivid memories. Perhaps it was an early dream of his? Whatever, I recognize the power of his memory.

It was a time before he was born on the Earth. He was in a great hall, made of marble and decorated very elegantly, and there were thousands of people lined up in rows. He was in one of the back rows, and smaller and shorter than most of the people there, who were both men and women.

Then into the great hall came a magnificent-looking man who Herr Müller recognized as the Archangel Michael. Everybody snapped to attention and assembled themselves into long lines, several rows deep and facing him.

"There is a battle coming on the Earth," Michael said. "It will be fought first on the most subtle of spiritual levels, and then on the coarser levels. I am looking for people who are willing to go to Earth at this time to take on this battle. Most of your work will be invisible, and you will suffer great difficulties. You may be tortured, or nearly put to death. You may often wish for death. But, if you persevere, you will sit with the Son of G-d at the wedding table. On the other hand, if you do not volunteer for this mission, there will be no penalty or punishment and you will be allowed to stay here in heaven and enjoy the life you have. Now, who will choose to volunteer for this?"

Herr Müller looked around and nobody was stepping forward.

"How can this be?" Herr Müller wondered: there were so many mighty and powerful beings here.

"Will nobody step forward?" Michael said, his voice now thundering. There was no motion.

Michael raised his hand, which held a flashing sword. "Then step back if you are unwilling to go with us!"

All around Herr Müller, people stepped back. There was a giant rush to step back, in fact. He looked about in wonderment. "How could anybody not want to sit at the table with Jesus Christ?" he wondered, as he stood in place.

After a few moments, everybody had moved back a few yards except Herr Müller, who stood alone at his end of the hall. Down the row, a few hundred yards and so far away he couldn't make out their features, there were other people who hadn't stepped back.

Michael looked at them and his face became filled with love and compassion. "I will send you help and I will send you helpers, although they will usually not be obvious. But you will know. And always remember, no matter how terrible it gets, that you are on a mission and your actions, if you are successful, will save humanity." Michael paused and looked around, then said, "And now I tell you what is your most powerful weapon: to commit tiny acts of compassion."

As Herr Müller nodded, Michael struck him on the shoulder with his sword. He winced from the blow, and then began to cry and struggle, trying to speak, but unable to: he was now in the body of a newborn baby, Gottfried Johannes Müller, in Germany, in 1913.

I later asked Herr Müller if he thought I, too, had chosen to incarnate on the Earth at this time for a specific purpose. He said that with me and others who were working to help the planet and the people on it the answer was a definite yes, and that probably we were there in that room with him, among those who did not step backwards.

"What about other people?" I asked. "All the other people on the Earth?"

"*Each* person is here for a reason," he said. "They have surrounded themselves with others who are there for a reason, each for himself and each for his circle. Always it is."

"And you and me?"

"We are brothers and teachers."

"What is my purpose? My mission?"

"To help prepare the world and the people in it for the new age."

"But there is a whole New Age movement," I said.

"This is different, from that. Those people do not know what they are talking about when they say 'New Age' and think it means that they should sing in a park and do yoga. This is the age of the Messiah!" He hit his fist on the desk, fire in his eyes. "This is the time of the rebirth of Earth and humankind, the return of ancient wisdom and knowledge."

"And how should I do my part in this?"

"You will have to wait to know that," he said in a tone that meant the conversation was over.

EXERCISE: FINDING YOUR TRUE PURPOSE

Since that time, I've often pondered my purpose. The importance of this was so great to me that I developed a mental exercise to help others discover their own purpose and bring it into their lives: it's in my books *ADD Success Stories* and *Focus Your Energy*.

Ask how you'd live your life differently if you knew you were going to die soon, then ask yourself who those people you admire are and why you admire them, and then ask yourself what was the most fun time in your life. The answers to these questions, when seen, heard, and felt, provide us with an open doorway into our mission, our destiny, our *purpose*.

Purpose, I now believe, is the foundation of a meaningful life.

Patience and Impatience

Let us, then, be up and doing,
With a heart for every fate;
Still achieving, still pursuing,
Learn to labor and to wait.

—LONGFELLOW

During that year in Germany, Herr Müller kept telling me that the biggest lesson I needed to learn was to wait. To be patient.

Waiting goes against my nature, and this was an odd nonsequitur coming from him, as he is often frighteningly impatient himself. When he's "on the hunt" or has an idea he's passionate about, he becomes an absolute fanatic, obsessed with that particular plan. Then, a week or a month later, he's off in some new direction. This week it's starting the natural health clinic, a month later it's opening a new program in China, and on and on. In that respect, he and I are very much alike, so it was interesting to me to hear him say that I must learn to develop patience.

As I watched him more closely, however, I discovered that he has the ability to be patient, even in his impatience. It's hard to describe: I'd know that he was mentally and emotionally screaming for something to happen, yet he'd sit back and say, "If it doesn't work out, or it takes another ten years, it's just G-d's will. We have to understand that, and be patient. We live in His time, not Him in ours."

So I practiced patience. It was as much a time of spiritual and emotional growth for me as was that summer in the tipi.

Nearly every morning I'd get up at 6:00 A.M. to catch Herr Müller as he went for his 7:00 A.M. walk up to his altar for his morning prayers. Every Friday night I'd join him with Sister Lotte and Frau Bethge as they lit the Sabbath candles and he read from the Bible. Afterwards, he'd often invite me back to his apartment to do the same with his family, only with bread, wine, and the Hebrew Sabbath blessings.

I was also working on several projects for Herr Müller. A physician friend of mine from California, George Than, had once shared with me how when he had to give injections to people, particularly of antibiotics, that he'd try to put them into specific acupuncture points whenever possible. "It seems to increase the potency or effect of the medication," he said. At the same time, the doctor at Salem's holistic health clinic, a Swiss M.D. by the name of Oswain Gierth, had shared with me many of the homeopathic remedies he was using, often by injection, with his patients. I'd studied and written about homeopathy for years and received a Ph.D. in it from Brantridge Forest School in England, and spent November of 1986 in Beijing, studying acupuncture at the international teaching hospital there. As I was learning those methods in China, the idea occurred to me to inject homeopathic remedies into acupuncture points.

I called George and asked him if he'd come over to Germany so we could discuss my idea, and he and I and Dr. Gierth got together in Stadtsteinach and brainstormed the idea. I'd developed a whole new model by that time, writing a short book about it and researching which points should work best with which remedies. I also saw a need for a product for the lay person, and so came up with the idea of combining homeopathic remedies with DMSO (dimethylsulfoxide, which rapidly transports other things across the skin barrier into the bloodstream) or alcohol and putting it into a felt-tip pen instead of ink so it could be applied noninvasively to acupuncture points.

I named this new medical technology Endochiliopathy from the Greek "endo" (within), the Chinese "chi" (life force), and the Latin "opathy" (science or study of). George and Oswain were both enthusiastic, and Herr Müller suggested that we start practicing this at the clinic in Stadtsteinach and begin to manufacture the remedies for sale to the public as a way of earning money for Salem. So I began meeting with German homeopathic pharmaceutical companies to try to develop products appropriate for injection into or application onto acupuncture points, and finished writing the book about Endochiliopathy.

Within a year of my meetings with the German pharmaceutical companies, two of them had come out with injectable homeopathic remedies and charts correlating the remedies to acupuncture points:

apparently the idea had merit, at least in their minds. And Dr. Gierth to this day practices the injection of homeopathic remedies into acupuncture points at the Salem clinic in Stadtsteinach. But the business side of it, the manufacturing of the remedies, we decided to set aside because it would have been too large an undertaking to compete with the giant German homeopathic manufacturers.

At the same time I was writing about Endochiliopathy, I was working to expand Salem's international work. I took trips to both Asia and South America to meet with individuals or groups who might be interested in starting Salem programs in their own countries.

And I was working on a novel about what I, as an outsider, saw as the incipient threat of the renewal of fascism in Europe and the United States.

Many interesting things happened during that year. One of particular note for this American was when my son, Justin, came home from the local German public school where he attended second grade.

"What did you learn today in school?" I asked.

"We learned that the American government killed 15 million Indians," he said. "It's called genocide."

Shocked, and assuming that this must be some sort of revisionist teaching in the German schools, I called my father, who was a history major in college.

"Dad, did our government kill 15 million American Indians?"

"At least," he said. "There were at least that many of them living here when we first arrived, and there are fewer than a million now. And it took many years. We were the first nation to use biological warfare, for example. When the smallpox vaccine was invented, the Army inoculated the soldiers and then traded smallpox-infected blankets with the Indians. We wiped out several states of them that way. And then the government declared a bounty on them, and the way you proved you'd killed an Indian so you could collect the bounty was by bringing in a scalp or a pair of ears.*

---

*There is debate in today's academic circles about exactly which practices the U.S. government initiated or used in herding and virtually exterminating most tribes of American Indians, but hardly anyone disputes that the extermination took place, amid a string of broken treaties, broken promises, and government-sponsored treachery.

That night, I went to Herr Müller and told him what I'd learned. "Germany is paying billions in reparations to Israel," I said, "but in America we're still taking land from the Indians. What do you think of that?"

He put his hand on mine. "And you brought slaves from Africa. Like Germany, your country has a heavy burden, spiritually. It began as a blessed place, but strayed from that. There will be a high price to pay."

"What can I do?"

"You must do what you can for the American Indians, to repay the debt of your family living on their land. Also, you must know that they have much to teach you, that your ancestors destroyed much important knowledge when they tried to destroy the Indians."

The subject was changed at that point and I thought he'd forgotten about it, but years later he brought it up several times again.

In the midst of all of this activity, though, things often moved slowly. I'd go to Herr Müller and express my concerns about the future, about the work we must do, about the difficulties we were facing. He always gave me the same answer: "Wait. Just worry about today: the future will take care of itself." I worked on that.

One high point was Christmas, 1986. I'd been in Stadtsteinach for Christmas before, and it was an amazing experience. In the early 1980s, government cutbacks in welfare programs had, in one year, cut by half the number of children placed in group homes in Germany. As a result, Salem had consolidated most of their children in the children's village in Kohval, Germany, in the north near Hamburg, and turned the Stadtsteinach property into a natural health clinic and conference center. But there was still a family of children with mental disabilities living in Stadtsteinach in 1986, and some of the children who'd lived there in decades past came "home" for Christmas.

On Christmas Eve, Louise, our children, and I went out of the Salem buildings—which cover about 30 acres and include room for over 200 people to live—and walked up the mountainside for several miles along an old dirt road. We were accompanied by about twenty people from Salem. In the distance, lit by star- and moonlight, we could hear a trumpet playing a Christmas hymn. As we made a turn in the forest, ahead of us was a large pine tree with hundreds of candles clipped to its branches. Beside it was Herr Müller with his old Bible, about a dozen children, the three horses, two sheep, and a few other assorted animals from Salem. The air was still and cold, sharp in the nose, and smelled of the pine forest and recent snow. The lit-up tree was a bright and rich green in a forest turned gray and colorless by the dim star- and moonlight. I felt like I'd stepped into an ancient time, a sacred and holy time and place, and my eyes watered in the cold air.

One of the children played a few Christmas hymns on the trumpet and another sang one, and then Herr Müller read the story of Christmas from the book of Luke in the Bible. Then he said a prayer and gave us all a blessing and we left to go home for our personal Christmas celebration.

By the end of a year, in July 1987, Louise and I were financially back where we'd been when we'd left Salem in New Hampshire: virtually all our savings were spent. With three young children, neither of us felt comfortable with this, although Herr Müller often pointed out that he was also the father of young children (Samuel and Nathan, his sons, were then in elementary school), and he only owned his clothing, his Bibles, and a few household articles. "Don't worry about money," he'd often say. "Money will come. It is nothing. Work on living today fully."

Louise and I, however, were longing to return to America. So, full of rationalizations about money and future and children and culture, we moved back to the USA.

When we arrived back in Atlanta, Louise and I started a business in our basement to produce magazines and newsletters for corporations. The business soon grew to where it could move to more formal quarters, and I was again back in the business world, although once a week for about five years I taught the meditation and insight techniques of Herr Müller at an Atlanta meditation center, run by an extraordinary woman named Rochel Haigh Blehr, in suburban Roswell. I also spoke at the New Age Expo in Atlanta, and gave speeches and did trainings in meditation in a variety of other venues. And I was continuing to visit Germany every few months, and to visit various parts of the world for Salem.

But I was feeling increasingly disconnected from Herr Müller and Salem, and soon that disconnection became unmistakable.

One summer morning in 1988, I noticed that the stone was missing from my lapis ring. I searched for it everywhere I could think of, but it was nowhere to be found: not in the house, on the way to or in the car, or in our offices.

The next morning, around 9:00 A.M., the phone rang.

"Thomas," Herr Muller's voice came from the other end. "You worry too much about losing things."

"I lost the stone from my Salem ring," I said, knowing that he knew it or wouldn't have called me, but figuring it should at least be said out loud.

"It did its work. Now you do not need it any more. It went away."

"But you blessed that stone!"

"It was the first tablet," he said. "When you begin your real work, you'll have the second tablet. The same as Moses, when he came down from the mountain. The first tablets had a purpose, but they had to be destroyed, to be lost, just as the stone from your ring."

"What shall I do?"

"Wait."

After some small talk, I hung up feeling very unsatisfied with the conversation. It was almost as if he was telling me that I was now divorced from him and the Salem work: the thought left a cold hole in me.

A few months later, my right ring finger naked, Louise and I were in St. Thomas in the U.S. Virgin Islands. I led her through the old city, a winding path through the back-streets and off the tourist trail, feeling an intuitive pressure. Finally we came to an old, unpretentious house converted into an antique store. "This is where we're going," I said to Louise, still not knowing why.

Browsing around the store, I felt pulled to the back, an old counter that was part of some built-in shelving and had knickknacks and jewelry under glass. In the case was an antique ring, inlaid with yellow-gold filigree in white gold, and a lapis stone. I knew it was the reason I'd decided to even get off the boat in St. Thomas, and what had drawn me through all those back streets. The woman in the store pointed out how such detailed inlay work wasn't done any longer: the ring was at least a century old, perhaps two or three. But it was also very expensive: more than the money I had with me.

I wanted to charge it on my credit card, but Louise insisted instead that I put down a deposit to hold it. "And if you can bring in a large account for the business within the next few weeks, then we'll have the money and you can buy your ring," she said. In the spirit of marital compromise, I agreed.

The next week I received a call from a man with a large hotel chain inquiring about our services. It turned into what was then, and is to this day, The Newsletter Factory's largest account. I called St. Thomas and had them ship me the ring.

A month later, I flew to Germany, anxious to have Herr Müller anoint and bless the ring. He looked at it with less than an enthusiastic eye. "This stone has been worn by others," he said. "It has their vibrations, which are good, but not yours. And, although it's a beautiful ring, the stone is not a very good lapis."

I pointed out that the setting was such that the stone could come in contact with my skin, as he'd suggested in the past (such settings are hard to find) and told him about how the ring had "called to me" in the Caribbean.

"In that case," he said, again enthusiastic, "I will bless this ring and try to clean it of its old vibrations." I left Germany feeling relieved, but that wasn't the end of the ring story.

In 1995, when I started to write this book, I asked Herr Müller what he thought of my ring. "It is not yours," he said. "The stone has the vibrations of other people. I told you that before, but did not want to 'press' you."

So I went to a jeweler in Atlanta and asked if it was possible to change the stone in my ring to a new one, recently mined. They indicated it would be easy, and quoted me a price. They ordered several stones for me to pick from, and I chose a piece of deep-blue lapis that was not artificially dyed (as are most lapis stones) and had it put in the ring.

When the ring was finished, I flew to Germany and visited Herr Müller, and he looked at it with a big smile. "This stone is without human vibration," he declared. Then he put a drop of his holy oil on it, said a prayer, and held it in his fist for a while before returning it to me. "That is your 'second tablet' stone for your 'second tablet' ring. Perfect."

Putting the ring on my finger, I immediately felt a sudden breathlessness, as if I'd touched an electrical circuit for a moment. That night I had an extraordinary dream about the transformation of humankind. It was the right choice, to replace the stone, and portended the beginning of my return to my "purpose" of working to change the world for the better.

Discovering and Writing
Books about ADD
Hunters, Farmers,
New Cultures and Old

Whenever a new discovery is reported to the world, they say first, "It is probably not true." Then after when the truth of the new proposition has been demonstrated beyond question, they say, "Yes, it may be true, but it is not important." Finally, when sufficient time has elapsed to fully evidence its importance, they say, "Yes, surely it is important, but it is no longer new."

—MICHEL DE MONTAIGNE

In 1992 we were living back in Atlanta, and our son Justin, whose 1978 birth had heralded the beginning of our full-time work with Salem, began to have some problems keeping up his grades in school. We took him to a psychologist to see if he had some sort of learning disability, and the fellow solemnly pronounced that Justin had a "brain disease" that he called Attention Deficit Disorder or ADD.

This sent me into a year-long research binge. I'd heard all about ADD when I ran Salem: the vast majority of our kids came in with that label, or the less charitable Minimal Brain Dysfunction or Hyperactive tags. We'd even done a study of the Feingold diet, which I'd published in *The Journal of Orthomolecular Psychiatry* in 1981. But my own child? It was startling.

The more I researched ADD, however, the more it became clear to me that Justin wasn't the only one in the family with it—whatever "it" was. Over and over again I saw myself in the diagnoses, and I was determined to learn everything I could about it.

175

The primary characteristics of ADD are easy distractibility, impulsiveness, and a love of risk or high-sensation. While conventional wisdom had it that these were crippling disabilities, the more I looked at it the more it seemed to me that in some circumstances these might be assets.

In a primitive hunting society, for example, a person constantly scanning their environment (distractible), able to make and act upon a decision instantly (impulsive), and willing and enthusiastic to go into the jungle where there are things that want to eat him as much as he wants to eat them (a risk-taker) would be at an advantage.

Conversely, as society moved more toward agriculture and industry, people who were able to focus on putting the same nut on the same bolt on the assembly line all day long (or picking bugs off plants, or hoeing the same row day after day, or doing tax accounting) would be valued. They'd be more compliant and risk-averse, and so they wouldn't talk back to the boss or change jobs, and they'd have enough control over their impulses that they'd not make rash decisions which could have season-long consequences in an agricultural society, or be disruptive in a highly controlled society where a firmly entrenched power structure doesn't like dissidence.

It seemed to me that ADD wasn't so much a disorder as a matter of people stuck out of time. Our schools were set up along the agricultural/industrial model,* as were most jobs, and certainly it would take the careful, methodical type of mentality to make it all the way through the traditional school systems to get a Ph.D. in, for example, conventional psychology. So, in a society which has persecuted differences since before even Cotton Mather or Joe McCarthy, the linear "farmers" pointed to the nonlinear "hunters" and labeled them as defective and disordered.

I'd seen firsthand how powerful labels are, particularly to children, during the years I ran Salem. If you could convince a child that his particular nature or destiny lay along a particular line, he would perform spectacular feats to live up to that expectation—even when it was a negative one, as most of the Salem children had learned when growing up ("You're bad"). And I wasn't enthusiastic about my son walking

---

*For an excellent analysis of how twentieth-century schools are set up on the "factory" model, see *Smart Schools, Smart Kids: Why Do Some Schools Work?* by Edward Fiske, former education editor of the *New York Times*. (Touchstone Books, 1992.)

around for the rest of his life with the badge of "psychiatric disorder" pinned to his jacket, or telling himself the story that he suffered from a brain dysfunction.

So I wrote a book about the hunter/farmer view, titled *Attention Deficit Disorder: A Different Perception*. I wrote the book mostly for Justin, but it found a wide audience, even being written up in *Time* magazine. (After that publication, I wrote four more books on ADD, while also collaborating on a book on the JFK assassination.)

I dedicated the book to my parents, who we now realized had raised four ADD boys and survived the experience (albeit with a few scars, no doubt), and to Herr Müller.

When the first edition came out, I flew over to Germany with a half-dozen copies of the book. I gave them to him, and explained my notion of hunters and farmers to him and his wife, Ursula. They agreed that he was a hunter as much as I was, and scoffed at the notion of this personality type as representing a "mental illness." If anything, Herr Müller said, people with what is called ADD are sometimes more spiritually aware than "normal people," although he readily agreed that they would have more problems with farmer institutions such as schools, churches, and factories.

It reminded me of Clark Stinson's comments about how agriculture was the beginning of the downfall of man. "What do you think of the idea," I asked Herr Müller, "that the agricultural revolution, and then the industrial revolution were not good things but were bad things, because they set the stage for mankind to begin to destroy the Earth?"

He stroked his beard and said, "It is possible."

Later I was thinking of how the Old Testament, in particular, was the story of the wrenching changes that a nomadic hunting and herding society went through as they made the transition to being a stable agricultural society. Moses led that charge, and it was at the time of that transition that the Ten Commandments had to be issued to the people.

Prior to that time of "stable and settled" living in one place for centuries, there were no "commandments" about how a person should live: could it be that written rules were now necessary because this lifestyle wasn't a natural thing for humans? Could it have been the beginning of our losing touch with our own connection to divinity and inner knowledge?

I asked Herr Müller about that, and he again said, "it is possible." (He said that the concept of older and younger cultures was interesting, but too academic for him. "I prefer to simply live life, fully alive each day." Interestingly, that's just what one would expect an older culture teacher to say if a younger culture theorist wanted to discuss theories in the younger culture point of view [science].)

Then he told me to go read the Sermon on the Mount in the book of Matthew. I was amazed to read, in this new light, Jesus's words that we should consider the example of the birds that do not "gather into barns" but instead live from day to day. He said:

6:24 No man can serve two masters: for either he will hate the one, and love the other; or else he will hold to the one, and despise the other. Ye cannot serve God and mammon.

6:25 Therefore I say unto you, Take no thought for your life, what ye shall eat, or what ye shall drink; nor yet for your body, what ye shall put on. Is not the life more than meat, and the body than raiment?

6:26 Behold the fowls of the air: for they sow not, neither do they reap, nor gather into barns; yet your heavenly Father feedeth them. Are ye not much better than they?

6:27 Which of you by taking thought can add one cubit unto his stature?

6:28 And why take ye thought for raiment? Consider the lilies of the field, how they grow; they toil not, neither do they spin:

6:29 And yet I say unto you, That even Solomon in all his glory was not arrayed like one of these.

6:30 Wherefore, if God so clothe the grass of the field, which today is, and tomorrow is cast into the oven, shall he not much more clothe you, O ye of little faith?

6:31 Therefore take no thought, saying, What shall we eat? or, What shall we drink? or, Wherewithal shall we be clothed?

6:32 For after all these things do the Gentiles seek: for your heavenly Father knoweth that ye have need of all these things.

6:33 But seek ye first the kingdom of God, and his righteousness; and all these things shall be added unto you.

6:34 Take therefore no thought for the morrow: for the morrow shall take thought for the things of itself. Sufficient unto the day is the evil thereof.

Reading this, the thought occurred to me: could Jesus have been warning the people of His time, and us now in ours, to beware of the dangers of the agricultural life and the type of culture and civilization that "dominating the Earth" would create? Perhaps He was even warning about the Pharisee mentality of organizing and legalizing and defining every little thing, planning out every action, and constantly measuring each other?

In another book,* I wrote about a discussion of this topic that I had during a trip to India for Salem. Two Indian businessmen and a physician told me that they thought that what we in the West call ADD was actually an indicator that a person was nearing the end of their reincarnational cycle, and therefore a good thing.

"In our religion," the physician said, "we believe that the purpose of reincarnation is to eventually free oneself from worldly entanglement and desire. In each lifetime we experience certain lessons, until finally we are free of this Earth and can merge into the oneness of what you would call God. When a soul is very close to the end of those thousands of incarnations, he must take a few lifetimes and do many, many things, to clean up the little threads left over from his previous lifetimes."

"In America we consider this a psychiatric disorder," I said. All three looked startled, then laughed.

"In America, you consider our most holy men, our yogis and swamis, to be crazy people, too," said the physician with a touch of sadness in his voice. "So it is with different cultures. We live in different worlds."

In 1994, a woman who'd read some of my writings on ADD sent me an e-mail over the Internet with the following comment: "Do you think it's possible that these are the last days, and that therefore many, many old souls have incarnated over the past four decades or so, and that these old souls—who are so 'non-normal'—are being diagnosed as having ADD and driving up all these numbers of diagnoses we're seeing?"

Beyond ADD, Underwood-Miller, 1996.

It made sense to me, particularly in the context of the Kogi Indians in Colombia, who consider themselves the "older brothers" to us "younger brothers" of Western society (and who have expressed alarm about our destruction of the planetary environment).

On my next trip to Germany, I put the question to Herr Müller.

"Certainly there are old souls on the Earth now," he said. "This is a critical time. Perhaps the most important time in two thousand years. And it may be that what this woman asked is correct." He touched his old Bible. "But that is all just the show."

"But so many spiritual people I meet are also people who could easily be diagnosed as having ADD," I said, persisting.

"Then honor and bless them!" he said. "I do not care about this label of ADD. That is the category of some doctor, some man who thinks he can put everybody into a box. I am not in a box, you are not in a box. ADD people are not in a box." He made a spitting sound.

I have to agree, although I also know that people "with ADD" are different from the average person, and do often have substantial difficulties fitting into our schools and culture. But that may not mean they're disordered: perhaps they're merely, as Harvard Medical School's Dr. Edward Hallowell says, "attentionally different."

So soon thereafter I wrote *Beyond ADD,* a book which had been rolling around in my mind for several years and strongly makes this point. The variety of human nature is so great that we do a profound disservice to the human race and to our culture by thinking that with a quick and convenient label we can explain a person in their entirety. People are not "in boxes," yet they must cultivate their awareness of mind, body, and spirit to reach their full potential and expand their consciousness enough to make positive contributions to the world.

Bogota,
1993 and 1995

*And I looked, and behold a pale horse: and his name that
sat on him was Death, and Hell followed with him. And
power was given unto them over the fourth part of the
Earth, to kill with sword, and with hunger, and with
death, and with the beasts of the Earth.*

—THE REVELATION OF ST. JOHN, 6:8

Herr Müller's prophecies predict deteriorating conditions that are worst
where overcrowding is worst and where governments stay in power by
force. The city of Bogota, Colombia is just such a place. And in Bogota
I was to find "deteriorating conditions" far worse than I'd have
believed: such severe overpopulation that there are human children
who live in sewers and are hunted for sport.

The consequences of overcrowding are no longer just theoretical;
they have already begun in many areas of this planet.

Here is the story of what happens when a culture and religion make
it easier to purchase cocaine than condoms, and population explodes
beyond available resources. It gives us a glimpse into a possible
Western-culture future, one which country after country is experiencing
now around the world.

In April 1993, I went with Herr Müller to Bogota. I'd gone there with
him two years earlier, when Elizabeth Bliklen had first moved there to
start a Salem project which was now taking shape in the La Paz slum,
and I had also visited the city in 1980, when it had about half the 8–10
million population it now is groaning under the weight of.

In Bogota, we again met with Elizabeth, a German woman who
then had just turned 40, and has lived all around the world. She speaks

fluent German, English, and Spanish, and was once, briefly, married to a Colombian, which is what brought her first to the country.

My first clue that something had gone terribly wrong in Colombia during the decade of the 1980s was the man at the Immigration counter at the Bogota Airport. When I handed him my passport, he asked me if I was in the country on business or as a tourist. (I usually list "tourist" because if you say "business" many countries then give you long forms to fill out which largely are only relevant if you're accompanying $100,000 worth of M-16 rifles or planning to steal high-tech secrets. Besides that, I don't consider myself to be traveling on "business," but as a "spiritual tourist.")

When I said I was a tourist in Colombia, he gave me a hard, cold laugh and stamped my passport.

"Mister Tourist," he snorted, now no sign of the laugh on his face. "Be careful."

The evening of our arrival, Elizabeth had a small dinner for us in her modest apartment. One of the people she invited was a German woman named Else (pronounced "Elsa"), who's on Elizabeth's Board of Directors. Else's husband imports products into Colombia from Italy, and has an office in Bogota. They've lived here 15 years.

Every time the doorbell rang, Else would jump as if she was expecting something terrible to happen. Finally, after two other guests had arrived, causing her to jump up from the table each time, I asked her, "What are you worried about?"

"Kidnappers," she said. "They may have seen you arrive. Did you come in with a suitcase?"

"Yes," I replied slowly, remembering the State Department advisory I'd received the day before, telling all Americans to stay out of Bogota because of murders, bombings, and kidnappings. The State Department had gone so far as to forbid all U.S. government employees from traveling into the region where I was now eating dinner. "I'm not a government official or a rich man," I said, trying to reassure her.

"They could take us all," she said, and then she proceeded to tell us the story of her husband's manager. Two months ago, 15 armed men showed up at his house, demanding to take away his 16-year-old daughter. The girl wasn't in and the husband was quite sick, recovering from hepatitis, so the men took his wife instead.

The kidnappers held her for a full month, forcing her to call her husband nearly every day, sobbing and describing in detail the unspeakable tortures they were inflicting on her. The husband gave them more and more money, selling his home, all his assets, and finally borrowing to the limits of his credit. Somehow the kidnappers knew when he'd hit his limit, and they returned the wife when he'd hit the limit of his ability to borrow.

"Now," Else said, "she is just a shell of a person. She cannot talk without breaking into tears, she trembles constantly, and she has developed several facial tics. She's also worried about AIDS from the many times she was raped. The family is trying to arrange to leave the country to return home to Germany, but they are prevented from doing so by their debts."

Horrified, I asked, "Was the man rich?"

"No," she said. "Just a middle-class manager. Kidnapping for ransom is now a major business here in much of South America, generating money both for the communist rebels and for the organized criminals. And they have spies everywhere, ordinary people they pay to tell them where the foreigners are. This man believes it was his groundskeeper who told them about him and how to break into his house."

The bell rang again, eliciting a twitch from Else, and Elizabeth let in a young Colombian man named Jose. He looked like he was at least half South American Indian, and was well-dressed in slacks and sweater, with a friendly smile and dark brown eyes.

Over dinner, Jose told us his story. When he was five years old, there was a political uprising in the area where he lived and soldiers (he doesn't know if they were government or rebels) came into his house and murdered the entire family, shooting them one at a time as they knelt with hands tied behind their backs, leaving only him alive for some reason known only to them. He watched as they shot his father and mother, and still wakes up with nightmares of it. His aunt took him in but, when he was six, she tired of being a surrogate parent and took him to a state-run orphanage, telling him she'd be back for him in a week or two.

She never returned.

At age seven, Jose escaped from the hellish orphanage, where the children lived in huge rooms and were regularly beaten and raped by the guards. Over the next two years, he lived as a street child, begging and stealing, and avoiding the "hunting clubs" of middle-class teenagers, soldiers, and off-duty police who go out at night with rifles to shoot street children for sport.

But finally, when he was nine, Jose was captured by police and put into another orphanage. Here he was "adopted" as the "foster son" of a family in Europe through one of the many programs where people send a monthly stipend of ten or twenty dollars to the child. This stipend allowed him to attend school for the first time, and he ended up graduating first from high school, then from college with honors and a degree in mechanical engineering.

He came by the apartment to meet Herr Müller and me because, he said, he now wanted to help other children in Bogota like him.

We were also joined by Osiris, a social worker who works with Elizabeth and had recently been robbed and beaten on a busy street in Bogota, and an elderly German Jewish woman who lived in an apartment downstairs from Elizabeth and who wanted to meet Herr Müller. She'd fled Nazi Germany in 1938 to come to South America with her husband, who died soon thereafter, and she was hungry for news of her homeland.

We had a pleasant dinner and despite my fears no kidnappers came for us. After the meal, Else called a taxi and escaped into the night, calling to let us know when she arrived safely at home.

The next day, Elizabeth and Osiris took Herr Müller and me via taxi to the slums where the first Salem building was just being finished. After an hour of fighting through the clogged traffic, our lungs and throats on fire from the auto exhaust that turns the air blue-gray, and our heads pounding from the thin air at the 8000-foot elevation, we emerged from the city of Bogota and into what was, just 30 years ago, the countryside. Here now, however, begin the true slums: for miles, as far as the eye can see, the mountainsides are covered with slum houses made of cardboard, asbestos, mud, or salvaged wood and brick.

The taxi had to stop halfway up a steep mountainside because the dirt road was washed away by a small river of black, stinking raw sewage which ran down through a narrow gully.

We climbed out of the taxi, jumped over the foaming stream, and walked about a half-mile up the mountainside along a dirt path lined on both sides by slum houses. The center of the road was muddy and wet with another, smaller stream of raw sewage and rainwater, from which scrawny wild dogs of the area gathered, to lap up a hurried drink. A newspaper blew across the street in the strong mountain wind, its front-page picture showing in graphic detail the exploded and burned bodies of the victims of a car bombing in downtown Bogota the day before.

The Salem building was built from bricks made in the area, and, while humble in its appearance, is solidly built and far more substantial than the shanty houses which lean on either side of it. Inside is a large room with a small stage on one end, an attached kitchen, and a wide tile floor. It's lined with new school-type tables and chairs—incongruously bright and colorful in this dreary and desperate slum—which Elizabeth had solicited as a donation from a Bogota company.

A crowd of children, mostly under six or seven, were clustered around a table with two women. One of the women, from her shabby dress and disheveled appearance, I guessed lived in the slum. The other was a teacher from Bogota who had come out to instruct them all (including the other woman) in how to read and write. The children squealed with delight at our arrival, clustering around Elizabeth and hugging her legs and holding her hands.

"We're giving these children a start in school," she said, waving around the room. "Most would otherwise remain illiterate, as is much of the country."

We spent a few hours walking around the slum, meeting people, viewing their simple "houses" (which were one-room boxes constructed from scavenged material that would make an American child's tree house look like a mansion) and hearing the plans for a second floor for the Salem building so it could serve more of the local children.

After returning to Bogota, we ate pizza at a restaurant in the northern area where the car bomb had recently gone off. "They won't bomb it again so soon," Elizabeth assured us, after telling us that she'd been just a block away from another bomb that went off several months earlier, killing more than a dozen people.

Over dinner, Elizabeth explained that there were two types of children in South America who needed help. The first are the children of the poor, those we saw in La Paz, the name of the slum where Salem is located. They have no hope and no future, no opportunity for education or job training, and die like flies from diseases ranging from polio to measles to cholera. But they have families.

The second type of child is what the South Americans call "Los Gamines." They are the street children of Bogota: there are hundreds of thousands of them, perhaps over a million. They live in the sewers, in abandoned buildings, old factories, under bridges and in tunnels. By the time they're eight or nine years old, they're often addicted to glue or drugs and are already hardened criminals. By that time, not much can be done for those children. The police hunt them as if they were coyotes: every morning more bodies of these children are found, shot by police or local teenagers during the night.

In much of South America there is little access to birth control, and no sex education. Women have few rights and no power. It is easier here to buy cocaine than it is to buy birth control devices. Back in the days of high infant mortality, disease, and no antibiotics, it was no problem, the nation's laws against birth control. People had children, but most of them died. No matter. But now all of South and Central America face a population explosion. This city's population has doubled in the past twelve years. There are too many people, too few resources. So people become disposable, and they will fight and die over a scrap of food. This, Elizabeth said, is the basis of Los Gamines.

Two years ago, Elizabeth had hoped to start a home for Los Gamines. In working with them, however she found that they were deeply involved in the kidnapping rings and the drug trade, and that the older children would kill an adult just for his or her clothes. So she decided instead to try to "save" the children of the families of the slums like La Paz, and that was when she started building the Salem building, which is a combination school, daycare center, community center, and, hopefully one day a clinic.

The next morning I got up at 6:00 A.M. for the long taxi ride out to the airport. Over breakfast I expressed to Herr Müller my frustration with the situation of the world, the exploding populations and insane wars, the senseless violence both explicit and subtle. It seemed like no matter what we did, we were shoveling sand from a huge beach with a tablespoon, and every lap of the waves brought in a new load of sand.

He said, "We must do what we can. Always. At night we must go to sleep knowing that we have done our best, and there is no more you can do than that. Do not let the problems overwhelm you. Start somewhere, anywhere, with just the smallest gesture of compassion, and you have made a dent against the evil in the world."

RETURNING IN 1995

Two years later I went to Bogota to follow up on my last trip. Two months earlier Herr Müller had gotten a crisis call from Else, about how the building was damaged in an earthquake and Elizabeth had had to go to Germany to have her baby.

I flew down and found the program in disarray, and Else's husband, 68-year-old Giancarlo, an Italian businessman, suggested as a solution that we pass management of the program to a local Catholic order, the Don Brunos, which was involved with teaching and children's work.

Neither Giancarlo nor I, however, were officers of the German Salem corporation, and so we couldn't sign the paperwork authorizing him to engage in or execute negotiations with the Don Bruno order. So I went to Germany to report on this, and then returned a month later with Horst Von Heyer to Bogota.

The Ride to the Slum

Giancarlo came by the church where we were staying to pick us up around 11:00 A.M., and brought with him the paperwork we'd negotiated the day before to give him a power of attorney to enter into negotiations with the Brothers of San Bruno to administer the program in the building in the La Paz slum that Salem had built.

We sat inside and talked for about twenty minutes, and Von Heyer signed the papers.

When we walked out onto the street, Giancarlo let out a shout. His car, a reasonably new Mazda, was parked in front of the church, on a main street, in full view of a relatively busy (albeit poor) part of town. And the hood was up.

Whoever had done the deed, however, wasn't in sight. We spent five minutes trying to determine if any vital engine parts were missing, but it appeared that the thieves had been more interested in trying to hotwire and steal the car itself than any of its parts.

Satisfied the auto was still serviceable, Giancarlo drove Von Heyer and me to the La Paz Barrio (slum) on the hillsides on the edge of Bogota. The ride took about an hour, through a city choked with beat-up autos and air so thick with exhaust it filled the backs of our throats with a metallic taste and turned distant buildings and mountains into gray ghosts in a dead mist.

As we approached the slum area, in the no-man's region where the middle-class death squads (they refer to themselves as "fraternal organizations" or "hunt clubs") go out at night with rifles to hunt street children, we passed a wide median in the middle of the street that had once, perhaps thirty years ago when the city's population was a tenth of what it is now, been a park-like strip between the two oncoming lanes of traffic. Fifteen feet wide and a block long, it now was mostly hard-packed earth and scraggly weeds.

In the center of it, a small pack of dogs, three or four, gaunt and scarred and covered with mange, were picking the last bits of flesh from dismembered bits of a skeleton. Little was left but wet, white bone and some red gristle around the hip and knee sockets: at first I assumed it was something they had dragged from a garbage can or a meat shop, the remnants of a side of beef. But as we drove by, I could see otherwise.

"Does that look human to you?" I asked Von Heyer as we drove by, passing within five feet of the struggling dogs.

"I had hoped not," he replied, looking away. "But obviously I was wrong."

Dinner

That night, Von Heyer and I decided we wanted to find a restaurant to get a good meal. (If you find it gruesome that I would mention "get a good meal" after describing that scene, you can understand how surreal the entire situation is in the slums of Bogota.) So far, we'd either eaten with Giancarlo at the private Italian Club of Bogota, an exclusive place filled with large expatriate Italian families and scenes that bore an eerie resemblance to an Al Pacino film, or we had been living on the loaf of bread, jar of pear jelly, and pound of cheese we'd bought our first day here. It wasn't bad, but for three meals a day became boring.

So we left our small cells (without doorknobs—a key was required to enter or leave each room for safety) and went downstairs to ask the nun who runs the church where we were staying if she had a recommendation for a nearby restaurant.

The look on the nun's face would probably only have been rivaled if we'd suggested having an orgy near the altar downstairs.

"This is Bogota!" she said, her tone shocked, as if that was all one need know.

"You mean it's dangerous out there now that the sun has gone down?" Von Heyer said, not patronizing, just doing a reality check. I thought back to the time when he and I were in Uganda: that wasn't just a dangerous slum, there was a war going on, and one of our biggest concerns was being intentionally or unintentionally shot. Or when he'd been in northern Iraq two years earlier, in the area referred to by the indigenous Kurds as "Kurdistan," and his car was sprayed with machine-gun fire by one of Saddam Heussein's men: he took bullets in the leg, arm, and neck. Gerhard Lipfert flew down to pull him out of the country, and I flew over to meet them when he arrived in Germany in an air ambulance.

She laughed bitterly. "You would not get two blocks from here."

"What about a taxi?" he said, nonplussed.

She put a piece of paper on the table in front of her and wrote a number. "Only call this company. Have them drop you off at the restaurant and then call only them to pick you up. If you must wait hours for them, wait. Do not hail a street taxi under any circumstances."

We went back upstairs and had another meal of bread and cheese, talked for a few hours, and went to sleep.

A Billboard Above Death in the Morning

The next morning we drove up to the slum and visited the Salem building, where the construction and repairs were nearly finished. It looked great, and Giancarlo took some pictures for Von Heyer to take back to the Swiss donors who made it possible.

Driving back from the La Paz slum we passed a concatenation of scenes that perfectly and sadly captured the reality of much of South America.

Along the side of the road to our right was a narrow sidewalk, and behind that a concrete-lined open sewer filled with slow-moving, fetid-smelling black water. At one particular spot behind the sewer was a slum community which stretched for a mile or so, made up of patchwork-quilt shacks assembled from scavenged corrugated iron and asbestos, car doors, bits of scrap wood, and a montage of red and concrete brick. High above this little roadside squatter slum was a billboard, at least seventy feet wide and thirty feet high, advertising homes in a new and secure community. It showed a picture of villa-like houses with spike- and razor-wire-tipped fences, rifle-carrying (and smiling) uniformed guards, and very European-white-looking children laughing and playing on manicured lawns in front of the houses and behind the fences and guards.

We stopped for a light as I gazed at the sign, positioned as if it were advertising the slum below it, and noticed about thirty feet to my right, on the narrow sidewalk, a small crowd of about ten people. Looking more closely, I saw that several were uniformed (I don't know if they were police or army), and they were surrounding a teenage boy (*not* European-white) sprawled on his back on the sidewalk, his arms outstretched, the crown of his head at the edge of the curb, unmoving, a pool of bright-red blood stretching a few yards down the pavement.

One of the uniformed men held a gun in his hand: apparently he had just used it.

The light changed and we drove on. We all looked, but nobody spoke. It was too familiar a scene for Giancarlo to comment on, and too intense for me to discuss at that moment.

An Older Culture Reaches Out to Ours

After Horst Von Heyer and I visited the La Paz slum, our host, Giancarlo, drove us by his office where we picked up his secretary and his office manager, both well-educated young women who look like they are of South American Indian heritage. The five of us drove to Giancarlo's club for lunch, a members-only place for Italians called the Italiano Centro de la Bogota.

Over lunch, his office manager, Maria, related to us a fascinating story. She told it in Spanish and Von Heyer translated it into English for me, so my characterization of her words may be somewhat less than perfect, but here is the gist:

There was once a tribe of Indians called the Kogi. They dominated

Colombia from the Pacific coast well into the Sierra Madre mountains of Bogota. Along with the normal aspects of society which you'd expect with a large and populous dynasty, they also had a secret priesthood, which had been given, in the dim mists of prehistory, an assignment of awesome proportions.

It is their responsibility to keep the Earth alive.

When Pizarro conquered the lands of this part of South America hundreds of years ago, he and those conquistadors who followed him were particularly brutal to the Kogi. By the end of the sixteenth century, all that was left of their civilization were the remains of ancient cities which had been so completely reclaimed by the jungle that only the occasional textbook on archaeology even made mention of them. As far as the world knew, the Kogi were dead, one of the hundreds of indigenous peoples wiped from the face of the Earth by the brutal and relentless march of Western civilization.

But the Kogi survived. A small band of them, fewer than a thousand, had retreated to a remote and inaccessible part of the Sierra Madres and created a walled city that was nearly impossible to find and, if found, could only be entered through one thin bridge over a deep gorge. For hundreds of years the Kogi protected that bridge and the entrance to their one last city, and the world knew nothing of their existence.

They had to do this, Maria said, because of the great responsibility the Creator had given them thousands of years before: to keep the heart of the Earth beating.

Ten years or so ago, however, they sent out across their bridge a solitary young man. His assignment was to make his way to our civilization and learn this alien tongue of Spanish, so that they could then deliver a message to the world. The priests of the Kogi had been given a revelation, had seen into the future and received an order from the Creator, and it must be communicated to their younger brothers who had taken over the world.

After a year, their young man returned, now the first person in three hundred years to speak both their language and that of the conquistadors. He brought with him a British journalist their priests had instructed him to find, a man whose spirit they had seen in the netherworld and who they believed would be their one hope of carrying their message to the other humans of the Earth.

This journalist recorded their words, and Maria had made a pilgrimage some years earlier to the city nearest the Kogi to learn what they had to say.

This is their message as she shared it with me:

The Earth is a living organism, not just a ball of dirt floating through space. It has a life and a consciousness. Therefore, humans upon the Earth must both live in harmony with and learn from the Earth, and, most important, feed and nurture the Earth with man's spiritual consciousness.

In various parts of the world, there are people who have been charged with this responsibility and taught the sacred techniques to accomplish this. The Kogi in Colombia, a tribe in Tibet, a small group of what we call the Aborigines in Australia, an ancient hunting tribe in central Africa, a group of Native Americans in the United States, the ancient Hebrews and early Christians, and a few others. The holy men and women of these groups know of and communicate with each other, as they have for millennia. Some have been lost: one was in that part of northern Africa we now call Egypt. Most have separated their holy ones from the remnants of their tribes so completely that the world, and in many cases even their own tribes, do not know about the existence of their priesthood.

Each of these groups is in constant prayer and meditation. This is their purpose in life, to be so in tune with the heartbeat and soul of the Earth that they can keep alive the delicate silver thread which connects the life and consciousness of the planet with that of its human inhabitants.

This has not been easy: to do such a great work has been a heavy burden and has consumed the lives of hundreds of generations of men and women. It was a work which had to be done in secret, even during the times when their civilizations ruled the Earth. They have survived the onslaughts of competing tribes, global changes in weather and the coming and going of ice ages, eruptions and cataclysms which created mountains and turned parts of the once-lush Earth to desert, and even the coming of what we call Western civilization, which has spread across the Earth like an infectious mold across the surface of a ripe fruit.

This has caused the Earth and the Kogi great pain, one felt across the planet by those peoples entrusted with keeping the heart of the Earth beating. But the Earth is resilient, and the ancient priests who have nurtured it and kept it awake so humankind could live upon it have persevered.

But now, the Kogi say, there is a true threat, which could mean the end of this cycle and the extinction of humanity. The Earth, of course, will recover, but its consciousness, manifested in man and other sentient beings, may take millions of years to return.

The threat, they say, is that the skin of the Earth is being torn open. A great wound has appeared in the heavens, and through this wound the Earth is being assaulted by the power of the sun and the forces of the stars. The Earth feels this as a pain as great as if a man's skin were torn from his back or stomach and he was then thrown into hot sea water or staked to a mountain ridge during the hottest part of the day.

The viscera of the Earth is being probed and torn out by "civilized" man in search of minerals and wealth, and the lungs of the Earth are choking with the filth belched forth from "civilized" man's technology.

But most dangerous is that the blood of the Earth, its oil and its water, are being drained out, burned and polluted, and discarded.

Unless this assault stops and these wounds are healed soon, even the efforts of the Kogi and their brothers and sisters across the world cannot prevent the death of humanity and much of the animal and vegetable world we interact with.

When Maria went to this area, it had been several years since the Kogi had made their brief appearance and shared their warning. Each year since, they have sent out their young bilingual man to tell those nearby that the wound in the sky is growing greater, and that the people of the West were ignoring their message at their own peril.*

---

*The British journalist made a brilliant video about this, available from Mystic Fire Video, 800-292-9001. If you watch the video, you may notice some inconsistencies between the video and the story as Maria relates it, but nothing that materially affects the basic message the Kogis are giving us.

Von Heyer and I listened to this story in a pained silence: it was disturbingly similar to a message Herr Müller had called several of us together to deliver nearly 15 years ago. We'd met in New York City just for this discussion, and he had talked about a vision he'd had of the end of the world, told us that there were groups of people around the Earth—the groups probably not numbering more than a dozen in total—who were keeping the Earth alive and preparing for the spiritual and physical renewal of the Earth that must occur in the next millennium. And that, among the people of the Western world, Salem was one of those groups who were given part of this responsibility.

He told us how he had a group of people, mostly elderly, whose job it was to spend some of each day in prayer and meditation. Over a 40-year period, he had brought them together, and at that time they numbered about 3,000. After dinner, when we were alone and back in Von Heyer's cell above the church in downtown Bogota, he told me that so many had died over the years that Herr Müller's prayer circle was down to only a few hundred people.

I confessed to Von Heyer that a decade earlier Herr Müller had told me to locate my "little flock" and communicate with them regularly, and that my flock, too, had never been more than only a very few: most people are simply too busy for such things. Or perhaps, looking at it in the cold light of self-examination, I found it easier to visualize such apocalyptic events as metaphor instead of reality.

CAN WE STOP IT?

The brain, as wonderful as it is, is not immune to ancient survival mechanisms. Much psychological research has shown that when overcrowding afflicts a population of lab animals, the brain sets about eliminating the overcrowding by the tidy expedient of having members of a species kill each other off.

It's a terrible thought, but I've seen it myself in more than one setting, in more than one city, in more than one culture—and in ways that are more frightening than I'd have imagined if I were writing the world's script myself.

As time goes by, the reality is coming ever closer, as the world's population soars out of control, resources are destroyed, and the organized religions and politicians dither about (comparatively) petty issues.

In Bogota I often remembered the prophecy of the African medicine man that his fate would one day, too, be the fate of the white man. More and more the streets of cities across the world resemble Bogota. In more and more countries, I've seen the deaths with my own eyes: we are approaching the edge.

The question I'm still left with is, what can we do? How can we understand what's happening, and what is a wise response?

Older and Younger Cultures
Understanding How
It Got This Way

*The man who sat on the ground in his tipi meditating on
life and its meaning, accepting the kinship of all creatures
and acknowledging unity with the universe of things
was infusing into his being the true essence of civilization.
And when native man left off this form of development,
his humanization was retarded in growth.*

—CHIEF LUTHER STANDING BEAR

In my earlier books on ADD, I pointed out how from the earliest times humans were hunter-gatherers, and that some of those behaviors that were survival skills for our ancestors are now problems in many modern schools or workplaces.

The picture that this model paints for some people is one of noble hunters who have been systematically tracked down and destroyed by the ignoble farmers.

While it's true that there are now only a very few hunting societies left on the Earth, as I discussed this with Herr Müller in more detail I came to realize that the real paradigm is deeper than just hunters and farmers.

While that does a fine job of explaining why some kids excel or fail in school, or why high-stimulation-seeking people are drawn to jobs like being an emergency medical technician while low-stimulation-seeking people are drawn to jobs like accounting, it misses a larger and more important point.

That point is the one that prophets from Jeremiah to Jesus to Nostradamus to Edgar Cayce have gone to great lengths to point out to us: "modern" (post-agricultural revolution, since 10,000 B.C.E.) human-kind is destroying the world in which we live.

One explanation often put forth for this is that there is a basic flaw in human nature. This concept of original sin is often pointed to as being demonstrated in the biblical story of Eve and the apple.

The problem with this concept, however, is that there have been human societies around for hundreds of thousands of years—people just like you and me—who did not destroy the world. Instead, they lived in harmony with it.

I first encountered this possibility as a teenager, reading Margaret Mead's book *Coming of Age in Samoa*. There were detractors and counter-arguments to her view of the noble primitive, however, and even when I first read her book it occurred to me that her Samoan "primitive" people were lacking basic and important things like advanced medical care and communications which, I assumed, would make their lives better if they'd had them.

My assumption was then, as it had been all my life, that our culture, what we call Western Civilization, was inherently better and more valuable than what we called the primitive cultures which preceded it.

Then while in Bogota for Herr Müller, at the Salem program in the La Paz slum, I first heard the story of the Kogi tribe, who live at the top of one of the Andes mountain ranges.

When I heard of the message of the elder brothers, I thought it an interesting spiritual story, but figured that the average person would have little interest in it. After all, how could a primitive people who live on simple crops have something important to teach us? We have, after all, conquered the Earth. We've conquered disease, hunger, space, and even the atom.

I also noticed that among the elder brother people, to use my hunter/farmer metaphor, they very much exhibit the characteristics of farmers. And it was the farmers who I'd been mentally blaming much of the mess of modern civilization on.

Yet these elder brothers lived in harmony with the world, and had for thousands of years. They tread lightly upon this Earth, and even in their architecture they didn't damage the ecosystems but instead guaranteed their survival over millennia.

And now I was being told that they are warning us, their younger brothers, that we are on the verge of bringing about a global catastrophe.

So, if the elder brothers, and other ancient civilizations who have lived in peace with the world, were farmers, and yet didn't create a civilization that (like other farmer societies of Europe, Africa, and Asia) would ultimately lead to the death of the world, what was different?

How could it be that some farmer peoples would leave behind a planet relatively unscathed, whereas others would wreak such incredible damage that it would put all life on Earth at risk?

I had similarly paradoxical questions about hunters. Many primitive hunting people (using my metaphor) left only gentle footprints on the planet. Elaborate cave paintings from 30,000 years ago in France, and 20,000 years ago in Australia are the remnants they have left us: not piles of nuclear waste which will be lethal for over a million years into the future.

But other hunting people were exploitative. They burned forests to drive out animals, or, more commonly, turned their hunting efforts against their neighbors and became hunters of humans. The Mongols and Tatars, originally nomadic hunting tribes, rose to conquer most of Europe and ruled it with a brutal iron fist for centuries, every bit as cruelly as had the Roman Empire which had evolved from an agricultural society.

So, with ADD it may well be something as simple as hunter and farmer material remaining in our genetic code. But from a larger view, the view of the past and future of the planet, there was a third picture that I only began to see after first visiting the Apaches in 1995.

This is the idea of cultures that are "old" and "young."

The old cultures, be they agricultural or hunting/gathering, live with an intrinsic connection to the Earth. For them, the planet on which we live is, itself, a living organism. It has its own life, its own destiny, and, in a way that the younger cultures could never understand, its own consciousness. Things that run counter to the Earth's nature will (naturally) not work in the long run—although the damage may be too slow to be noticeable on the younger culture time scale. All we have to do, to tell which is which, is look at what's happening on the planet.

And that's why what I've seen in my travels is so disturbing.

The younger cultures live quite different lives: they view themselves as separate from the Earth, with "dominion" over it, and see the resources of Earth only as things to be used and then discarded. Nature is the enemy, not the mother, father, or brother/sister of these younger peoples, and their disregard for it is so visceral, so intrinsic to their world-view, that many live their entire lives without ever once questioning their own cultural assumptions about humankind's place in the universe.

The older peoples are so clear in their understanding of humankind's place on Earth that they often pray for the soul of an animal as they kill it for food. Daily they thank G-d for the life given them, and the life around them, all of which is viewed with reverence.

The younger peoples, on the other hand, are so egocentric that in the recent past they tenaciously fought—killed and tortured—to preserve their belief that our planet was at the center of all creation. Many of these younger culture descendants still argue that the creation of humans marked the creation of all things, and even today fight to insert such teachings into public schools. They are so ethnocentric that they make it an article of faith to seek out and convert older cultures to their view of the world . . . or to obliterate them entirely, as was done across much of North and South America, Africa, Australia, and Europe. Their view was so short and their arrogance so great that they believed their "conquest" of disease and hunger with modern medicine and agriculture were signs of a blessing by G-d.

Older cultures the world over are warning younger cultures of the danger and stupidity of their ways. I was told by the Apaches and received the message in Colombia. Tribal village elders in Africa asked me to "warn the world" that the famine I was seeing there in Uganda in 1980 would one day be worldwide, the fate of the white man as well.

I cannot imagine it is mere coincidence that *the same message* would come from all these disparate cultures, who have no conventional way of communicating with each other.

And all I'd seen of death, famine, children suffering, warfare, extermination . . . all because of the arrogance, the limited vision, the greed, and, ultimately, the immaturity of the younger cultures. We discovered and developed technology, but do not have the wisdom to consistently use it responsibly: we've infected the Earth's land-masses like an encrusted sore, and now we're filling the seas with the pus of our waste.

Herr Müller pointed out to me how Jesus warned against this. The earliest Jews had been an older culture, and we can see this in the story of Cain and Abel. The farmer (Cain) killed the Earth-respecting herder brother, and so his future agricultural efforts were cursed by G-d. Surely this was the story of an older culture peoples, and a warning to those who would follow.

But along the course of time, the ancient Hebrews encountered more and more younger peoples, and began to adopt their ways. The prophets railed against this, and warned over and over about the inevitable results . . . but as the record of the Bible tells us, the prophets were almost always ignored.

Then came Jesus who, it now appears from the Dead Sea Scrolls and other sources, was a member of the Essenes. The Essenes were an older culture Jewish fragment that still remained in His day, which was dominated by younger-culture Judaism. And His message, not at all well received in His time, was an older culture message: stop worrying (G-d will provide), trust others to the point of not fighting them in court, respect and see G-d in everybody, forgive people no matter how many times they harm you.

> Then came Peter to him, and said, "Lord, how often shall my brother sin against me and I forgive him? Seven times?" Jesus said, "Not just seven times: but seventy times seven."*

Absolutely, the older culture message is one of harmony and living together. It is not a message of separation, of "us or them," and it has not a word about dominating others—despite what His "followers" would later do to others in His name.

He directly challenged the younger culture notions of destroying one's enemy, exploiting the Earth by intensive agriculture, and the ultimate younger culture idea: that man is independent of G-d and that human "thinking" is the same as "consciousness."

These teachings showed older culture insights that man is *not* separate from G-d and nature, and that even our thoughts have meaning and impact—and are known to G-d. We are all part of a larger, more encompassing consciousness.

---

*Seventy times seven equals 490 times, which is more than once a month for forty years.

In a younger culture, it's assumed that G-d is distant, that heaven is far away in time and space, that humans are separate and unique and have to grab what they can, and that the ancient laws that protected the Earth, such as a Sabbath for the land, are merely quaint. Jesus challenged all of these, and did so with such conviction that it led to his being sentenced to death.

But after His crucifixion, a man who was an enthusiastic member of the younger culture of the then-modern Jews, and circulated freely and comfortably in the younger culture of the Roman conquerors, was visited by the Holy Spirit or Christ Himself or both, and began an aggressive ministry. This man Saul, later renamed Paul, took much of Jesus's messages to the far parts of what was then his known world, and the messages he carried became the basis of what was to be today's Christian church.

But there were also parts of Jesus's message—those older culture warnings and admonitions—that Paul could not understand because of his own cultural upbringing. So he overlooked or ignored them.

Some years ago, Herr Müller commented to me that he preferred to read the four Gospels, the Psalms, and the Prophets over the writings of Paul.

It wasn't until I understood this fundamental difference in worldviews that Paul's writings represent that I understood his comment. A man who worries about the life of a worm certainly has an old culture view of the world—a view that's now nearly extinct planet-wide.

How many pastors of today, for example, would survive in their position if they preached that people should not have savings or charge interest, should not gather into barns, should trust G-d totally for tomorrow even if it meant their death, and should not only not fight against their enemies but should help them and pray for them?

In the small view, those are all recognized as good words and often cited from the pulpit. But they're only cited as quaint stories, or perhaps metaphors, or lessons in humility—not as instructions to an entire culture about how it must reform itself if it is to avoid destroying itself and the world.

Herr Müller's commitment to peace (that's what "Salem" means, after all) is so complete he will not eat the products of violence. His older culture understanding teaches that food must be grown organically—not just to be healthier, but out of respect for the Earth itself. As we pollute and destroy the Earth and ourselves (from our drunken-like consumption of oil and energy to the very personal pollution of our bodies through nicotine and other drugs), we show how totally disconnected we are from the life we were bred for, and the spirit that's part of it.

Once when Herr Müller embraced a huge pine tree, hugging it, talking with it, giving it his blessing and asking it for its blessing, I asked: "Do trees have souls?"

He shrugged. "I do not know. But the light of G-d's life is in all living things."

"So you see G-d all around you?" I said.

"Yes, of course."

"But some would call that animism, or say that you're worshipping nature spirits, or something like that."

"We are humans, in the image of G-d, but we are also part of nature," he said simply. "I save the life of a worm, I have saved life. I touch the life of the tree, I have touched life. Of course, we have a highest obligation to human life, but it is the stupidity of people who do not see the light of G-d in all living things that has led to this." He waved his hand above his head, at the browning pine trees, victims of acid rain and pollution. "Who could kill off a forest for a few dollars if he knew that the forest was alive with the light and presence of G-d? Only a stupid man, and that is what we have become. Because people do not see the light of G-d in all life, they are so ready to destroy the world for profit and power. And this is what will end with the end times: in the new times to come, people will know that all life is sacred."

And so I saw it clearly, at last.

As an enthusiastic member of our science-worshipping modern culture, I'd felt a shock when I first realized as a youth that there might be buried within my religion and education the remnants of an older and wiser culture. This older culture seemed inexplicable and odd: its most famous ancient spokesperson (Jesus) said that we should forgive people regardless of what they did, that we should not worry about the future, and that we should bless and love those who have hurt and used and exploited us. Nobody I'd ever known lived that way.

At the time I didn't know what to make of this, and I carried the dissonance with me as the years went by.

You can imagine the effect on me when I later did meet a human who actually lived the principles of that older and more mature culture: Kurt Stanley. The things Master Stanley did and taught were inexplicable in the context of my scientific world-view: they were miracles or madness. Yet I knew what I'd seen, whether or not I could explain it. And I later met Herr Müller, who had similar insights and powers.

As I delved into Master Stanley's and Herr Müller's lives and teachings, I saw that their older culture beliefs were firmly anchored in things I had always told myself were the basis for our younger (Jewish and Christian) culture: the words and acts of Jesus and the prophets who preceded Him.

But I also discovered that even *these* teachings had been turned by the younger culture into machines, mechanistic steps and rituals to be manipulated to suit the purposes of those in power, into "do-this-and-you'll-get-that-result" formulas.

We had kept the information, but we'd lost the wisdom.

This loss of wisdom has led to terrible human suffering in our past, and has set up potentially severe difficulties in our future.

The early colonists of the United States were fond of the Calvinistic notion that those who won in battle or commerce did so because it was manifest destiny or the will of their god. This rationalization satisfied their consciences as they slaughtered the natives who already occupied the land the colonists had "discovered," and as they bought, sold, and used human slaves—as had their younger culture dominator predecessors all the way back into the earliest records of human history.

It's clearly a story of younger, immature cultures, interested in themselves (like any immature entity) to the exclusion of the larger community in which they live. The view was well articulated by Aristotle and Descartes. It holds that those who survive are, *ipso facto*, better suited for survival. By this logic it follows that those who conquer, who destroy, are superior; otherwise they wouldn't be around to write the history books.

Further, since better machines make better conquerors, a culture that views the entire universe and all of life as a machine will make the best machines and thus be the best conquerors.

Unfortunately for our culture, this only works in a world of abundant resources. When human populations and their needs outstrip the resources available to them, this cultural viewpoint most often leads to war and famine.* If our standard way of interacting with the world is to dominate and subdue it, then our first response to other people competing for resources is to dominate and subdue *them,* too.

Older cultures, on the other hand, view living things as interrelated and interconnected. The world, in the words of an Apache medicine woman I met, "flows from the web of life." The Earth is alive and all humans are part of its life, not separate from it. And the valued skills are not machine-building or conquest, but love, mercy, forgiveness, and a connection to the power of life.

In a younger culture, consciousness means *thinking,* considering with a purpose in mind.

In an older culture, consciousness touches an *experience beyond thought* that has to do with *being,* with the way we are—the power of life.

Let us return, now, to the search for understanding of how life works: how we can achieve our fullest potential in a seemingly overpowering world.

---

*Language reflects culture. Consider the metaphors we use when we face problems: we have the "war on drugs," the "war on cancer," the "war on poverty," and the "war on crime," among others.

Living on the Edge

The universe is eight billion years old, the last two billion of which have produced intelligent life. During this time not one hour of absolute equity has prevailed. It should be no surprise to find this same basic condition applying to your personal affairs.

—JACK VANCE, *THE HOUSES OF ISZM*

A common reaction, when people hear about the worst places on Earth, is to think "How on Earth can we do anything about this??" It's common to feel powerless, especially if you view it from the mechanical "engineering problem" view.

In the engineering view, massive problems require massive solutions. I knew this approach, and mastered it, in my schooling and in my technical businesses.

Individuals tend not to feel powerful against massive problems.

But teachers such as Herr Müller counsel that *there is power in small actions.* This was hard for me to understand until I learned what happens at edges, at points of transition. They are points of great power, and I'd like to explain why, and invite you to bring yourself to the edge of whatever change you'd like to create in the world.

EDGES, TURBULENCE, FRACTALS, AND CHAOS

It appears to me that the world is approaching an edge.

I hear it in the words of the Kogi Indians, warning us, from our written history and from their ancestors, about the path we're going down. I feel it when I walk through cities like Kampala and Cairo and Beijing. I see it when a truck passes me on the highway in Bogota and the back of the truck is stacked with the bodies of dead children.

It's an edge of threat and, perhaps, an edge of promise.

Edges are interesting places: they're where everything is happening. Edges have unique forms, which can only be described with fractal geometry.

Mind you, this is a field of study that literally didn't exist when I was born. This is new information, information that simply wasn't available when our culture and our shared attitudes were developed. It is our responsibility, now, in our generation, to build this news into our shared view of the world, because when we got the idea that there's nothing we can do, we were wrong: something was missing.

Fractals, and the related field of chaos theory, have only come into existence during our lifetime. But as in so many areas, younger-culture science is finally discovering and documenting a "technology" that's been used by older cultures for ages. (As every well-educated scientist knows, the fact that something hasn't been noticed or explained yet doesn't mean it's not real!)

Edges are essentially unmeasurable except in terms of infinite possibilities, yet they *are* measurable for practical purposes. The classic example is the question, "How long is the coast of Britain?" If it's measured by a person with a yardstick, the answer will be quite different from somebody using a match-stick. There's an infinite variety of "ruler lengths" you could use, so there's an infinite variety of answers to the question—yet the answers are also limited!

Edges are points of intersection, and the intersections cause unique energies and forms to arise. For example, the rainbow sheen that you see on the road after a rain is the result of the intersection of water from the rain and oil from the road, which will not combine with each other. Instead, an edge is created, and the fractal structure of this edge brings forth the rainbow colors from the "white" sunlight that strikes it.

The science of chaos—the turbulence that happens at fractal edges—has been the demise of the last original hope of science, the belief that we could control everything *"if we can just gather enough data."* As mentioned earlier in this book, researchers have now proven that it's not possible to gather enough data to be certain about most natural processes. What happens at edges is too complex to control.

What a powerful place to be!

CREATE EDGES;
KEEP YOURSELF AT THE EDGE

While working on this book, Louise and I rented a house on the South Carolina seacoast. Walking to the water's edge, we saw an entire ecosystem contained in the changing of the tide as little birds ran back and forth anxiously pecking at stranded snails and crabs, and dozens of types of creatures, predators and prey, struggled with or profited from the changing nature of the sea's edge.

A few weeks earlier, we'd spent a weekend at The Farm, a community founded in the 1960s by Stephen Gaskin. Outside the Eco-Village where we stayed there was a small plaque by the side of a man-made pond which was labeled "Edges" and talked about how important and interesting edges are in natural systems, and therefore how at The Farm they try to maximize biological and ecological edges.

Similarly, in human terms, edges are places of great activity. Be they the front lines in battle, the point of customer and vendor interaction in business, or the places of disagreement and difference between individuals, cultures, or nations, edges are dynamic, alive, and inherently unstable.

Societies without edges become stagnant. This had happened so profoundly to Japanese society during the Meiji era that they wouldn't trade with the outside world. It took Admiral Perry parking his "Black Ships" off the coast of Japan and threatening war if they wouldn't talk with him to shock the Japanese into rejoining the world. Perry created an edge, and the dynamic energy of that edge reinvigorated Japanese society.

I've always been a risk-taker, a "hunter" as I use the term in my books on ADD. As a child and teenager, it got me into considerable trouble, but it also led me into situations where I learned things that have been of considerable value to me all my life. When Master Stanley said I should go teach (a new edge between me and others), I said "yes," when Herr Müller said I should quit the business world (three times) and start Salem work (creating new edges), I said "yes," and I've said "yes" to hundreds of other things, both good and bad.

This has always been my intuition: to say "yes." And, I've observed, it's Herr Müller's, too. I've seen him agree to some of the most harebrained schemes—and seen a few of them work out beautifully. He always astounds me with his willingness to trust both other people and that whatever is happening, good or bad, is all the unfolding of G-d's will. (And, of course, it's also G-d's will that we make decisions and continue on through life!)

Living on the edge, in fact, is a central part of his philosophy.

I remember one time I was in Germany and sitting in his office with him. His bookkeeper came in and, with a serious look on her face, informed him that in two days they had to make payroll and were 54,000 German marks short. She was speaking in German, and apparently assumed I could not understand her: she spoke to him quite harshly.

"We cannot borrow any more from the bank," she said, "and if you do not pay these people they will quit and you may even be committing a crime."

"Don't worry about it," he said, waving his hand across the front of his face as if to shoo off a pesky fly.

"What?" she said, her voice now shrill. "I am the one they will come to first!"

"Please!" he said in a sharp voice. "You must learn to trust in G-d."

She wagged her finger at him. "G-d does not have a checking account I can take money from to pay the staff. And we must send another shipment of food to the starving children in Uganda."

"Ah, but G-d has wealth," he said. "Look out the window. He owns it all."

"Where is our share of it?" she demanded.

"Wait."

"I cannot wait! I have to make a deposit now!"

"Just wait," Herr Müller said. "Has G-d ever abandoned us?"

She paused and sighed. "No." Then she cocked her head to the side as if she had a sudden thought. "Do you know of a donation that is coming and you haven't told me about?"

"No," he said. "But G-d will take care of us. Do not worry."

She spun on her heel, stomped out of the room, slammed the door behind her.

"Whew!" I said. "She's upset."

"You must have a strong person as a bookkeeper," he said, shaking his fist in the air in the "strength" gesture. "But there is a price to pay for that." He laughed.

"What are you going to do about the money?"

He put his wrists together as if they were handcuffed. "Wait. And pray."

"Do you know anybody you can call for a contribution or a loan?"

"Not necessary," he said. "G-d will provide. Trust in Him and he will honor your trust. If you do not trust in Him, then He will not perform miracles to strengthen your faith."

"In the Bible it also says something like, 'Thou shalt not test the Lord thy G-d.'"

"This is not a test. This is trust. We should go for a walk."

We walked for about two hours, up and around in the mountains along his Prophet's Way, finally, around sunset, ending up at his altar. "Dear Lord," he prayed, "you know my situation, so I will not say it again. Only know, that I trust you, and praise you, and love you, and do my daily work for your honor. Amen." And he bowed. We walked back to Salem and had dinner together, then we both went to bed.

The next morning I was in his office. We were discussing something, as I recall, having to do with the startup of Salem in New Hampshire. And in marched his bookkeeper, her eyes on the floor as if she were embarrassed, three envelopes in her hand.

"Herr Müller," she said, having a difficult time looking directly at him. "I have here in my hand three envelopes that came in this morning's mail. Each contains a check. Together, they add up to 54,000 German marks. Exactly."

He clapped his hands, to make a single loud sound and said, "Of course! I told you to trust in G-d!"

She turned around and marched out of the room without saying a word, although this time she didn't slam the door.

"The exact amount?" I said. "That's cutting it close."

He smiled. "G-d's little joke. So often it happens that way, just exactly what you need, and just exactly at the last minute."

"That's been the story of my life, too, and when I ran Salem in New Hampshire it was the way things always worked. But people tell me that I'm nuts. They say, 'Why wait until the last minute? Why not plan in advance and make sure you have the money?' I always tell them that I just do it the way I do it, that my way is not to store up and hoard, but instead to *do*."

"You are right," he said. "Planning like that would mean storing up money in the bank while children are starving and people are dying. It would not be right. Whenever I have extra money, I know that I am not doing what I must."

"And you like living on the edge?"

"*Ja,* of course!" He laughed again, then became serious. "To trust in G-d is the most important lesson, Thomas." He leaned forward. "Always you must trust in Him."

In other words: live on the edge between this world and that of Spirit.

My trust in G-d was tested many times when I ran Salem in New Hampshire. Dozens of times we were on the financial edge, but always it seemed that something miraculously came through. I've seen this even in my business work, which has caused me to wonder if it was protected because I was using the money from it for my Salem work.

In January 1996, when I went to visit Herr Müller for a week while his wife was in Rwanda, both of our abilities to trust were tested again. The week before I arrived, somebody had fired a high-powered rifle through the window of his office during the night. The trajectory of the bullet was a perfectly straight line through the window's two panes of glass, across the top of his chair right where his head would have been had he been sitting at his desk, through a painting on the wall (with no living images), and into the wall.

"That the shooting was so precise indicates this is a warning," the police told Herr Müller. "Clearly if they wanted to kill you, they would have."

Tracing the trajectory back out the window, they found that the gunman had to have climbed a tree a few hundred feet down the road. This was no accident.

But why?

Nobody knew. We were operating a program in Russia, and had not involved the Russian Mafia in the contracting work: perhaps that had something to do with it. Or it could be German nationalists (a rising force in modern Germany and all across Europe) offended that Salem wasn't promoting German nationalism in Russia the way many other organizations had done. Or maybe somebody who had a grudge for some reason we couldn't even imagine. Or somebody associated with factions in one of the other countries where Salem was operating:

Uganda, Rwanda, Colombia, Taiwan, Austria, Israel, or the United States. Nobody knew.

"What do you think?" I asked Herr Müller.

He shrugged. "I stand under the protection of the cross of Jesus Christ, under the cross of Golgotha. If they kill me today, so be it. If not, I continue my work. I cannot worry about this. It is not the first time my life has been threatened." He looked out the window, thought for a moment, then continued. "For the past weeks I felt an order to recite the Ninety-first Psalm very frequently. I did not know why, but I was obedient to the order. Now I know why. I needed the extra protection."

"Who do you think did it?"

"I will not give it that much thought," he said. "You know, Thomas, when you begin an important work, the enemy sends his army against you. They will pull at your pant-legs and tug on your shirtsleeve. If they do not get your attention, they will shout at you and create obstacles for you. Or try to shoot at you." He waved his hand as he had when the bookkeeper came into the room on my visit 17 years earlier. "You cannot think of them too much or you give them a power they do not deserve. Never be afraid to do the Salem work. Never be afraid to take a risk for G-d or His children. Always know that the beginning is half the battle, half the work, and we are now in the beginning. The birth pains are starting as the times of the Earth will soon change. And so we are under attack. Of *course* we are under attack." He pointed at me, and then the sky. "We should thank G-d that we are under attack! It means we are on the right path!"

TO CREATE CHANGE, GO TO THE EDGE

I've observed that people tend to live at one of two extremes in the spectrum of life: those who live on the edge, and those who avoid the edge. Those who live on the edge are hanging out in the most dangerous and unstable places—yet they're also often the most powerful agents of change, because the edge is where change happens; away from the edge, things are naturally unchanging.

Ben Franklin, Thomas Jefferson, and George Washington lived on the edge. So did Thomas Edison and Ernest Hemingway. Their willingness to challenge norms and conventions and governments led to the creation of new inventions, institutions, and even the United States of America.

One of the things the military loves to point out is that many of the major inventions and innovations of our time, both mechanical and medical, have come about as the result of war. Being on the edge, where conflict occurs, brings about a new, dynamic, unstable, and innovative consciousness (for better or worse).

Everybody is familiar with the edge between normal waking consciousness and sleep: it's often a time of extraordinary feelings, sensations, and insights, particularly as we move from sleep into wakefulness.

In a similar way, mystics are aware of the edge between the physical world and the world of spirit.

Understanding edges was, for me, an epiphany.

The physical mind is a function of the body/brain, and, as Skinner, Pavlov, and the Behaviorists showed, the manifestation of a rather predictable bioelectronic computing machine.

On the other hand, the consciousness which is the universe is so deep and profound and all-pervasive that no mind could possibly contain it. How can the body/mind contain or express that which is essentially not of the body/mind?

The answer for me is that it cannot. Instead, the body/mind touches the edge.

When the brain is brought to the edge of the world of G-d, the place of "true" consciousness, a fractal intersection occurs. An unstable and dynamic system is created, and, like the rainbow colors of water and oil, new energies and visions are created.

This insight, then, led me to wonder about the question the woman had asked me years earlier about whether it was possible that "hunters," people with ADD, could be more spiritually evolved or older souls than "farmers." I didn't (and don't) think the answer is anywhere near that simple. However, my experience has been that a willingness to approach edges, to live on the edge, will increase the probability that a person will approach a spiritual edge—the intersection point between the world of matter and the world of spirit where extraordinary breakthroughs in consciousness can occur. And those people "afflicted" with ADD are, by their own neurochemistry, drawn to edges . . . as are many without ADD.

If you want to bring about a change in the world's consciousness, my advice is that you bring your mind to the edge: bring yourself into contact with the larger consciousness of which we're all made.

Look for *your* edges. They may be in work, relationships, life—or, as you'll see in the next chapter, you may even find yourself moved to find an orphanage or leper colony to help.

India, 1993 and 1996

Do not wait for leaders; do it alone, person to person.
—MOTHER THERESA

When many Americans think of India they picture a world full of holy men, honoring life so much that they won't eat beef. This is, after all, the origin of the expression "sacred cow."

But visiting India, like Colombia, showed me the truth of the message of the Kogi. Each country has a time-honored heritage of an older culture, but as younger Western values have run wild across the country, the older culture values have become hidden in mountaintop retreats or monasteries, and poverty and disease have exploded where the younger culture has taken over.

My trips to India solidified my certainty that we are, globally, on the wrong path and that only a change in consciousness and culture can save us.

My trip to India in 1993 was my second for Salem. The first time had been back in 1980, when an Indian businessman offered to donate land to Salem for a children's village, and Horst Von Heyer and I went to Bombay to see what could be done. The project ended up hopelessly tangled up in red tape, however, and we had to forego the program.

Von Heyer and I had left India quite unhappy that we'd been unable to organize a Salem program there, because, we learned, the plight of orphans in India is particularly brutal (as in much of the Third World, particularly in tourist areas). Often they are taken by organized criminal gangs who will maim them—cutting off an arm or leg, or gouging out an eye—and then put them onto the street to beg. Another problem is with child slaves, most often in the silk and textile industries, but also in prostitution and as domestic servants. Orphans are bought and sold for this work, and even children of poor families often end up in these situations as they are given as "security" for small "loans" which will, of course, never be repaid.

Thirteen years after my first trip to India, a small group of Swiss families contacted Herr Müller. They'd been supporting an orphanage for many years in the interior of India, run by a local Lutheran minister, Rev. Yesu Ratnam. They were now getting old enough (in their eighties) that they were concerned about the future fate of the orphanage if anything were to happen to them. Would Salem consider taking over the project, they asked?

Since nobody had visited the orphanage in years to make sure it was legitimate and the money was being used appropriately, Herr Müller told them he'd only consider it after "somebody from Salem" had gone there to check the program out and audit their books. (Phony charities are also a problem around the world, and siphon off many well-meant dollars merely to enrich the people who operate them.) It turned out the "somebody" he had in mind was me, and he called me the day after they contacted him. Fortunately, at the time my business was doing well enough that I could afford to go, and to pay for the trip.

BOMBAY

I arrived in Bombay on a hot August evening and took a taxi from the airport to the Taj Intercontinental Hotel, one of the hotels in the city which cater to a foreign business clientele, so you know the water is purified and the food well-cooked. In the lobby there were several men from one of the Middle-Eastern Arab countries sitting in a large area covered with Persian rugs and expensive furniture. Obsequious Indian men brought them teenage girls, one at a time, and as I checked in I watched the Arabs inspect the girls as if they were inspecting bits of meat in a market. Most were dismissed with the flick of a hand: when one was chosen, the man would head to the elevator with several of his underlings, their long white robes flowing; the girl and her keeper would follow a few discreet minutes later.

After checking in, I went outside and asked a taxi driver how much it would cost for a quick tour of Bombay. It was about 1:00 A.M., but I was wide awake with jet lag. "You want girl?" he asked. "No," I said. "Only I'd like to drive around the various interesting sights in town. I must leave very early in the morning."

He took me first to a series of government buildings. All were dirty and the streets everywhere were filled with sleeping people: sleeping on rags, on box bits, on the bare cement. Men, women, children. The streets stunk of human excrement and the exhaust from cars and trucks which invariably sprayed out thick gray or black exhaust. Then we drove past a few museums . . . all also populated by street-sleeping people. It all was depressing: you could see that many of these buildings, when built 50 to 200 years ago, were palatial and beautiful structures. Now they were decaying remnants of a desperate and overpopulated society.

On the way back to the hotel, he took it upon himself to make one last sales pitch and drove me through the "red light" district (my guess is that taxi drivers make a commission). This was particularly depressing. Cars and taxis cruised slowly along back streets, while hundreds of girls of all sizes and ages stood in the open doorways of little five-by-eight-foot rooms. The air hung heavy with the smell of raw sewage and sweat, the girls talked among themselves or stood sullenly, men in rags ran among the cars soliciting customers. "There is much disease here," the driver said. "But the girls are only one hundred rupees." That's about $3 US. I asked him to return me directly to the hotel, where I drank a beer to try to get the smell of the area out of my nostrils and went to sleep.

Early the next morning, I took a taxi to the domestic Bombay airport and picked up a flight on a local charter line called East West. After the interminable waits in the airport, continually swatting mosquitoes, I remembered that I'd forgotten to get any quinine (to prevent malaria), and found a pharmacy and picked up some tablets, taking one with some bottled water. After a few hours, the oft-delayed flight left for Hyderabad, a city in the interior or India.

In Hyderabad, I took a taxi to the Oberoi Hotel, another business hotel with safe food and water, and asked the customer relations woman at the counter how to get to Dowleswaram. She'd never heard of it, and we couldn't find it on any maps, but she did check the train schedule and found out that the next morning there was a 6:45 A.M. train that went directly from Hyderabad to Rajamundri, which seemed to be in the area I was looking for. She sent a boy to the train station and secured me a first-class ticket for the 12-hour ride. The cost was about $10 US.

The Train to Dowleswaram

The next morning at 5:00 A.M., I headed to the train station. It was a riot of people, lepers begging, hawkers selling tea and coffee from jugs they carried on their backs, cleaning the used cups with a spit and a wipe on their shirts. The tracks smelled like a sewer: the train-car toilets empty directly onto the rails. Along the side of the train station was a little shanty-town of shacks made of corrugated asbestos, tar-paper, scraps of cardboard and rags. Dogs and naked children competed for scraps as they scavenged among the piles of trash near the tracks.

The trains themselves were a startling sight. The insides had wooden benches and floors, covered to overflowing with people, who stood down the center aisles, on all the benches, and even hung out the doors as the cars filled up. The smell, mostly of urine and body odor, but also of incense and tea, was overpowering. The train cars had once been painted a military green or brown, and a few were orange, but the paint had long ago become so covered with filth that they looked like refugees from some late-nineteenth-century dump.

I walked along from car to car, noticing that on the outside of the "sleeper" and "first-class" cars, there were pieces of paper with lists of names on them. I finally found mine, after two very pleasant business-men stopped me to ask if I needed help (which help I accepted), and entered the car.

Although "first class," the car was covered with dirt and black greasy grime. There were four fans in the ceiling, and the two windows were open to the flies and mosquitoes and sounds outside, with beggars' hands occasionally sticking in. As a small consolation, there were horizontal steel bars on the windows, at about three-inch intervals.

The compartment had four "seats," each a long plastic-covered bench. Two were at normal sitting level, and two hung from the ceiling. Each small compartment held four people, so, with the agreement of my compartment-mates, I took one of the upper benches, tossed up my carry-on bag and jacket, pulled out a book I'd picked up at the hotel, and settled in to read. My three companions were all apparently businessmen, who would take this train as far as Rajamundri. Although curious about what I was doing on the train and why I was going to Rajamundri (I was the only non-Indian I'd seen among all the thousands of people in the train station: I told them, as I always do, that I was a "tourist, visiting a friend"), they were very circumspect when asked what they did for a living, but, it turned out, two were business-men and one was a physician. After the train left, the one of the three who was dressed in a business suit—a strikingly handsome man in his fifties with a handlebar mustache and an uncanny resemblance to Omar Sharif—undressed and put on a traditional Indian wraparound in two pieces, one around his waist and one around his chest. Even so dressed, he carried an aura of great dignity

After I finished my book, one of my companions offered me the *Times of India.* It was both an insight into the soul of India, and also into what an entire world could be like if it was desperately overpopu-lated and ravaged by poverty. I read a story with the dateline of Hyderabad, my destination:

"Viral fever and other water-borne diseases are sweeping through-out the state since the past couple of weeks. These include influenza and cholera, jaundice, Japanese encephalitis, measles, typhoid, gastroenteri-tis, and TB. Government hospitals, private nursing homes, and clinics in the city and other parts of the state have been flooded with hundreds of cases . . . the country of Pakistan is currently under water, and thou-sands of people a day are dying in this region from their homes and vil-lages being swept away, and from the water-borne diseases."

I put down the paper and took a short walk through the train car.

I discovered that the toilets on the train were "not Western," mean-ing they were just a hole in the floor of the "latrine room," with a small spigot of water next to them. After squatting and using the hole, which looked down onto the tracks, one was expected to use one's hand to clean oneself, then to press up against the water-nozzle to produce a trickle of train-water to clean the hand. I shuddered, and left the room as quickly as possible.

Around midday, my three traveling companions each produced from their bags containers of rice and curry with small bits of vegetable. It smelled quite appetizing, but each ate with his fingers. After a few dripping mouthfuls and licked fingers, each in turn offered me a bite, but I passed, and took a few swigs of my bottled water. Today would be a fasting day, I decided.

Along the way, the countryside was mostly rice-paddies, being farmed by families standing in the knee-deep water planting or pulling rice bundles. Water-buffalo were a common sight, as were large Brahman cows. The countryside was lush and green, with large flat-lands punctuated by rocky hills about 500 feet high and running like spines along into the distance. The sky was cloudy all day with the promise of monsoon rain, but it didn't rain and the air blowing into the car through the open windows must have reached around 100° during midday.

Rajamundri

When we arrived in Rajamundri, I stepped off the train, thinking that now was the time to begin my inquiries. As I was looking for a local policeman or train official who might have heard of the supposedly nearby town of Dowleswaram, a group of a half-dozen young men and an equal number of barefoot boys ran up to me. Assuming they were beggars, I first looked away, but the one in front said, 'Thomas C. Hartmann?"

"Yes, that's me."

They all began to applaud and the children threw garlands of fresh flowers around my neck. "Welcome, welcome!" the young man said.

"Are you the Reverend Yesu Ratnam?" I asked.

"No," the man said. "I am Devadanam. The director, Ratnam, went to Hyderabad to meet you."

I'd sent a telegram a week before my departure, telling Ratnam that I would be in Hyderabad at the Oberoi, but had never received a reply, so I assumed he hadn't gotten my telegram. Apparently, though, he had, and now the unfortunate man had spent the money and time to take an all-night train to Hyderabad to pick me up and accompany me here. "I'm very sorry I missed him," I said.

Devadanam shrugged. "He went with Emmanuel, the director of the seminary school here. You did not get our telegram?"

I shook my head.

Devadanam produced a receipt for the telegram, which had my correct home address. "It went out before the first of the month. I don't understand. We thought you had received it. The telegram company said you had."

"I'm sorry," was all I could say.

Devadanam smiled. "Don't worry. Emmanuel and Ratnam arrive in one hour on the next train. They missed you in Hyderabad by one hour, so they hired a car to try to beat the train to the next town, but, unfortunately and unusually, the train was on time, so they missed you there by ten minutes. So they called here to the seminary and told me to meet you, and they took the next train."

Six of us crowded into a car that looked like it had been built before World War II, and we chugged our way to the Garland Hotel, the newest hotel in the city of Rajamundri. "Vegetarian Hotel" it said outside, which in India is not at all uncommon. I was given a first-class room, meaning it had an air conditioner. The bellboy sprayed perfume on the dirty and blood-stained sheets and pillowcase, and in the bathroom, which was an Indian-style hole in the floor with water bucket beside. I closed the windows and spent the next half hour talking with my hosts while they engaged in the sport of trying to kill the many mosquitoes which infested the room. Later, I discovered that most of the mosquitoes were coming up out of the toilet, and if I just kept the bathroom door closed, the sleeping room would stay relatively mosquito-free.

Ratnam and Emmanuel arrived after an hour or two, and we ordered up a vegetarian curry and vegetable cutlets for dinner. As there was no restaurant in this "vegetarian hotel," the bellboy would run outside and find what we wanted from some local street vendor, then bring it back to the room.

Ratnam was a thin, intense man with an honest, friendly smile and a direct approach. I would have guessed his age at around thirty, although I could be off by five years in either direction. He spoke with a quiet sincerity, and wasn't at all the "self-righteous" type that I have so often met in mission work, and who seem so full of their own self-importance. He struck me as a truly humble and very hard-working man.

Over dinner, my hosts explained their efforts to meet me. I had put them through considerable expense and difficulty, although they were most gracious about it and only told it as a "funny" story. I later learned that the money they had, because of the telegram's failure to reach me, wasted on the train trip was an entire month's budget to feed 30 of their orphaned children.

Arriving at Dowleswaram

The next morning they picked me up and we drove to Dowleswaram along a broken and potholed "road" through the rural countryside. We came to a compound about an acre in size, surrounded by a brick wall, and with an entrance arch. Children and adults created a path a hundred feet long, and put garlands around my neck and threw rose petals on me and in front of me. "In India, we have a saying," Ratnam explained when he noticed my embarrassment. "The guest is G-d. And so, we always must treat our guest as if he were G-d."

I later learned that Ratnam had paid for my hotel room, my meals and beers, and even bought my return train ticket himself. When I tried to reimburse this very poor man, he said, "Absolutely not." It would be very bad for a guest to have to pay for his being a guest, he explained emphatically, and he would only accept money from me if it were a gift given for his work in G-d's name, and not for my trip. I tried to give him money that way, but he wouldn't accept it. "I will not take your money now," he said. "You are my guest." Their hospitality and grace made me uncomfortably aware of how arrogant my own culture is.

I walked up to the front of a building about 60 feet long and 25 feet wide. There was a ribbon across it, and Ratnam asked me to cut it. "It is our new dining hall and kitchen facility, donated by our friends in Switzerland, and they said that we must wait for your arrival to dedicate it in G-d's name before we use it." I straightened my shoulders and cut the ribbon to cheers from the hundred or so adults and children there.

Inside, Emmanuel (who, in his sixties, was the senior director of a nearby Lutheran seminary, and a Lutheran minister: Ratnam had been one of his students), Ratnam, two of the teachers, and I sat at the front of the long room, while everybody else came in and sat on the floor in front of us. Ratnam gave a speech welcoming me, which he read from a prepared text, and told me about their work.

There were 30 orphans living in the compound. They stood up, little girls and boys from around 5 to about 12 years old, expectant, smiling, innocent faces. There were 35 local children whose families were destitute or homeless, and these children lived or studied and ate here. There were about 20 or 30 widows living there, old women who sat to one side of the room, many very elderly and feeble, and about a dozen "churchmen," men in their twenties to forties who went to local villages to teach literacy and sanitation, feed people, and, of course, spread the word of G-d.

"Because this is officially a Hindu country," Ratnam told me later, "we are not eligible to receive any assistance whatsoever from the government. This is a government with an official religion, unlike the United States, and so for us to be Christians here, we have a somewhat difficult time."

Emmanuel said a few words welcoming me and telling everybody what a great work he thought Ratnam was doing, and Ratnam's wife and three young children were introduced to me.

Then they asked me to say a few words. I quoted from the Bible the story of when the young children came to Jesus and the adults tried to shoo them away, and told the children that they were the most important of all of us, and the most special in the eyes of G-d. They smiled proudly. I told the widows and "churchmen" that I would do whatever I could to help them, and they thanked me. And then I said a prayer of blessing that Herr Müller taught me in Hebrew, telling them that they were the words that Jesus probably sometimes used to pray. Finally, since they'd all sat through about a half hour of other people's speeches (and about five minutes of mine), I told them that if I were them I'd rather be outside playing than sitting inside listening to some strange fellow talk on and on, so I was finished.

Then Ratnam produced a handful of small envelopes, each with a name on it. The paper was thin enough that I could see that each envelope contained a 100 rupee note (about $3 US), and asked me to call out the names and hand out the envelopes. They were for the widows. I called the names, handed them the envelopes as they came up one by one, saying a silent prayer for each as I handed her the envelope. "It is their monthly living stipend," Ratnam told me, when he thanked me for distributing the money.

After this ceremony, we went to the front porch of the girls' dormitory. It's across the dirt compound from the remains of Ratnam's home, which was destroyed by a cyclone. He told me that he and his family sleep in a tent in the central area of the compound, and keep their possessions in a box in one of the girls' rooms.

We sat in chairs on the front porch, and Ratnam's wife brought me a plate with fresh tomatoes, onions, toast, and jelly on it, along with a glass of beer. Apparently, having seen me drink beer the night before, word of my preference had preceded me. "I don't drink coffee or alcohol," Ratnam said. "But you are welcome. I think it is safe for your stomach."

I agreed, remembering to take another quinine tablet, and made a simple sandwich out of the food. When I noticed I was the only one eating, Ratnam said that he would eat when I was finished, because I was "the guest." I explained that in my country it was best manners to "eat with the guest," so he ordered his lunch be brought—a rice curry with nuts and hot peppers—and ate it with his fingers in traditional Indian style. The children clustered around, fascinated to see me eating with what was probably the only fork in the village.

After we were finished, several of the widows approached us, heads down, as if they were very embarrassed. "They would like you to pray for them," Ratnam explained. "It would be a great honor for me if you would." He pointed to a toothless woman. "Her back is damaged, for example."

I put one hand on the woman's head, another on her back, and silently prayed that G-d would send some of my vitality into this woman. She wept.

After her, there was a long line of old people, and then the children. On each, I placed my hand and said a simple prayer, feeling all the while terribly self-conscious, yet praying that it would do some good for them. I'm no holy man, nor even particularly pious, so this was a very humbling experience.

From the "Christian Mercy Children Welfare Association" center (where we were located), we then took a car about ten miles away to another town, where we visited a home for blind children. All the teachers were blind, too, and Ratnam explained that one of them, the senior man, white-haired and in his sixties but very robust, was Ratnam's uncle. The children ranged in age from around 4 to about 13. There were about 20 of them, along with a few blind adults. They sang several songs for me, and then two of the boys read brief passages from Braille Bibles: one in English and one in the local language. Outside, under another "Welcome Mr. Thomas C. Hartmann" handmade sign, they clustered together so Ratnam could take my picture with them.

The children were so beautiful in this harsh and poor land. I fought the lump in my throat as we left.

"You support this organization?" I asked Ratnam as we drove away.

"Partially. The government will pay for their rent of the building, a poor house here in this slum, because they are blind. But because we and they are Christian, they are not allowed to take any other sort of assistance. So I pay for their teachers, their houseparents, and their food."

"How much does this cost you?" I said.

"About one thousand rupees a month," he said simply. Thirty dollars US.

"And your budget for the larger center?"

"That is about fifteen to twenty thousand rupees a month, for the children, the widows, the food, the doctor who comes every week, everything." Five to six hundred dollars.

Because I had to leave that night to take the overnight train back to Hyderabad, there was no time to go visit the leper colony which Ratnam also supports out of his $600 monthly budget. It would be a half-day's drive away, and he asked me to return, with my wife, to see it.

I took the overnight train back to Hyderabad, sleeping fitfully with four other men in the small compartment, and then caught an Indian Airlines (the domestic airline) flight from Hyderabad to Bombay. There was a 20-foot sign behind the ticket counter that said, "25,000 Employees of Air India and Indian Airlines Are On Agitation Against Privatization." While wondering what this meant, I was sent from line to line. There were any number of airline employees sitting idly behind their counters, but when I approached, I was told that it was not their particular job to issue my ticket, or approve my credit card, or assign me a seat, or tell me if or when the flight would leave, and that I must go stand in another line. I spent most of my time standing in line, shooing off the mosquitoes that seemed to have a particular fondness for me.

As I stood in the airport, watching the bustle of businessmen and families traveling to far parts of India and the world, I reflected on Yogananda's descriptions of this country in the 1920s when the population was a quarter of what it is now, and the older culture values of respect for the Earth and other living things were widely practiced. I felt a deep sadness for a time and place so recently lost.

INDIA, 1996

In 1996, I returned to India to visit Ratnam at Herr Müller's request. This time I took Louise and Kerith with me.

Part of the reason for the trip was that Herr Müller and I had been getting increasingly urgent letters appealing for money from a "Mrs. K," who said she was running an orphanage about 200 miles away from where Ratnam was located. She claimed that the orphanage had been started by an American woman, who was later killed in a car accident, leaving Mrs. K. stranded with the children and no money. When we tracked the American woman down, however, we found her alive and well in upstate New York. She said that she'd visited India once on a business trip and had probably passed out a fair number of business cards, but had never visited, or supported, an orphanage there. Suspecting fraud, and worrying about whether it might have anything to do with Ratnam or his project or people working for him, Herr Müller asked me to promptly go to India in May, just a few weeks before the beginning of monsoon season.

Parts of the following are written in present tense because they're directly transcribed from the report I typed for Herr Müller, using a palmtop computer as the events took place.

Returning to Bombay

Our first stop was Bombay, where again I was overwhelmed by the human misery. We arrived at night and everywhere people were sleeping on sidewalks, stacked side-by-side like cordwood, and using the streets as toilets. When we walked around the next morning, many of these people had vanished from the sidewalks, presumably to go off to do manual labor or beg. Most heartwrenching were the many families: at least half, if not three-fourths, of the people we saw sleeping on the streets were families with children.

One particularly poignant situation was a little boy about ten who was blind in one eye. He was carrying four or five handmade drums and approached us as we walked along the street in Bombay. Kerith made the mistake of asking him the price, and he then followed us for six blocks or more, pulling on our clothes, drumming his drums, and yelling at us.

I was torn between feeling sorry for him and being irritated at him. We ducked into several stores to avoid him, but he always waited for us and then began his sales pitch again. Yelling "No" at him only made him more persistent. I thought about giving him some money, but what we'd discovered at this point, to our chagrin, was that when we gave money to beggars they only became far more aggressive, demanding more and getting more physically demanding, pulling on our clothes and grabbing our hands. In a country where toilet paper is virtually unknown, this can be quite disconcerting and scary. So finally we found a shopkeeper who came out and yelled at our little drummer boy and we were rid of him. Today, writing this, I think back on yesterday and wish that I had given him some money, even knowing that it would have increased the inconvenience to us.

May is a bad month to visit the interior of India. It's brutally hot the temperatures on the train were over 110 degrees for most of the day, and the newspapers in Hyderabad were filled with stories of people who had died from the heat, reported at 50° Celsius (105° F) on average. The hot air was a palpable thing, a hot blanket that surrounds and stifles you and from which you cannot escape.

In addition, May is the month when most Indians go on vacation. This made it almost impossible to get a train reservation. We spent an entire day in Hyderabad just waiting for a confirmation to Rajamundri, and then were told that all the return trains were full—we would have to travel on the overnight train back, perhaps sitting on the floor, certainly in a second-class car with no amenities or glass windows.

Ratnam and about a dozen people met us at the station in Rajamundri with much noise and flower garlands and a photographer. My wife, child, and I refused to wear the garlands, and he became far less enthusiastic: apparently I had embarrassed him in front of his followers. To honor the guest is an ancient tradition in India, but I told him that I would rather that the money from the garlands go to the children, and that Jesus washed his disciples' feet rather than the other way around. He was graceful but not smiling any longer.

Once again we were told upon arrival at the Rajamundri train station that it would not be possible to get a return train. Since we had left most of our luggage in Hyderabad, and I already knew that our flights were sold out, this presented a substantial problem, which Ratnam said he would solve. We went to a hotel in Rajamundri recommended by a businessman on the train and got a relatively clean room for about $12 per night.

Visiting Mrs. K.

As I type these words, we are in a taxi with Ratnam on the way to visit Mrs. K. The roads are impossible and the driving is very dangerous. We just passed into the town of LalumPeka (phonetic) and are now driving out of it.

Yesterday when I said that we must visit her, he was strongly against it. I insisted, however, and so now here we are in this ancient taxi with a truly crazed and perhaps suicidal driver.

In the last three hours, we passed several wrecks, one recent and quite bloody: the rural roads here are treacherous—more so than any I've seen in the world—I'm thinking that I shouldn't have brought my daughter along and subjected her to this danger.

We turn off the "main road" onto an ox path and follow it for several miles to a little town in the middle of nowhere. No cars, few bikes, filled with semi-naked people and utter poverty.

In the middle of this town, we come to a dirt-floor building with a tiled roof (a major luxury—most have thatched roofs) and one brick wall. The other walls are made of newspaper glued together to resemble papier-mâché. It's almost noon and brutally hot—we are all covered with a slimy sweat. We get out of the car and see the sign on the building: "Werner Child Welfare Home."

Ratnam leads us into the building where there are 14 children assembled, all apparently between five and ten years old. They begin singing and clapping—reciting over and over again what I assume are Bible songs. More arrive as we sit and listen, older children, probably preteens. It seems as if half the village will soon be here. The recent arrivals don't seem to know the songs, so I suspect they're more local kids.

Louise asks who the children are and where they live and Ratnam says that they are orphans or children of poverty who live here on the reed mats on the floor. One of the children opens one of a dozen boxes (each the size of a briefcase) and takes from it a book, but inside I can see clothing: I suspect he is one of the "true residents" of this place.

Ratnam sits at a table with a Bible and has Louise, Kerith, and me sit beside him in chairs. The children are smiling and well-behaved and clean, but most are wearing clothing that is frayed and torn.

After twenty minutes or so of singing, Ratnam begins to call on children, who then stand up, Bible in hand, and read passages to us. I recognize the words "Jehovah," "Israel," and the "Hallelujah" that ends every song.

Then Ratnam gives a sermon, and then he asks me to do the same. So I tell the story of the Sermon on the Mount and the importance of love, forgiveness, and to pray to G-d instead of just as a big show for people.

Just before the sermon, Mrs. K. arrives. She is 25 years old, nicely dressed with a nice purse, and attractive in a somewhat plump Indian fashion. She speaks no English whatever, but only Talu, which is the language of the region: Ratnam will translate.

I ask her if she has any questions for me and she says, "Please help us."

Ratnam then tells me that she said it costs her $20 per child per month for food. I calculate that at 680 rupees, or over 20 rupees per day, which in this part of this country is a lot of money (the average per capita income for the entire nation is about $10 US per month). When I point this out, Ratnam says that that amount included the bank's exchange fee, books, clothes, etc., and went far beyond food.

Before we left the United States for India, a friend who wrote a chapter for one of my books gave us $5 to give to a needy person when we arrived at our destination. As we are now as far into the interior of India as I can imagine being, I write a check on our personal account for a larger sum and give it to Mrs. K. along with the $5 bill from Sharon.*

Driving back in the taxi to Rajamundri, it is now well into the hottest part of the day. This car was built in 1950, and is far less than

---

*We gave her this money during our visit, but overall, her claimed spending seemed out of all proportion to what we'd seen it actually takes to care for a child in India. We had been concerned when her letters claimed that her benefactor in New York had died, when in fact the "benefactor" had never heard of the orphanage; now, these inflated statements of financial needs seemed to confirm our fears. We decided not to offer further support to this well-dressed woman.

comfortable. The air from outside hits me like a blast from a furnace. And yet at least we are in a car and not walking along the roadside, or rolling ourselves on a small platform with wheels as used by the beggars in Bombay who have lost their legs.

26 May 1996

Reverend Yesu Ratnam picked us up in our hotel at 7:30 A.M. Kerith was eating a breakfast of fried onions, and I had some sort of thin fried bread that had slices of fresh onion and deadly hot little peppers wrapped up in it. The coffee was undrinkable: black like motor oil with grit in it, and smelling of sewage; I feared for the water it was made from, boiled or not. Mosquitoes nipped at our ankles.

Ratnam had hired the same driver as the day before, and he gave us another harrowing ride the 15 kilometers from Rajamundri to Dowleswaram. We arrived at Ratnam's place, which faces the road, around 8:00 A.M., just as the sun was midway up the morning sky and getting very hot. The air was still and dry, cutting into my nostrils; the temperature was well over 90° already. My skin was covered with sweat, tickling as it trickled down my back and stomach, and when I wiped my forehead on my white cotton shirtsleeve, just the ride from Rajamundri had covered me with so much grit, dust, and diesel exhaust that it left a dark stain on the shirt.

Ratnam had erected a hand-painted fabric sign over the entrance to his compound "Welcoming Mr. & Mrs. Thomas C. Hartmann & Family," and, as we passed under this and through his gate, we faced a double row of children and adults stretching half a city block to the back of his buildings.

Children rushed up and reverently put flower garlands around our necks and threw rose petals over us and in our path, laughing and shouting welcome. Some of the children looked at our white faces and Louise's blonde hair in slack-jawed amazement—in this most rural part of India they may have never before seen a Caucasian person—but most were giggling and jumping around as if they'd been invited to the world's biggest birthday party.

Deciding that this was their culture and Ratnam's show, we went along with good graces and accepted the garlands and waved and thanked them for the attention.

The women took 14-year-old Kerith off to the girls' dormitory as Louise and I stood talking with Ratnam and the men. Shortly later Kerith emerged, very self-consciously wearing a beautiful Indian sari of rich orange and red, trimmed in gold. She looked like a princess, and the children all clapped in delight: the expressions on her face caused me to assume she was feeling both pride and embarrassment.

To the left of the compound, a large tarp was set up on poles to keep the sun off the ground. Squatting on the hard red dirt under it were about 60 people. The first three rows were men, ranging from old age to teenage years, with a few small boys. The fourth and fifth rows were women and girls.

As Ratnam led us over to them, I wondered what was special about them and why they were sitting off to one side rather than participating in the welcoming festivities. As I got closer my stomach dropped as I realized the situation.

The man closest to me had no fingers on either of his hands, and his left foot was a bloody stump. The man next to him was missing the first two joints of all his fingers, and both feet. The man next to him had lost his entire right hand and most of his nose and chin: his feet—or what might have been left of them—were wrapped in pus-soaked bandages. Every person in the group—men, women and children—shared the same fate.

These were lepers.

Meeting and Serving the Lepers in Ratnam's Colony

Four folding chairs were set up in front of the group of lepers, and Ratnam gestured for Louise, Kerith, and me to join him in sitting with them. We sat and Ratnam gave a short speech in Talu, the local language. Then he asked me to speak, so I said a prayer asking for G-d's blessing and grace on each of them and then sat down. They applauded, clapping stumps and bloodied limbs together.

Ratnam then pulled from his pocket a pack of ten rupee notes (thirty cents US) about a half-inch thick, and asked me if I would give two notes to each of the lepers. As I walked along the rows handing each leper two notes, each handed back to me a small, red, carnation-like flower he'd been holding. Many cried as they did so: all were clearly grateful with what I was to learn was their monthly stipend.

Soon my left hand was overflowing with the lepers' flowers, and an assistant of Ratnam's relieved me of my burden.

I was ripped with emotions. On the one hand, these people had a terrible and highly contagious disease which takes five years of daily medical treatment to stop. Ratnam later told me that none could afford the medications, as a week's treatment cost could exceed three months worth of food and all were desperately poor. All these people had active cases of the disease, and using their pus-infected stumps and limbs they were handing me flowers.

On the other hand, I remembered Jesus's admonition that we must always strive to help the least among us, that this was the most holy work we could do. He Himself went out of His way to heal lepers. And so mixed in with my fear was a certain joy at the opportunity to be on the front line, as it were, of help to humanity.

When I finished with the men, Ratnam suggested that Louise and Kerith should distribute money to the leprous women and children, which they did. Kerith conducted herself with aplomb, but I could see glistening in her eyes, as in Louise's, the intense emotion that this experience was causing them.

After passing out the money, Louise, Kerith, and I all passed out three cupfuls of rice and a handful of vegetables to each of the lepers. It took a half hour to finish the job, sweat soaked my clothes, but still I was conscious of how much more fortunate I was than any of these poor souls.

After feeding the lepers, Ratnam led us to the second floor of his main building. When I was here almost three years ago, this had been a bare roof, but now it was complete with rooms, doors, and ceiling, all made of durable concrete. The bottom floor was the girls' dormitory, Ratnam explained, and the upper floor was to be the boys' dormitory. While the floor was finished, it was unoccupied: Ratnam had been waiting for us to arrive (perhaps for several months?) for the ribbon-cutting and ceremonial prayers.

We cut the ribbons—me the first room, Louise the second, Kerith the third—and after each ribbon cutting the entire community walked around the inside of each room chanting a prayer to bless the room and its future occupants.

Following this, it was time for Sunday morning church services.

Ratnam is an ordained Lutheran minister, and the main feeding hall doubles as a church on Sundays. In addition to the orphanage's children, which seemed to number between 30 and 50, at least another 50 people from the local community came for the service. Hymns were sung, prayers said, and then Ratnam asked me to give a sermon. I told the story from Matthew 6 in the Sermon on the Mount about the importance of praying in secret, which Ratnam dutifully translated, and then the service ended with one of the lay pastors giving a long-winded prayer (in an ironic contrast to my sermon).

After the church service a long line of old women assembled in front of me asking for a blessing. Remembering Herr Müller's teaching about giving spiritual light and power from your right hand, I placed my hand on each person's head and said a prayer in Hebrew. I could feel an energy flowing through me, from head to heart to hand and out, and it was interesting to see a number of these people visibly straighten, smile, and/or sigh loudly at the exact moment I could feel heat or power flowing out of my hand.

After the old women, many of the children lined up for a blessing, and then the men. This was all spontaneous and I spent altogether about a half hour in this process. Throughout the trip up to this time, I'd been practicing giving people light when we encountered beggars and others on the street.

From here we went to sit in the shade with Ratnam. He introduced us to his wife and his two sons, and his wife handed Louise their 14-day-old daughter, who they just adopted. The child was born premature, her mother died in childbirth, and she was so tiny and delicate it was like holding a baby bird. I took her in my arms and she immediately fell asleep. In this country where a substantial portion of children die before they reach puberty, I felt a painful emotion of joy and sadness that this child, if we can help Ratnam to continue his work, will have a chance to live.

Next the bookkeeper came over. After seeing my interrogation of Mrs. K, Ratnam had apparently anticipated this. Louise (who is, herself, trained as a bookkeeper and has done it for several of our companies) and I went through, page by page, line by line, the past three years of Ratnam's books. Not only did everything seem in order, but we were impressed by how carefully and meticulously every expenditure was documented. I asked to see the bank's records, and the bookkeeper brought out the actual printouts from the bank. We spent a half hour comparing line-items from Ratnam's hand-done books with the bank and they agreed perfectly. When I commented on this, the bookkeeper said that because Salem International/India was a registered charity with the government, everything must be exact to the last penny or there could be severe penalties . . . in addition to his desire to be accountable to Salem and the Swiss donor family.

Nearly all the moneys spent went to food and clothing for the children, and about $1000 US per year was spent for the expenses of his evangelists, which paid them $3 to $5 per month each to travel from city to city to preach, plus the cost of Bibles and literature.

After this, we met with the evangelists and the "Bible women" in a small room just behind where we had given the food to the lepers. Several told me that their families were hungry because Ratnam no longer had the money to pay them their $5 per month allowance, and they were worried about their children. One man in particular held onto my feet and told me that he was afraid that one of his children might starve.

In response to this, I told them the story of Jesus telling his disciples that when they fed the hungry, clothed the naked, healed the sick, and visited those in prison that they were feeding, clothing, healing, and visiting Him. I said that some religious organizations, particularly those following the writings of Paul, put great emphasis on spreading the word of Christianity, and that while Salem respected and honored this work, we are not a proselytizing organization: instead, the mandate Herr Müller had given us was to feed, clothe, heal, and visit the least of the least: that in these, we were seeing the face of Christ.

This didn't make them particularly happy, and so I told them that I would write a letter of recommendation about their work and send it for reproduction to Ratnam along with a listing of the mail addresses of Lutheran churches in America, since Ratnam was ordained as a Lutheran minister and they may be interested in helping him.

After this meeting, we took a car back to Rajamundri. At 10:00 P.M. we left for the train station, but the train to Hyderabad was late. At 2:30 A.M. it arrived and left, with us jammed into a second-class compartment, wall-to-wall poor people, stinking of body odor and urine and filled with flies, for the twelve-hour ride to Hyderabad where we would pick up our commuter flight to Bombay for our Delta jet flight to Frankfurt.

On our return to America, we stopped in Germany to see Herr Müller and share our observations and the stories of our trip. He said, "Of course, the situation there is terrible: it is India," and then, "Of course, we must help." And so something that, to a young culture mind, would be a contradiction, now makes sense to me as my world-view is changing.

EPILOGUE

While this book was in production, I heard a conservative talk-show host say it's a joke that people in America are sending money to help the starving poor in India. Why? "Because," his reasoning went, "India has become a net *exporter* of wheat." If India is growing wheat that it's shipping out of the country, why should we send food money in?

One response would be, as Herr Müller points out, that the right thing to do is to do what's right: there is power in taking the right step, however small, and regardless of the situation. The Sermon on the Mount teaches that we should feed the hungry, and there are millions of hungry in Bombay.

Nonetheless, the situation in India is a sad irony, worth examining for a moment. How could it be that India is exporting more wheat than it imports while so many of its people starve?*

The wheat growers in India grow and export wheat because that's how they make money. There's never any money to be made by feeding the penniless; the export transaction has nothing to do with the starving neighbors. The starving people simply don't enter the equation.

I have no objection to profit. I've started and run several successful businesses. But I've come to understand that the profit motive flour-

---

*Of course, one might ask the same question about hunger in America. The biggest privately-owned corporation in America is a highly profitable grain producer (with a billion dollars in sales per week), and another grain company paid a fine of $100 million in 1996 for illegal price fixing, while millions of people in America are malnourished.

ishes only in younger cultures—the cultures in which people see themselves as separate from each other and from the rest of existence.

Profit exists only if you draw a circle between "me" and "not me," then measure how much goes out of your circle and how much comes in. That simply doesn't happen in the older cultures where people don't isolate themselves but instead feel "we're all in this together."

The talk show host identified a nasty irony in India. But he didn't notice that it's caused by the people in that ancient land who've adopted *his* younger-culture ideals.

Coincidences

Small Lessons for the Future

*I do not think that any civilization can be called
complete until it has progressed from sophistication
to unsophistication, and made a conscious return
to simplicity of thinking and living.*

—LIN YUTANG, *THE IMPORTANCE OF LIVING*

When I visited Germany and Switzerland in 1993 to make my first
report on India, I had a fascinating conversation with Herr Müller
about my trip. I mentioned the many odd coincidences that seemed to
happen during that journey, as well as all the ones that had filled most
of my life, and had recently had a conversation with a friend who'd
read a "New Age" book that said that coincidences were a sign of
spirituality.

"Some people say that coincidences will increase as the end of the
old age comes and the new age begins," I said.

He shook his head. "Coincidence has always been with us. For the
average person, they are random acts. For the spiritual person, they are
evidence of the Holy Spirit."

"But what about people who claim that there are more coincidences happening now?"

"There are more spiritual people on the Earth now. Many do not
even know yet their own spiritual identities: it may take a shock for
them to wake up, or they may discover it gradually because of the
unusual things they experience in their lives, things they may not tell
other people about for fear of ridicule. These people have lives filled
with coincidence."

"So there is more coincidence now because there are more spiritual
people on the Earth now?"

He smiled. "*Ja*. But there is also more not-coincidence now, because there are also more not-spiritual people on the Earth." Of course, I thought: there are more people on the Earth, overall.

I believe that both numbers and coincidence—bound together by the laws of mathematics and probability—are somehow an "edge" between the physical and the spiritual. (To be sure, it's an edge that we don't understand.)

It was the total discarding of the spiritual, of virtually all edges, which led to the destruction of Russia, as I was soon to discover.

Russia

A New Seed Planted Among Thorns

Every second of existence is a new miracle. Consider the countless variations and possibilities that await us every second—avenues into the future. We take only one of these; the others—who knows where they go? This is the eternal marvel, the magnificent uncertainty of the next second to come, with the past a steady unfolding carpet of denouement.

—JACK VANCE, THE HOUSES OF ISZM

There are a few more spiritual lessons in this book, but in some ways they grew out of my experiences in the world, particularly in those places fermenting with change.

Traveling to Russia for Salem taught me another important lesson. I saw how the communist concept—once embraced by the Russians as the solution to the problems of the West—destroyed the human spirit because it detached people's actions from any response.

I have come to conclude that the natural way of being, for any alert sentient creature, is to sense its surroundings, act, and directly experience the result. Consistently, around the world, this is the way of older cultures. Wherever this process is disrupted, the spirit goes out of being and people's natural power degenerates in atrophy or destruction of harmony.

Divert a person's attention away from the "now" and they get out of touch with their inner reality. Convince them that there's no point in acting, and they become depressed.

Similarly, what happened in the Soviet Union, for generations, is that although people acted (did their jobs), it made no difference in how their life went; whether they worked hard or not, there was no change

238

in their standard of living. With no connection between initiative and outcome, their productive spirit died.

Children need to grow up learning that their choices make a difference. In Russia, even the parents—and even *their* parents—had rarely ever seen a situation where they had choice and could learn from it. In this chapter you'll see what effect that has.

I was in the Scandinavian Airlines twin-prop plane that landed at about noon on a gray, blustery, raw-cold December day in Kaliningrad, Russia. The airport is about 20 miles outside the town, surrounded by now-unused barbed-wire fences and empty guard stations. Inside the terminal there was no heat, and only about half the overhead lights worked. Remembering the lengthy interrogations I'd been through when entering and leaving East Berlin years earlier, I was expecting rigid formalities on entering, particularly since Kaliningrad was and still is a "special zone," an area of secret military installations and one of the former Soviet Union's most sensitive places. Even normal Russians aren't allowed to travel into the region, but on this day the immigration inspector just looked at my visa, stamped my passport, smiled, and said, "Welcome to Russia." Nobody was even checking luggage for contraband in the customs area: I just walked outside, carrying my shoulder bag and the five liters of water I'd brought from Copenhagen.

Outside, Gerhard Lipfert waited with the blue Volkswagen bus he'd driven from Germany. He greeted me with a huge hug, saying, "Welcome to Russia!"

Inside the bus was a man named Herr Burkhardt, who'd been a foot-soldier in Hitler's army, captured by the Russians, and spent decades as a prisoner of war in Russia. Finally he was released and returned to Germany, where he now worked for Salem as a Russian/German translator. His appearance was a bit of a shock to me: I'd been reading a book about Martin Bormann and Odessa, and his face looked so much like Bormann did back in 1944 that I did a double-take. Burkhardt's face, though, creased in a wide smile as he welcomed me.

The next morning we set out for an area about 200 kilometers from Kaliningrad, near the Polish border, where Salem has undertaken a project in Russia. It was bitterly cold, and the sky was so dim, the clouds so thick, that the world looked like an old black-and-white movie from the forties.

Gerhard barreled along at high speed once we got to the edge of the city, when we were flagged down on the highway (a two-lane potholed road) by four men dressed as police or military. They stepped into the road in front of us and waved us over with a black-and-white-striped baton.

One came to each of the front windows while the other two inspected the outside of the bus. The man at Gerhard's window began shouting in Russian, waving his finger, and then his fist at Gerhard. The man on my side stared across me at the tableau. Herr Burkhardt, in the back seat, leaned forward and shouted back in Russian, waving his fist. Now both Russians were shouting, one hitting the bus with his fist, all very animated and emphatic. But, somehow, it seemed like it was all a performance of some sort: I couldn't figure out what was going on.

Herr Burkhardt opened the side door and jumped out, ran around to the driver's side, and put his arm around the Russian who'd been most loudly abusing Gerhard (who understood nothing of what the man was saying in Russian). Burkhardt whispered something in the man's ear, and they walked off behind the bus, with the other three Russians in tow. The back of the bus opened, and we heard soft discussion, then the back closed, Burkhardt came back to the side door, got in, and brushed his hands together in a "that's finished" gesture. The four Russians crowded around the two front windows to shake our hands and, in German, to say, "Have a good trip." They smiled and waved as Gerhard put the bus into gear and we pulled away.

"What was that all about?" Gerhard asked, bewildered.

"They had a radar gun," Burkhardt said. "The speed limit here is 60 kilometers per hour and you were going 140. They said that the penalty was for us to go to jail."

"And?" Gerhard said.

"And I gave them each a chocolate bar from our storage in the back," Burkhardt said. He slapped his hands together with a smile. "End of discussion."

Gerhard laughed, but I could tell in his reaction that he, like me, saw something terribly wrong and tragic about the state of a nation where four police officers would consider a chocolate bar worthy of setting aside their sworn duty. On the other hand, we weren't going any faster than most of the other traffic, but we'd been singled out to be stopped: most likely the whole thing was a setup to squeeze such a bribe from "rich foreigners." I'd had to pay such bribes in the past to get out of the airport in Entebbe, Uganda (at gunpoint, no less), in both Sri Lanka and the Philippines to get a seat that I'd already reserved on a state airline, and in Mexico to get out of a "speeding ticket" when I was going slower than the rest of the traffic.

Nonetheless, the experience really brought home to me how much of a third-world-country Russia is. How could we Americans have ever thought otherwise, I wondered, as we drove through the countryside and I watched the passing parade of fallen-down fences, broken-down houses, ancient cars, potholed pavement, and the steady stream of old men and women hitchhiking. (Von Heyer once remarked to me that you can tell the poverty of a nation by the age of the hitchhikers. I've found this to be so very true, all over the world.)

It was close to 10:00 P.M. when we arrived in a little town whose name I never managed to get straight. In the midst of rolling fields and gentle hills, the Russian farmlands, was this little collection of box-square houses, each identical to the other, each just a bit larger than a double-wide trailer home. There were perhaps 60 houses that made up the town, maybe five streets.

We stopped first at Erika's house. It was her mother's birthday, a little old lady with a scarf over her white hair, her face wrinkled with age and weather, and a birthday celebration was in full-swing. Twenty people packed the house, fifteen or so of them in the living room, where a long makeshift table had been set up and was covered with food and drink. There were potatoes and carrots, next to a bottle of vodka. Beans and some sort of meat next to another bottle of vodka. Several piles of Salem-bread from Germany, sitting by a bottle of peach schnapps. Red beet soup and sauerkraut next to the bottle of wine.

People were laughing, the women were singing long songs, rocking from side to side together, hugging each other. Each person wanted to shake my hand, and every time anybody walked by me, they put their hand on my shoulder or back. At first it struck me, a rather reserved American, as overly demonstrative, but I then saw that this was how everybody was with everybody. Here was the soul of Russia, the heart of the people: touching, laughing, kissing, hugging, singing maudlin songs while holding hands.

We were given places of honor at the table, and Gerhard gestured for me to eat the food. "This is a rare occasion," be said. "And most of the food is what we've brought here recently. You can eat it safely, but don't drink the water."

I didn't have to worry about drinking the water. First a glass of sangria was put in front of me, we all toasted, and everybody downed theirs in one gulp. Next was a tumbler of straight vodka. Then the schnapps. Then back to the vodka. I was accumulating half-full glasses in front of me, to the great amusement of my hosts, but my explanation that I was sick from the airplane seemed to soften the blow of my lack of participation.

In addition to the friendliness of the people, I noticed something else was oddly different about them. It took a few minutes for me to realize what it was, but when it hit me, I took a look around and saw that it was a universal constant. Not a single one of the Russians had a full set of teeth. Most had several prominent gold or silver or steel teeth, some an entire mouth of such false teeth. And most simply had huge gaps where there had once been teeth.

There was another surprise at the party: it was Horst Von Heyer, the Salem employee who was shot in the Kurdistan region of northern Iraq two years ago when Salem was trying to set up a program to help the Kurds there. Von Heyer, having survived the loss of his assistant in Namibia to a crocodile, and five bullets in his body in Iraq, was again up and around, a distinguished man in his late fifties who stands well over six feet and speaks perfect British English (and a half-dozen other languages). It was great seeing him: he'd taken me into Uganda the second time I'd gone to Africa, and we'd spent many an evening together talking long into the nights the year our family lived at Salem in Stadtsteinach. Now he was helping the Salem project here in Russia.

Around midnight the party broke up, people bundling up to trudge out into the cold, black night (no streetlights, dirt streets) back to their homes. Several liters of vodka had been consumed, along with the schnapps and wine: I was amazed anybody could stand up, much less walk home. Later, Gerhard told me that alcohol was a major problem in Russia. In this small town of 400 people, 22 have died in the past year from alcoholism. Two deaths a month, in a town of 400! Vodka is cheaper and more readily available than bottled water, and as Von Heyer said, with the "morale of the people so utterly destroyed, with nothing to do or strive for," all they do is drink. Gerhard blames it on communism, Burkhardt says it's part of the Russian psyche, and I just watched, observing it and trying not to judge it.

Herr Burkhardt and I spent the night in the house next door to Erika's, inhabited by Olga, her husband Sergei, and their two children, a boy about 13 and a girl around 7. The two kids share a room with a small bed on either side, and Olga moved them onto a mattress in the kitchen and gave Burkhardt and me their beds. I went to sleep, exhausted.

SATURDAY

The next morning I woke up still a bit jet-lagged around 10:00 A.M., dressed, and joined Olga's family in the kitchen. They all sat on little stools around a small metal table with a new German-made tablecloth, and there was bread from the bakeries at Salem in Germany on the table, along with tea so dark it looked like coffee and homemade plum preserves filled with large pits that you scooped around. I brought a liter of Danish bottled water and shared it with the table.

Twenty minutes later, Gerhard and Von Heyer arrived from next door where they'd been sleeping, and told Burkhardt and me to get dressed up to go out. In my jet-lag daze, I forgot to put on my long underwear, and just pulled on a jacket, hat, gloves, and boots. Outside it was snowing so hard I couldn't see more than 100 feet and the wind was howling down the streets like a rabid wolf. We bundled into the bus along with an old woman who I soon learned was the "book-keeper" for the Salem Russia operation, and drove off along frozen, pitted dirt roads into the countryside.

We drove for an hour or so through the countryside. For about a half-mile, there was a high double barbed-wire fence on our right. "It's the border with Poland," Gerhard said. I tried to place it on the map in my mind, but was lost.

The heater in the Volkswagen microbus was only effective enough to melt the snow that had covered my clothes, and I was now both cold and wet, shivering. We crested a hill, and, pitching wildly from side to side, came down into an area in the midst of desolate miles of empty land, punctuated only by two houses under construction and a small wooden shed.

"This is the beginning of Salem here," Gerhard said, turning off the bus.

We all climbed out and walked through foot-deep snow to the first of the two houses. They were two-story brick-and-wood homes with steeply-pitched roofs. The outsides were covered with scaffolding, no windows or doors were yet in place, and the wind hooted mournfully as it whipped through the skeletal buildings.

In the first house we found four men, bundled against the cold in thick coats, Cossack hats, thick black boots. One was listlessly driving nails into a wall, the other three smoking cigarettes and apparently supervising the first man. All four were mostly toothless, with aged and lined faces, wind-burned skin, thick and cracked hands. Men in their thirties who looked like they were in their sixties, their bones and teeth ravaged by malnutrition, their livers and skin devoured by vodka and cigarettes.

Von Heyer became very upset when he saw their work. The wood boards didn't fit together: you could see outdoors through the cracks in the walls. The carpentry looked like a kid's treehouse, constructed of scrap wood. The electrical wires weren't recessed into the brickwork or the walls but stapled haphazardly across walls and ceilings. And the chimney (as with most all the brickwork) had no mortar laterally between the bricks, only above and below them (and they were uneven at that). The result was that as I stood on one side of the chimney, I could see clear through the other side and get a glimpse of Von Heyer between the bricks.

I shook my head and started to say something; Von Heyer put a finger to his lips. "You be the silent one," he said. "And try to look upset."

Gerhard and Von Heyer brought over Burkhardt and, with loud and angry tones, pointed out the deficiencies, waving their arms and hitting the flimsy walls with their fists. The workers yelled back, and it seemed that the winner wouldn't be the person with the greatest logic but the loudest voice. Then Burkhardt pointed to me and said something in a low and menacing voice, and they all got quiet.

We marched out of the first house and walked through the snow, leaning against the wind, to the second house, where the scene was repeated, although this time the workers kept glancing furtively at me, and didn't yell back so much. I looked around, wondering if I'd been cast in the role of some sort of building inspector. There was the same central heating with no room controls in each room as at Olga's house. The walls were made of a crazy-quilt of fiberboard, pine board, and plywood. The window and door frames were obviously prefabricated and put into place, and the wood was uneven, showing big gaps. In some places, where a piece of wood wasn't long enough to complete a seal, smaller pieces were nailed into place, willy-nilly.

After the showing was over, we stood by the old stove and I said, "What's going on with the houses?"

Von Heyer snorted. "The materials are pathetic. We have to buy them as prefab houses, because everything in this country is made in huge central factories. You wouldn't believe the size of the factories, or the ancient machinery they have in them. It's pitiful."

"So the walls and doors are prefabricated?"

"And the concrete for the foundation. Those big slabs of concrete out there with the holes running lengthwise through them."

"But what about the assembly? The men putting the houses together? They don't seem like happy workers."

He shook his head. "They don't know how to work. And even when you can get them to work, they don't know how to do the job."

"What do you mean?"

"The brickwork is all wrong, you saw that."

"Yes," I said. "Looked to me like the house would burn down the first time somebody started a fire in the furnace."

"Exactly," he said. "But when we pointed it out to them, they said that we should hire somebody else to redo it. And still pay them!"

"They don't know how to lay bricks?"

"They said they did, but their work gives the lie to that. Same with the carpentry and electrical work. One's drunk and the other three are incompetent."

"Why not fire them?"

"I already did that once. They work for a local contractor, and I fired him last time I was here, last month. We hired another contractor, and he brought out these same men. They don't care. The work ethic here has been totally destroyed. That's the doom of this country. They've been ruled by kings, czars, or communist dictators for a thousand years: they have no understanding of individual initiative, of pride in workmanship, of climbing up through hard work.

"I suggested to the bricklayer that we could bring a master mason from Germany, or send him there for an apprenticeship. He asked how long it takes to become a master mason in Germany, and when I told him it's a three-year apprenticeship he told me I was crazy. That's impossible, he said, anybody can learn how to lay bricks in a few days. I tried to tell him that he doesn't know about the subtleties of mortar, how to plan the bricks, how to select them, what tools to use, how temperature affects the way the mortar sets, and on and on. He just shrugged. There are no apprenticeship programs left here, there's no status to being a craftsman, and they don't care!"

Over in the corner, another argument had erupted. I moved a step closer to the stove, which Von Heyer eyed with consternation. "So, what do you do?" I said.

"Well, first we yell and scream and jump up and down. That gets their attention. We threaten to not pay them, but they know that's an empty threat because the government will back them up in their claim for wages. And finally we brought you in."

"Me?"

"Traditionally, in Russia, particularly under the communists, the 'big boss' was the guy who stood quietly in the back and said nothing. If he didn't like things, he was very quiet, which is a very dangerous sign to the workers. They can't imagine that somebody like Gerhard or me, who are out working with the people, helping plant the fields, getting our hands dirty, living in the houses with the farmers, could possibly be 'big bosses.' But you, you're quiet. You stand in the back. You wear nice clothes, and only stay for a day or two. And you're from America. They know that Yeltsin has many friends in America. Maybe you have influence with the government, and that could be dangerous to them. We're hoping your presence will encourage them to do the job right."

I looked over at the men, again shouting and waving their fists, and saw now the fear in the way they glanced at me.

"Seems like a pretty damn poor way to have to get things done," I said, feeling resentful about the role I'd been cast in without consultation.

"This is a pretty damn poor country," Von Heyer said, his voice thick with frustration. "I had an easier time getting the natives in Uganda to help build our hospital. Straight from the bush, never a day's school in their lives, but they were eager to learn and to work. But not these people. Their spirit has been totally broken."

We went back out into the snow. My clothes were now soaking wet, and the sky had darkened and the wind picked up. The snow had let up: perhaps it was too cold to snow.

We piled into the bus and Von Heyer put me in the front by the heater. Back on the rural back roads, the windows closed and the heat on, I asked Gerhard to explain to me exactly what the Salem work in this area was.

"As you've seen, many skills have been lost," he said. 'These include not only construction skills, but also agricultural skills. As when you went with us into Africa in 1980, you know that if people are starving we will feed them, but our goal is to leave. To make them self-sufficient. We built the children's village, the hospital, and the farm in Uganda, and now we're turning it over to the people who live there. Here, we'll start with the farm, because in this climate that's the first basic of survival."

"You're teaching farming?"

"Small-scale, organic, low-tech agriculture. What will work in a country like this with so little infrastructure. Seven families back in the village where we are staying are being helped by us. Herr Müller heard about their plight from one of their relatives who wrote to him about them. When we arrived here, they had no food, no work, only the clothes on their backs. There was the very real risk that first winter that they might die of illnesses related to malnutrition. So we brought in food, blankets, clothing, cooking utensils, and helped them rent the houses they're living in, in the village.

"Then we rented some land, and they farmed it last summer, using our techniques. The result was such a huge harvest, the largest in this entire state, that they could make a profit selling it, and the government came in and honored them with an award. In the past few months, 120 families have formally applied to us to 'join' our project. They still have this collective-type thinking, and we're trying to tell them to just imitate what we're doing, on a small scale, with only a few families at a time. It's re-creating the family farm, which built Europe and America. Now Herr Müller has committed to build them seven houses on land that they're buying and some land that we've gotten from the government to teach agricultural methods, and you saw the first two just now. We'd hoped to have all seven finished by now, but things take very, very long in this country."

"I think I'm beginning to understand why."

"It's not just the workers," Gerhard said. "It's also the materials. If we could just truck materials in from Germany, it would be easy, but the government won't let us do that. You saw what we went through just trying to bring in a busload of household goods. So we have to buy locally, with hard currencies, and what we get is so substandard it's almost impossible to build with."

"So what do you do?"

He looked at me with a grin. "We persist, of course. Nobody ever said doing a good work is easy."

As we were driving back, Gerhard turned on the headlights, illuminating the dusty snow the wind was whipping across the plains. Trudging along the street toward us were two children, bundled up and leaning against the wind; I recognized one of them as Anna, the teenage daughter of Tamara, one of the seven families. "What's she doing out here?" I asked Gerhard.

"They walk to and from school," he replied simply. "It's only nine kilometers each way."

Back at Olga's house, the TV was on in the living room. The show looked oddly familiar, although all the words were in Russian. "What's that?" I asked Olga.

"Twin Peaks," she said. I've never seen the show, but American TV is instantly recognizable anywhere in the world . . . even here in the frozen hinterlands of Russia.

Olga moved a rug and raised part of the hallway floor, then lifted up a jar of pickles from the dirt crawl-space under the house. She brought out some bread and wine, and I got one of my bottles of water, and we sat with the old woman and Herr Burkhardt and watched the

TV. They were absorbed in the show; I was trying to warm up, and to pick up a few words of Russian.

When the show ended, a man's face filled the screen. He was giving some sort of speech, and his face was twisted with an insane anger. He pounded his fist and shook his finger at the camera, then became soft and soothing in his voice, then began shouting again. He was followed by a news anchorwoman, sitting behind a desk, making commentary.

"What's that?" I said to the room in general.

"Vladimir Zhiranovski," said Olga. "He's a candidate in tomorrow's election, and he said that if he's elected then we should work more closely with Germany, reestablish our old border with them."

"Isn't Poland in between you and Germany?"

"That's what he means," Olga said, shaking her head in disbelief. "Get rid of Poland."

I shivered.

An hour later, Gerhard and Von Heyer came over, having changed their clothes. "Tonight is another birthday party," Gerhard announced. "Not one of the Salem families, but another family down the street, and they've invited us to come. It'll be very high status for them if we drop in, so we really should."

So we set off through the absolutely black night to the house a few blocks away.

There, a family was gathered: Mom and Dad and two sons just short of their teenage years. Von Heyer, Gerhard, Burkhardt, and I were the guests. Mom put a liter bottle of vodka on the table and poured shots for all of us, then gave a toast and downed hers in one gulp, as did her husband. The boys, who weren't invited to sit at the table but only watched from the couch, observed the ritual with sad eyes.

The conversation over dinner, punctuated by rounds of the vodka (Mom was now drinking it out of a water glass), was mostly about the election. I got up to use the bathroom, and discovered that, unlike in the houses of the families Salem was supporting, there was no toilet paper in this house. Instead, next to the toilet, was a pile of computer paper torn into four-inch-square scraps, and next to that a basket for the used paper. When I tried to raise the toilet seat, it fell off.

SUNDAY

The next morning was the day of the Russian elections. When I woke up, Olga's family was clustered around the TV watching Zhiranovski make another speech. He seemed charismatic to me, a fighter, a "true believer." I reminded myself that while those qualities could describe JFK, they could also describe Hitler.

"What's he saying?" I asked.

Olga turned, shaking her head with an amazed look on her face. "He says that everybody who votes for him will get a liter of vodka and a turkey after the election."

"People fall for that?" I said.

She nodded. "Remember, Russia has been here nearly a thousand years. And this is the first democratic election ever. Ever! People have no idea what to do, how to do it, or what to believe."

I went into the kitchen and made myself some rice and lentils, and finished off a bottle of Danish water. Around noon, Von Heyer and Gerhard came by to collect me, and, my bag packed and a final water bottle under my arm, I said goodbye to my hosts. The ten Danish chocolate bars I left for Olga, and the small airport-bought toys for her kids, brought tears to their eyes.

We drove through a blizzard for six hours to Kaliningrad, finally arriving back at the ship, Hotel Hanza.

We went out into the city, which was unnaturally dark. All the "official" stores were closed, but in the area around Lenin's Square, a central park in the city, were a series of kiosks the size of New York City newsstands. All were open and doing a brisk business. "These are the stores the Mafia runs," Burkhardt explained as we parked the car. "Therefore, this is the safest part of town."

At the first kiosk, there was every imaginable type of chocolate. Swiss, Danish, German, French, Austrian . . . but nothing Russian.

The second kiosk had booze and cigarettes. Johnny Walker, Marlboro, Winston . . . again nothing Russian, except vodka. Even the maps and souvenirs that they had were printed in German, and referred to the town as Königsberg.

And on down the line we found toys, gum, candy, more chocolate, more booze, but nothing Russian. "The country is dead," Burkhardt said as we climbed into the bus without having found a Russian souvenir of any sort. "Their only product is vodka."

MONDAY

At 6:00 A.M. the next morning, we drove out to the airport. It was a crisp, cold morning with a high cloud cover and an inch of dusty snow on the ground from the night before.

The airport gate was closed, but the guard station and machine gun turret was empty, so I got out of the bus and opened what was once the high-security gate myself; we drove through.

The building was unlocked: an old woman with a homemade broom of straw tied to a stick with wire was stooped over nearly to her knees, sweeping the floor. No heat, nothing open. There was nothing to be open except a small café off to one side.

We walked around and told each other stories for two hours, as Gerhard and Von Heyer were concerned that Aeroflot might cancel the flight, and the phones didn't work. They didn't want me stuck at the airport while they were driving back to Germany.

A few minutes before scheduled departure time, the flight crew arrived. "Check their breath," Gerhard said to me, adding that he'd recently been on a domestic Aeroflot flight and the pilot had shown up so drunk that he'd apparently passed out in the pilot's seat, as he was snoring when the copilot landed the plane. "It probably won't be so bad on an international flight," he said, referring to my flight which was scheduled to fly to Berlin. "They'd have to deal with the German airport authorities."

Gerhard and Von Heyer left and I went through security. The metal in my jacket fired off the metal detector, but the people at security just waved me through anyway. They didn't even bother to watch the screen as my bag went through the X-ray machine: perhaps it didn't work.

We walked out across the frozen and slick ramp to the plane and climbed ice-covered stairs. A de-icing truck came out and two men began to listlessly spray something on the plane, blowing off the accumulation of snow and ice from the previous night. It took them an hour, and I cringed as I watched one of them walking on the wing, one foot on the flaps, walking all over areas that, on US planes, are clearly marked "NO STEP" and, on this plane, had a similar-looking marking in Cyrillic. At one point, one man's truck's engine began to billow steam from around the hood, and he climbed up onto the tank on top and dropped a bucket down into the de-icing solution. Lifting the bucket up, he then took the fluid to the radiator and refilled it with a satisfied look.

Finally, we took off for Berlin. The plane smelled musty and my seat kept falling back into the lap of the man behind me, but we wobbled up into the air, and two hours later landed in Berlin during one of the heaviest blizzards I've flown through in years. Stepping into the Berlin airport, with all its shops and signs and products and well-dressed people going one place or another, I remembered the people back in Russia. How long would it take them to rebuild their country? Von Heyer thought it would be at least two generations; Olga was more optimistic, and thought ten to fifteen years. And the politicians, of course, are promising to do it in two. And could they avoid being destroyed by the commercialism all around me in the "developed" world?

Salem is a start. The impact we've had on a small region is already startling, with 120 families going from being suspicious and skeptical to enthusiastically wanting to jump on the bandwagon. Because the media are so centralized and pervasive in Russia, it's possible that once the Salem program is up and running at full speed it could be a model that will quickly spread across the country, teaching the basics of free enterprise, agriculture, food storage, and nutrition.

In my visit, I'd seen people whose spirit was destroyed by centuries of repression, by alcohol, and by a total lack of hope. I'd also seen and come to know those who believed change was possible, that there could be a future for Russia, if only the "older" wisdom of the peasants could be brought back and enough people could see and sense the possibility of success.

The next step, Gerhard says, is to help upgrade the local hospitals and change the way the orphanages are run, moving them to the Salem family model. With enough help, and if the government doesn't turn in on itself or experience a total economic collapse like the one that, in part, led to World War II, I believe it just may work.

To flourish, the human spirit needs to be allowed to do its natural work. It needs to be *present* in its surroundings (tuned in to Now, not unconscious or living in another time); it needs to touch the wellspring of the creative spirit; it needs to act on what it knows is possible; and it needs to experience how its actions affect the universe.

When that happens, people get the sensation of personal power: "I perceive, I conceive, I act, it works." When the sequence is blocked, whether by government oppression or material distractions, people get the idea that there's no use in trying.

When I realized this I began to see why "The right thing to do is to do the right thing." When you're alive in the Now, it doesn't make sense to do anything else.

My experience, though, has been that most people don't get it. They feel powerless. And, as I was about to realize, this frequently keeps everyday people—including me—from acting on their deepest wishes. Often, that wish is for peace on Earth, but people are afraid to stand up and lead. Until someone wakes them up and asks them . . .

"Where Is a Leader for Peace?"

This world is but canvas to our imaginations.

—THOREAU

The years after the first World War saw great shortages and even famines and plagues (particularly cholera and tuberculosis) in Europe. Out of those shortages (that imbalance between population and resources again) came nationalism among many nations. In the world view I've developed during these travels, I now see nationalism as being a manifestation of the younger culture view: "us versus them."

Germany was particularly afflicted by this, and very hard-hit by the wild inflation of the 1920s and depression of the 1930s.

When we were living in Germany in 1986, I became fascinated with the phenomenon of the Nazi movement. How could these people have done what they did? How could the German people and the world have allowed it? One day, after I finished reading a book about the Third Reich, I visited Herr Müller in his office and asked about Hitler and how Herr Müller could have been part of that machine that was the German army.

He told me that he'd been a patriotic young man, that that was the reason he'd joined the army and even volunteered for a special assignment in the Middle East. "Thank G-d I was captured and spent the war in prison, so I could not have harmed anybody and nobody could have killed me," he said.

"But how could you have even been part of it in the beginning?" I said.

We were in his office: I was sitting on the sofa and he was sitting on a chair facing it. He moved to the edge of his seat, his back ramrod straight. "I met Hitler twice," he said. "Not one-on-one like that, but in two public events where I was part of the line of people who walked by him or shook his hand or saluted him. There was a power and magnetism to that man that is indescribable. Many of us thought that he was the savior of our nation, that he would lead us to a time of prosperity of peace, and it looked, at that time, like this was true."

I expressed some skepticism and he leaned closer to me. "In seven short years," he said, "one man rose from obscurity and conquered nearly all of Europe. He altered the course of history. Look at that power, at that accomplishment, regardless of your opinion of whether it was right or wrong."

He stood up. "Now, forget about those times—they are gone. What is important is the question for *today!* Where is the man who would have that kind of power for *good?* Everybody complains about Hitler, but he is dead and gone and that time is over. But where, today, is the 'Hitler' for peace? Where are the great leaders who will fight the war against all the pain and suffering in the world?

"It is so easy to complain, to whine, to point to the past. We must instead create a mighty army *now*, a conquering army of angels, of people committed to peace and good. And then conquer the world with acts of compassion and mercy, give blessings to people, and, reach within ourselves to see the face of G-d, to know Jesus Christ as you and I know each other, and to know the Name of G-d. Where is the movement that is doing this?"

"Here!" I said.

"*Ja!*" he thundered, hitting his fist on the table top. "This is our work, to create a worldwide network of points of light, places of peace, to teach those who want to know how they can know G-d, to spread the word that Jesus taught, not this lukewarm oatmeal they spoon out in the churches." He sat down, leaned over, and put his face a foot from mine. "Thomas, do you have the courage to be a great leader for G-d?"

"Yes!" I said, unhesitating.

He smiled. "Then begin with the smallest work, a tiny act of compassion for the least of the least. And do it in secret."

HUMBLE ACTIONS CAN MAKE GREAT CHANGE

Years after we had that conversation, I was listening to a discussion about fractal geometry and chaos theory. One of the early examples put forth to explain this new type of mathematical modeling is that a butterfly flapping his wings in Brazil could cause a hurricane in the United States. In incredibly complex and dynamic systems—such as the world we live in—very tiny changes can have massive consequences in faraway places.

This is no longer disputed in scientific circles. As mentioned earlier in this book, no matter how minutely most natural processes are controlled, an even tinier difference can throw off the outcome.

As I listened, I realized another level of the truth of what Herr Müller had said: one person *can* change the world. In fact, as any student of history knows, over and over again the world has been changed in massive ways by what first appeared as small, seemingly insignificant events.

I can change the world and you can change the world.

We don't need to wait until we're nominated as Pope or President: tiny acts of mercy, small changes in our lives, gentle transformations in the world, all will affect the entire world-system in ways that are impossible to predict but may have profound and longlasting impacts.

Will you be a leader for peace? For G-d? Or do you feel there's no use in trying because you're not "big" enough to make any difference?

Consider what has been done, starting with literally nothing, by a man with no money and no position of influence, a man most people have never heard of, Gottfried Müller. A deeply religious man with high moral standards, he nonetheless never tells another what to do and never seeks obeisance; he leads by example, and lets others discover their own potential in their own time. And he has no more desire for power than does any droplet in an ocean wave.

THE POWER FOR CHANGE IS IN INDIVIDUAL ACTIONS

Herr Müller has taught me many "techniques" to change myself and the world around me, most of which are in this book. I asked him in 1996 if he'd considered organizing them into some sort of system and teaching them to people.

"That would be creating a religion," he said. "That is not my job." Instead, he said he sees the job that G-d and Michael gave him as being an example of how to live in the coming times: to set aside poisons like tobacco, to avoid violence and death and flesh foods, to commit little acts of mercy every day, and to tell people to wake up: time is short and "Already they are saddling the horses in heaven."

"So what can people do if they come here, or want to meet you?" I asked.

"They are welcome to come here and stay in our guest house," he said. "Learning in the heart does not need words. Just being in this place, or the other Salem villages, is a transformational experience. They will feel it in their hearts. People come here and they are changed: they don't need to hear a speech from me for that to happen. You know that the same happens to people around you, and the same is true of other people doing spiritual work on themselves. So, sometimes we may offer some advice or an idea, but always people are free to come and go, to do or not as they will, and those with an open heart will have it filled."

The guest house and community at Salem in Stadtsteinach is unique. Much attention has been put into the design and furnishing of the place, and into respecting the Earth's energy fields. The carpets are all natural fibers, the wiring in the walls is shielded so there is no detectable electrical radiation, and there is a thin layer of silk under each mattress to insulate people from the currents of the Earth. Virtually all the food is grown in one of the Salem organic farms and a gourmet vegetarian fare is served in the guest house restaurant.

A few years earlier, I'd been staying for a week in the Salem guest house, visiting daily with Herr Müller, and there was a Catholic priest visiting. He and I had lunch together one day before he left, and he told me an interesting story.

"One day Herr Müller and I were driving near the Bavarian Alps," the priest said. "It was about five years ago. We were going to visit some people who were supporters of Salem. And as we were driving along, and I was looking out of the window, I saw a place in a large field where there was the crumbled foundation of a building, and beside it, from the Earth, I saw a bright light shining up into the sky. At first I thought it must be an optical illusion, or perhaps something shiny reflecting sunlight, except that it was an overcast day in the late winter. And this light was so bright, and it had a golden color. So I started shouting to Herr Müller as we drove by it, 'Stop the car! There's a light coming from the ground over there and I want to see what it is!' And Herr Müller said to me, 'Don't worry about that. It's only where I built an altar.'"

"Did you go back there later?" I asked the priest.

He nodded. "Yes. I couldn't find anything, and didn't see the light again. There was a small pile of bricks where I'd seen the light, but that was all."

So that night, I asked Herr Müller about the man's story. "What happened?" I said. "And why did you build an altar there?"

Herr Müller smiled. "Some years ago, about ten years ago, I happened to be driving through the Alps between Bavaria and Austria. One day I drove by this place that I knew was one of Hitler's command centers. It was built on a place of spiritual lines of power across the Earth. And so I went to the ruins of the building and collected 12 of the bricks and built a small altar next to the building, and gave it a blessing that would cause it instead to become G-d's holy place forever. And that is what the priest saw."

Later, in my visits with the Apaches in America, a medicine man would tell me of the significance of lines of power and piles of stones. He taught me a specific technique for building fires for sweat ceremonies, which also involved stacking stones within the wood in a particular way, always using the same sacred numbers Herr Müller referred to.

I think of this like radios, in some ways. You're sitting in a field and the only sound is that of the breeze and the bugs and the birds, and then you throw a switch on a box and "out of the air" comes information, power, a voice or a sound. An altar may be a similar sort of spiritual receiver or tuning mechanism.

We can have holy places in our homes, and on our properties, which we visit daily, even if just to nod a quick thanks. And we can build altars in our hearts, on the memories of those we love and our experiences of the divine. Those altars we can build within, as David referred to so often in the Psalms (and the Hindus call the hridayam or "heart cave"), are always with us and always unassailable.

These are the beginnings of the "small works" which stir the wind which eventually create the hurricane of change in the world.

Rwanda, 1994
The Most Powerful Tool to Save the World

Perhaps we cannot prevent this world from being a world in which children are tortured. But we can reduce the number of tortured children. And if you don't help us, who else in the world can help us do this?

—ALBERT CAMUS,

QUOTED IN 1968 BY ROBERT F. KENNEDY

JUST BEFORE HIS OWN ASSASSINATION

In traveling the world I've seen more and more desperation. I've also been unable to avoid learning a lesson I'd rather not acknowledge because of its consequences: there's an ancient biological imperative to control resources (such as food), and that imperative becomes strongest during times of strife.

The result is a killer spiral: where resources are thin, war often sets in, and war is the most common cause of famine. The following is evidence that Herr Müller's grimmest prophecy can already be seen unfolding.

One day in 1994 I was visiting Herr Müller when Frau Bethge came into his office with a telex in her hand. She gave it to Herr Müller, who read it and then passed it to me. It was from Uli Bierbach, the man who runs the Salem program in Uganda:

I just came from Goma, on the border of Rwanda and Zaire. There are over 1.5 million refugees here, and hundreds of them are dying every hour from cholera. In another city I visited, Bukavu in Zaire, there are about 500,000 people, in the same dire straits.

In Goma on the Virunga Vulkane the earth is so hard that we cannot break it with shovels and so cannot bury the dead.

The suffering I saw myself is so terrible that I feel that I must shout about it to you. Salem must help the surviving people, particularly the many orphans who have lost family and clan and are huddling alone and starving. First of all we must send another 7.5 tons of relief goods for the orphans I have taken under our wing in the area of Byumba and Ruhengeri. I also need 12,000 German marks immediately to pay for the transportation.

For the victims of cholera all help is now too late, but in G-d's name let us help those children who have survived to begin a new life!

Herr Müller responded with the food and the money. But two weeks later, Uli sent this follow-up telex:

Our first project to help the Rwandan refugees was successful, but the situation in the camps continues to deteriorate. Here's a short report:

Last Tuesday, together with a reporter for Austrian radio, I drove from Kampala, Uganda, toward Kabale, a trip of 430 kilometers. We were driving a truck loaded with 7.5 tons of relief materials (food, medicine, blankets, etc.) from Salem. Wednesday we passed through the Rwandan border at Gatuna and were cleared by the soldiers of the RPF (Rwandan Patriotic Front).

On the way to Byumba, along the main road to Kigali, we saw a mile-long snake of men, patiently standing and waiting for food to be distributed from the International Red Cross. Because most of the refugee camps are located on the mountaintops (the only available land, because it's useless for anything else), the big trucks from the Red Cross cannot get to them, so they distribute food along the main road right off the trucks.

Thursday we arrived at "our" camp in Kisaro (actually, it's four camps, located on four hills, at an altitude of about 6,000 feet). We now have over 24,000 people in our camps, and we distributed to each person four ounces of beans, twelve ounces of corn, and 25 grams of oil. We also gave every two people one blanket to share.

This will have to last each of these people a period of 15 days,* as it'll be that long before we can get more supplies in here. I knew as we handed out these materials that some of these people would die of starvation before we returned.

Yesterday two of our children were killed by mines as they went out into the fields near the camps to scavenge for food. Over 55 percent of all the people in our camps are orphaned children. We from Salem must help for a longer period, in order for these children to survive.

Thursday night I returned to Kampala, and Friday returned to Kisaro to try to organize more food for our camp. The situation is terrible, I keep crying when nobody is around to see me, and I cannot eat anything after seeing the misery and distress. I promised the people in our camp that I would return with more food and medicine soon, but could not promise when, as the situation is so unstable and it is so difficult for us to get supplies.

Please send us more money and supplies as quickly as you can. I will work 24 hours a day to get them to our children!

The telex reminded me of my first time in Uganda, and the "joke" an old Ethiopian priest had told me to break the tension and my sobbing after we'd spent a day helplessly watching children die of starvation. The priest had said, "What do you get when you feed a thousand starving refugees?" and I said I didn't know and he said, "Ten thousand starving refugees!" and began to laugh hysterically.

I had been crying and I started laughing uncontrollably along with him; for both of us it was really just some sort of bizarre hysteria. But the question haunted me ever since: overpopulation is the engine driving much of the destruction of the planet and, therefore, the human race.

I also know from first-hand experience that, worldwide, very little is being done about it on the scale necessary to avert disaster (or even to soften the already-happening disasters).

---

*Each person was given the equivalent of one quarter of a can of beans, one package of frozen corn, and one fluid ounce of oil. That's all the food each person would have to live on for two weeks.

"Be fruitful and multiply:" from Jacob's desire for many children, to Solomon's desire for many wives and concubines, this ancient saying *was* an imperative when population density was low and resources were everywhere. Tribes with the highest population conquered their neighbors and had the greatest probability of cultural survival into the future, just as described earlier in this book.

"When in trouble, reproduce" is so much a "hard-wired" part of our physical and cultural beings that we usually don't even notice it. But when you think about it, it's inevitable: there have been famines throughout history, and only the tribes who reproduced have survivors today. Every single one of us is descended from a people who succeeded in reproducing! Not one of us has a single childless ancestor.

The problem is that *we are adapted to survive in a world that no longer exists*—a world of few people and plentiful resources.

Now that the equation has reversed itself—plenty of people, scarce resources—religious and political leaders do not have the courage to face the new realities.

For example, in 1972 President Indira Ghandi started a birth control education program in India which unleashed a political and religious firestorm: both the Moslems and the Hindus claimed it was an attempt to diminish their numbers and, therefore, their political power. She was accused of cultural genocide, and after her assassination—which many believe was a direct result of her instituting the educational programs—the programs were shut down and the topic has never again been raised in India with any success.

So when that second telex arrived, after I read it, I said to Herr Müller, "Often people ask me why must we do this social work when all we're doing is feeding people so that later they will starve someplace else or die in a war."

"Everybody dies," Herr Müller said. "Even you and I will die."

"But it seems that sometimes relief agencies do more harm than good."

"More harm than politicians and armies who create famines?"

"You know what I mean. Wouldn't it be better, long-term, if we were teaching birth control?"

"Thomas, often my teacher, Abram Poljak, told me that the most powerful tool we have in our work to save the world is *Barmhetzigkeit*. Do you know this word?"

"'Mercy,' isn't it?"

"Not quite. It is a small act of compassion. A small act of compassion, particularly when it is done with no desire for recognition or fame or praise, creates an explosion in the spiritual world. It is a mighty artillery. There is nothing more powerful and therefore every day you must look for *Barmhetzigkeit,* even if it is picking up a worm from the street. And when you do it in secret, it is a thousand times more powerful. This is why in the Sermon on the Mount, Jesus referred to this so many times, in prayer, in giving, in doing good deeds, in helping your adversary. It is all *Barmhetzigkeit.*"

"And so we feed people because it is a spiritual act?"

He made a fist. *"Ja!"*

"Even if they will die later?"

"Everybody will die, sooner or later. But if we can save a life, even for only one day, then we must. We have been given our orders by G-d, and we must follow them."

When I left Germany at the end of that trip, I was changed. More than ever, I had come to realize the inexorable spiral of death and overpopulation, and that it's a force of nature. It's also the result of our culture, which views nature as something to be dominated.

But at the same time, more clearly than ever, I came to see that despair is a useless place to spend time: it gets you nowhere, and it denies the Spirit. The right thing to do is the right thing to do. . . even when the situation looks desperate.

Who *will* be a leader for peace? What is holding you back, right now, from acting on behalf of humanity as a whole? Perhaps nothing. But many people hold *themselves* back because they feel unworthy, or think they're not "pure" enough to do good things.

The belief that you're not good enough (because of your errors), and you should therefore insult yourself and not accept that you do have the power to help, is an artifact created by Young Culture power-grabbers who've told people they're bad. It keeps people apart from their spirit.

But who are you to deny your own spirit?

Since this point keeps so many people stuck in the past (not Now), and stuck in not trying, it's important to talk about it for a moment.

"My Lord Is a Loving G-d"
Forgiveness and Compassion as Therapy and Hope

The best way to know G-d is to love many things.
—Vincent Van Gogh

On a walk with Herr Müller through the forest one day, I talked to him about something I'd done that I deeply felt was wrong. I asked him how he thought I should clean my spiritual slate. I'd already worked it through as much as I could with the person I'd hurt.

'My G-d is not some old man who is sitting on his throne with a stick in his hand, just waiting for you or me to make a mistake," he said. "We bring pain on ourselves, when we act like you described. But G-d always forgives, and His forgiveness is instant. As soon as you have turned from your wrong deed, you are forgiven. You do not need to tell me or anybody else about it: just tell G-d. Remember the story of the prodigal son? Remember the prayer of Jehoshaphat that I taught you in Hebrew? *'Praise G-d, for His mercy endures forever.'*"

"But doesn't that philosophy give people license to do anything they want, wrong or right?"

"We all, always, have such choices before us. But when we choose wrong, we are punished by natural law, by the natural consequences of our acts, not by G-d. He is love, not anger. Remember in the Bible? 'G-d is love.'"

"But what about free will?"

He laughed. "The Bible says that everything was decided before the foundations of the Earth. And yet we think we can make decisions. It is one of the great mysteries of life. If G-d makes us do something because it was ordained before we were even born, did we sin? Must we ask for forgiveness? Of course. And yet, not one hair is lost from the head without it being G-d's will."

This reminded me of a discussion I'd had with a psychologist two decades earlier when I was Executive Director of the Children's Village. I'd recently hired him to work with our kids, and we were sitting at his home, after dinner, chatting about psychology and various therapeutic systems.

"I've discovered something new," he said, "and it seems to be one of the most effective techniques I've ever used to help people heal from psychological wounds."

Intrigued, I asked him what this "new" technique was.

"Forgiveness," he said. "If I can get them to truly forgive the people who have harmed them, or to forgive themselves for the harm they've done to others, the results are startling."

AN EXERCISE IN FORGIVENESS

I smiled and agreed. About two years earlier, when I was teaching meditation techniques in Michigan, I'd used a guided meditation with people wherein they imagined themselves in a comfortable room of their own creation, and invited into that room a person with whom they have "unfinished business." They then internally, mentally talked out their unhappiness or upsets with that person, and then forgave them or asked for forgiveness.

The experience often left people in tears, but invariably those people who experienced it strongly also later came back to thank me for helping them resolve issues that they thought would haunt them forever, particularly if the person they were "stuck" with was dead, lived in a distant place, or was noncommunicative.

Doctors will tell you that it's not uncommon for dying patients to express the belief that they "deserve" to die, and there is a growing body of evidence that our immune system becomes less active when we experience negative emotions. Shame, guilt, and anger are the blackest and most destructive emotions we can experience, which I believe is why Jesus, and other spiritual teachers, have so emphatically gone out of their way to tell us the importance of forgiveness.

When I taught classes on these topics, I loved to use the Uncle Remus story of Tar-Baby. The clever fox built a figure out of sticky tar and placed it on a log, and when Brer Rabbit walked past, the fox yelled insults at him from behind the tar baby. Brer Rabbit, assuming the tar baby was the source of the insults, began to hit and kick it, and the more he did, the more he became stuck to it.

Similarly, when we carry around guilt, anger, and shame, we become stuck. Asking the forgiveness of G-d is an important step, because it opens the door for us to begin to forgive ourselves and others. And when we truly forgive, we become free of the "tar" that darkens our lives, slows our spiritual growth, and can even lead us to mental and physical sickness.

Forgiveness is an exercise in compassion, and G-d is a specialist in compassion. Each of us, coming from the same spiritual well, is capable of being absolutely godlike in compassion. The spiritual benefits of doing so are real.

To be like G-d, be forgiving.

Small Miracles

A Lesson about
Making Ordinary Life Miraculous

That best portion of a good man's life,
His little, nameless, unremembered acts
Of kindness and of love.

—WORDSWORTH,
"LINES COMPOSED A FEW MILES
ABOVE TINTERN ABBEY"

Sometimes our best lessons are the simplest. My father recently had a heart attack, and I thought of how bereft I would feel if he died. That experience caused me to reconsider my own life, and to look more every day for opportunities to experience my aliveness, to share myself with my own family, and to stay in closer touch with my father and mother.

A far less dramatic lesson provided the opportunity for Herr Müller to teach me a similarly important lesson, one that is so easily lost in the day-to-day of life, yet is so important.

During a visit to Stadtsteinach, Gerhard Lipfert, the director of the Salem program in Höchheim and the man who started the Salem program in Russia, stopped by to visit with Herr Müller and me. We sat around the table in the kitchen of Herr Müller's modest apartment drinking dark coffee with cardamom in it and eating thin slices of the heavy brown bread they bake in the Salem bakery.

"Tell Gerhard the story of your flight over here," Herr Müller said.

It was a funny story, so I related it to Gerhard.

Two days before my flight from New York to Frankfurt, New York City was hit by one of the worst blizzards in its entire history. The city was shut down for two days, the airports closed, even the streets closed to all but emergency traffic. I was in the city for three days to give a speech to a New York group about ADD and, by coincidence, was scheduled to fly to Frankfurt on one of the first planes to leave the city after JFK airport was opened.

When I arrived at JFK, the airport was a madhouse: three days worth of travelers, tickets and reservations in hand, jammed every line. People were shouting and screaming and cursing, and the airline employees, many of whom had been working long hours through the blizzard or were even stuck at the airport unable to get home themselves, were doing their best to accommodate people.

At the gate, as my flight was about to board, I was standing by the counter waiting for my row number to be called. Next to me, a well-dressed man in his fifties pushed his way up to the counter and began to berate the gate agent for the fact that his flight hadn't departed the day before. The man behind the counter was gracious, but the passenger wouldn't be mollified. "You should upgrade me!" he demanded. "I have been abused by your airline, and I'm sick and tired of people like you blaming it on the weather."

On an impulse, I turned to the passenger and said, "Hey, lighten up. He's doing his best, and you wouldn't want his job on a day like this."

The passenger looked at me like I was a speck of dirt: I was dressed in jeans and an old leather jacket, and I hadn't cut my hair for several months. He ignored my remark and went back to shouting at the airline employee.

The gate agent was reasonable with the man, but firm, and finally the man turned and stalked away in apparent disgust.

"Sir?" the gate agent said to me, startling me out of a daydream as I watched the passenger stalk away. "May I see your ticket and boarding pass please?" His voice was all official and spit-and-polish, and I wondered if I'd offended him by interjecting myself into the argument. Without saying anything, I handed him my ticket. He typed a few keystrokes into his computer, shaking his head as if something was wrong, and I heard the printer running. He reached down and took out a new boarding pass, tore up my old one, and stapled the new one to my ticket. "There was an error on your reservation," he said, smiling for the first time as he handed me my ticket. I looked at it, worried that I had been relegated to the smoking section or even to a different flight or date, but instead saw that he had moved me to seat 1-E, the first row of first class.

"Thank you . . ." I said.

He waved me away before I could say anything more. "It's nothing. I'm glad I could fix your reservation." He turned to the next person in line, an angry woman who wanted to yell at him about the fact that our flight was scheduled to leave at 7:00 P.M. and it was now nearly midnight. "Next?" he said to her as she simultaneously started screeching at him.

So here I am, back in Herr Müller's kitchen with him and Gerhard, and after I tell Gerhard the story, they both laugh until there are tears in their eyes. "You must put this story in your book," Herr Müller said.

"But why?" I said. "It's not anything special. I defended the man, and he returned the favor. What does that have to do with spiritual stories?"

Herr Müller leaned forward and wagged his finger at me. "Thomas, Thomas, Thomas. People must know that life is not about the big miracles. It is about seeing the small miracles in everything. The sun comes up: it is a miracle!" He slapped the table with his hand for emphasis. "You are kind to a man, you make a small act of mercy, and a kindness comes back to you. Not because you expected it, not because you wanted it, but because you did an unselfish act with no expectation of reward. That is in accordance with the laws of G-d. So of course a reward would come to you, one way or another.

"And that, too, is a miracle. It is a miracle that we are here together at this table. That we are friends. That we love each other. That I would give my life for you, and you for me. We are spiritual brothers: that is a miracle. That we can breathe this air. That there is bread and wine in front of us. That this is Shabat." He raised his finger and pointed at the sky. "That is the biggest miracle: Shabat. That we are here together on this most holy day of the year.

"And so you must put that story in your book, so that people will know that they must look for, and see, the 'everyday miracles.' Because that is the most important thing. That is how a man can know and see G-d: when he sees the hand of G-d, His miracles, in everything, every day."

This lesson came back to me vividly when I first met some extraordinary and wise people among the Apaches of the American Southwest.

A Visit to
the Apache Nation

Face-to-Face with an Older Culture

What is life if we are imprisoned like cattle in a corral?
We have been a wild, free people,
free to come and go as we wish.
How can we be caged?

—VICTORIO, AN APACHE LEADER

In 1995, with this book already started, I experienced my first true encounter with an older culture.

As I now know is typical, this older culture has been beaten, pillaged and slaughtered by a younger culture. But enough of the culture has survived that I was able to experience their way of being first-hand. The encounter taught me several important lessons about living in the Spirit.

Earlier in the year I had been invited to Harrisburg, Pennsylvania to speak to a group of school principals and superintendents about ADD. Oddly, a few days before I left for the trip, I received a fax from Herr Müller which said, "You must visit the American Indians." It was completely out of context and I couldn't figure out why he'd say that, particularly then, other than that he often does seemingly inexplicable things.

While I was in Harrisburg a local physician, Dr. Jane Shumway, invited me to visit her home and meet with her, her husband Clare (a retired professor of pediatrics and also an M.D.), and a few local psychiatrists and pediatricians. Jane and Clare are an amazing pair: both over 70, they're active and passionate about life. Both are avid birdwatchers, and Jane has become one of Pennsylvania's experts on ADD (she's still in private practice).

Over dinner with them and their doctor friends, Jane said, "Have you ever thought about visiting the Apache Indians?" I nearly choked, remembering Herr Müller 's fax.

"I've thought about it," I said.

"Clare and I are going out to the San Carlos Apache reservation in October if you'd like to join us," she said. They were going to be doing in-service work with members of the community and the local physicians, and thought that my perspective on ADD may be of some use to the social workers and teachers. (As it happens, minimal work was done with physicians, due to lack of interest.)

I made a tentative commitment and penciled it into my calendar.

In the meantime, the exigencies of business forced me to cancel. I had to give speeches in Cleveland and Detroit the week that Jane and Clare were going to be in Arizona, and so I told them that I'd not make it.

This was particularly distressing because I was hoping to meet Paul Nosie, a descendant of Apache Chief Nosie, whom Jane had spoken of very highly. On the other hand, though, Jane hadn't been able to get any commitment of any sort from Paul to meet with us. "He operates on what he calls 'Apache time,'" Jane explained. "Things just seem to happen when and how they should, and he dislikes planning things."

Then a few weeks later, Herr Müller came to the United States for a board meeting at the Salem children's village in Maryland. I organized my schedule around it, and flew out to spend a day with him.

While we were there, he took me for a long walk up the side of the mountain on the backside of the Maryland property (it's in the Allegheny mountains in western Maryland). Up to this point, I hadn't mentioned to him my planned and then aborted trip to visit the Apaches with Jane.

(Pardon the digression, but as I'm typing these words a hummingbird with a red head and a gray-speckled body just came over and is hovering about two feet just behind and to the left of my head. I'm sitting in a folding chair outside Jane and Clare's travel trailer on the edge of a canyon here on the Apache reservation, typing into a Sharp Zaurus hand-held computer. The little bird is just hovering there, making soft squeaking noises as if he's trying to tell me something. I'll have to ask somebody about this.)

Anyway, as Herr Müller and I were walking along an old logging trail through the forest in Maryland, he put his hand on my shoulder and squeezed me hard. "Why haven't you visited the Indians yet?" he said, a slight hint of reproach in his voice. "There is an important lesson there for you, and important people for you to meet and know."

I told him about Jane and the invitation.

"And you're not going?" He narrowed his eyes. "Don't you recognize when things are organized by G-d?"

I shrugged. "G-d also organized that my business would be struggling now and I'd have to take on the teaching responsibilities of several of my former employees."

He looked at me for a moment as if deciding something, then said, "Probably it was only for this reason—that we have this conversation—that I had to come here."

"What do you mean?"

He shrugged, smiled, and changed the subject. His "It was only for this reason that I had to be here" comment was one I've probably heard 100 times in various circumstances over the past 18 years.

Our conversation lingered with me, though, and so, without telling Herr Müller, I booked a flight to arrive in Arizona a week late (the earliest I could work out), but didn't order the tickets. I'd wait and see what came out of it all.

Then, a week later, I received another fax from Herr Müller reminding me that I should go visit the Indians. I called Delta, and learned that in order to get a discounted price I'd have to order the ticket then and there. I called my travel agent and asked her to print and mail me the ticket.

I arrived in Phoenix Wednesday night and drove out toward the Apache reservation in the dark. A nearly-full moon hung low in the sky just off my left shoulder, throwing the mountains across the desert into sharp relief, like broken teeth jutting from a dinosaur's jawbone. The air was cold and smelled of creosote bush, and the two-lane highway was empty. I found my hotel in the town of Globe, just a few miles from the Apache town of San Carlos, got a room, and went to sleep.

Thursday morning I went for a walk on the edge of the desert as the sun came up. I recognized the familiar desert speckled with sage, cholla, tumbleweed, and giant saguaro standing, arms out and up to the sky, like mute guardians over this ancient land. Near here is Mt. Graham, an Apache holy place, a confluence of spiritual lines of power, which the University of Arizona has used political influence and money to take from them to build an observatory.

On the drive out to the reservation police station where we would meet with several social workers, I saw ahead of me, above the road, a giant black bird, flying in the same direction I was driving and holding an altitude of about 20 feet. With slow, graceful sweeps of its wings like I'd never before seen a raven do, it bobbed along in the air ahead of me. The car caught up with it, and, as I slowed down, it just kept flying down the road, right above my lane, just above the car. I passed under it and it seemed not to notice me: in the rear-view mirror I followed it until it was just a speck above the highway, out of sight.

I arrived at the lake above Coolidge Dam and found where Jane and Clare were camped. They were supposed to take their travel trailer and drive back home that day, but decided to stay two extra days to show me around and introduce me to people. (I'd called them just two days ago to say that I was coming. "You operate on Apache time, too," was Jane's comment.)

I told Jane of the experience with the bird over my car and asked her opinion. She told me that birds are her messengers, bringing her information about situations and the future, and often protecting her from danger. Just a few days earlier, she said, a raven had appeared out of nowhere and dove at her windshield. It woke her from her reverie and she slowed down in response to it. Moments later a truck roared by and cut in front of her. Had she not slowed down in response to the raven, she could have been seriously hurt.

From their trailer, Jane and I went onto the reservation, where we met with a woman named Velda who works with Tribal Social Services. The tribe had recently taken over social services functions from the Federal Government's Bureau of Indian Affairs, and Velda was horrified to discover that in all the years that BIA had been running their foster parents program, there had never been a single bit of training of foster parents. She was looking for resources, and Jane brought me along to talk with her about ADD.

"This is a very bad situation here," Velda said. "This tribe has over 60 percent unemployment, and you can trace so many problems back to that."

Jane had found a partial set of parenting instructional videotapes to take to Velda from the local Catholic school. Velda was wishing out loud that she could get such resources for the tribe, when I looked at the videocassette box.

I was startled to see that on it was the picture of Dr. Michael Popkin, a close friend who'd written the foreword for my first book on ADD and owns an Atlanta company called Active Parenting Publishing. I looked in my Zaurus to get his address for Velda, and also discovered that tonight I would be missing a previously scheduled dinner with him in Atlanta. I'd completely overlooked it!

The coincidences were startling: I excused myself to go call Michael to apologize for missing dinner. In the phone conversation, he offered to send to Velda a new and improved set of instructional videotapes at no cost, and so when I returned to the meeting I told her about that.

"This is a real blessing for us," she said, telling me that for a tribe of 10,000 people there were 50 foster homes, none had any training, and all were totally full.

After the meeting, as we went to lunch, Jane was fretting that I might miss meeting Paul. She hadn't seen him for several days, and couldn't get in touch with him. Finally, she shrugged as we drove to the San Carlos Café (the only diner on the reservation) and said, "Well, if it's meant to be it'll happen."

"Apache Time?" I said.

She nodded thoughtfully.

The café was a dutifully air-conditioned building. We retired to a Formica-topped booth in the back of the room after ordering our meals (I ordered an Apache Taco, which, it turns out, is vegetarian).

As our food was coming, Jane looked over my shoulder at the front door with a startled expression on her face. I turned to see a huge bear of a man, tall and muscular with a mustache and black hair in a pony tail down his back, with a friendly-looking Apache woman at his side. They came to our table.

Jane whispered, "I guess it was meant to be," and introduced me to Paul and his wife, Marilyn, who sat down at our table with us.

Looking at Paul up close, I would have guessed he was in his early thirties, but I had to recalculate that when their daughter and grand-daughter came in a few minutes later (their granddaughter's name is "Blessing").

We talked about the situation of the Apaches and of tribal politics: small talk, really, and then Paul said something that startled me.

He was describing a visit he'd made on behalf of the tribe to a drug rehab training center in Minnesota. He's partly responsible for the drug and alcohol programs for the Apaches, and so had gone to meet with other drug and alcohol program administrators and counselors.

"I noticed that the walls were covered with flags and emblems from the countries and organizations of the people who'd visited there in the past," he said. "And in the center of the main wall, right over the fireplace, there was a glass frame that held a dream catcher and an eagle feather. I asked the people there if they had any idea of the importance and spiritual significance of their wall decoration, and none did. That gave me an opportunity to talk with them about the importance of knowing your purpose in life, of being grounded in the Earth, and of connecting to your spirit and the planet's."

He paused for a moment and got a faraway expression on his face. "Probably it was only for that reason that I had to be there."

I was shocked. His voice even sounded like Herr Müller's. So, when he invited us to join him for a sweat, and to see the Crown Dancers, local ceremonies which are normally forbidden to non-Apaches, I eagerly accepted.

After lunch, we went back to Jane's trailer and I wrote the following note:

It's mid-afternoon on Thursday, October 12, and I just returned from lunch with the descendant of a famous Apache chief, a man Herr Müller had sent me to see, although neither of them knew or had ever even heard of the other.

As I'm writing these words, I'm sitting on the side of a mesa overlooking a small valley, with cactus and scrub-brush-covered hills rolling off into the distance. This is the desert about 100 miles east of Phoenix, Arizona, and it's over 100 degrees in the shade: it's the most desolate and unyielding land Uncle Sam could find to herd the Apaches into, and not a mile from where I'm sitting Geronimo hid from government soldiers after they (after signing a peace treaty with him and his tribe) slaughtered his wife, his parents, and all but one of his children in an unprovoked attack.

Friday night I attended a sweat ceremony with Paul, Marilyn, and a few other Apaches and Jane.

This was a deeply powerful experience for me; it was the first time in my life I'd participated in an age-old ritual from an older culture. I can't describe the ceremony because it's profoundly personal, and the man who taught me the ceremony was concerned that putting it into words in print would profane it.

I will say this: it confirmed everything I'd intuitively known about the power of connecting to your spiritual source.

The next morning I got up at 4:30 A.M. to go to the Sunrise Ceremony with Judy, a friend of Jane's. Judy is one of the planet's good souls, a wonderful mother and grandmother to her three children and grandchild, and struggles with the many economic and social problems facing other Apaches.

The morning of the Sunrise Ceremony, she'd invited me to first "walk the mesa rim" with her. We set out at about 5:30 in the morning from the edge of the desert.

Judy walked the six miles along the mesa rim so rapidly I occasionally got out of breath or had to run to keep up with her. It was dark, and the road was strewn with pebbles: the desert was absolutely silent. She'd read the first chapter of my book *ADD Success Stories* the night before, and wanted to discuss it.

"You wrote that Native Americans like us Apaches are more likely to have ADD than Anglos," she said.

I didn't know if she was offended or not, so just said, "It was a speculation. A few others have told me that that was their observation." I shivered in the cold, wearing only my jeans, dock shoes, and a long-sleeved white shirt.

"I think you're absolutely right," she said. "My people were hunters and warriors, and you can see that in everything they do. My son is a great hunter, but he's stuck in a farmer's high school and he's having a miserable time. I think you'll see this throughout our tribe, and it may be why the Indians are so easily snared by alcohol."

I told her about the teachers we'd met with a few days earlier on the reservation who said that they'd seen incredible amounts of high-energy activity from the Apache children. One teacher, an Anglo woman who'd come here recently, had said, "These children have a power, a force, that's hard to describe. If I try to restrain a child, to hold him back from running toward something, and grab his arm or put my hand on his shoulder, and he's only eight or nine years old, I feel the strength of a teenager or a young man. They are incredibly powerful, and when they make a decision it's nearly impossible to stop them from acting on it."

Judy agreed. "Your concept of hunters and farmers was an insight for me. It was a revelation. All of a sudden so many things made sense. We've always thought it was just my son with a problem, but now I realize that we're an entire family of hunters, living among a tribe of hunters, and that the problem is as much with the Anglo school as it is with us. You've given us a way to understand why and how we don't fit into white society, and done it in a way that leaves us our dignity and self-respect."

I thanked her, and she kept bubbling about the insights she'd gotten, and how one led to another, and we managed to work each other up into an enthusiastic lather about the wonders and pains of being a hunter in a farmer's world.

As the sky was turning first pink then light blue, and the edge of the sun came over the mountains to the east as if it were melting off their tops, we arrived at the Sunrise Ceremony.

In a large dirt area surrounded on all sides by desert, seven men stood in two rows, four ahead of three, beating drums and chanting. I recognized one of the chants from what I had heard sung the night before in the sweat ceremony.

Standing in front of the men were two women. On my left, facing them, was a girl around 12 or 13 years old, dressed in the most elaborate and beautiful buckskin dress I'd ever seen, completely covering her from neck to toes, with a blue shell or stone fastened to the center of her forehead and elaborate beadwork and decorations. To her left was an older teenage girl, also dressed in an beautiful buckskin dress but nowhere near as elaborately adorned as the younger girl.

The young girl held in her right hand a staff with a curved handle on the top; there were eagle feathers and bells hanging from it. With each beat of the drums, the girls bobbed up and down, flexing at the knees and ankles. The men behind them danced, too, lifting first one foot, then the other, with each beat.

In front of the two girls was laid out a square of buckskin, and there were things on it that I couldn't make out. To either side, flanking the medicine men and singers, were four men, two on either side, and they were dancing with the drums, too. One man on each side held a burden basket, tassels swinging to the dance, and the other man danced with his hands held in half-fists in front of his stomach.

The girls and the singers and medicine men faced directly into the sun, which was now fully above the mountains. The air had changed, in about 30 minutes, from below 60 degrees to above 80. Stretching down from the singers to the sides of the medicine men, creating a three-sided rectangle, were two rows of people, about 20 in each row. They were dressed in normal fashion, and were the visitors who'd come to participate in the ceremony. All were dancing, in a step just like the men and the girls. The two rows faced each other from a distance of about 70 feet.

Judy led me over to the row on our right, and the line parted to let us in. We began to dance along with everybody else, gently moving from foot to foot with the beat.

"This is a rite of passage," Judy whispered to me as we danced in the bright sunlight. "When a girl gets her menses, the Sunrise Ceremony is scheduled. A partner (or friend) who has already been through the ceremony is chosen to assist the girl during the ceremony. The godmother is chosen by the mother of the girl having the ceremony. For four days her family and her godmother's family camp on opposite sides of the ceremonial area, in huts they make specifically for this purpose. The girl is kept from contact with anybody, and has been preparing for this day for the previous four days by building all fires and cooking all food. She has her own little hut to stay in during the four days of the ceremony, built just for her and for this. The ceremony runs from Thursday night until Sunday night, virtually nonstop."

"It's what we were hearing last night during the sweat?" I said.

"Yes. There was a ceremony last night. This is the girl's first full initiation, though. You'll see. And tonight will come out the Crown Dancers. It's awesome."

Each chant the medicine men and medicine singers did lasted about 15 minutes, and we all danced through each one. There was a minute or so pause before they'd launch into another one.

We danced like this for an hour, and then two.

I was becoming tired and my feet and legs were sore: the sun was now fully 30 degrees above the horizon, the air temperature was over 90, and the girl in the buckskin dress hadn't stopped dancing since before sunrise. Judy noticed that I was sweating. "It's an endurance test, isn't it?" she said with a smile. I nodded. She inclined her head toward the girl in buckskin. "It's really a test for her. This is a very difficult four days. But if she comes through it, she knows that for the rest of her life she will be able to survive anything. And she'll have a great blessing because of this."

A group of four women in their sixties broke out of the line opposite us and danced slowly over to our line, stood in front of a man down the row from me, and danced facing him for a minute. They backed up and he danced out of the line as if attached to them by an invisible rubber band.

"If they come for you, you must dance with them," Judy whispered.

I swallowed. I'd been warned several times that these ceremonies were "Apache only," and felt very self-conscious, surrounded by these people who had been so viciously crushed by my people.

Women broke out of our line and danced with men from the other line.

The morning continued; it was now 10:00 A.M., and the sun was unbearably hot. It had to be in the 90s in the shade; in the sun I guessed it was well over 100 degrees. The girl in the buckskin was visibly exhausted, but she kept dancing and pounding her staff into the ground, shaking the bells in perfect beat with the drummers.

Two elderly women danced over to our line, heading straight for me. "Your turn," Judy said with a giggle.

They danced in front of me, eyes locked on mine, then began to move back. I danced forward without even thinking about it: it was as if a huge invisible hand had put itself to my back and propelled me forward. We danced all the way across to the other line and then back. When the chant ended, they both smiled and said, "Thank you." I bowed and said the same back to them, which made one of them laugh, a friendly gesture. They turned and walked back to their line and I rejoined Judy.

Another chant began and we started dancing again. "The women here say you did a good job. Much enthusiasm and spirit."

"Thank you," I said.

"Were you praying for the girl?" Judy said.

"No, I was dancing."

"Dancing is praying," Judy said. "Maybe it would help if you knew the words to the chants, but this entire ceremony is one long prayer for this girl. So now when you dance, pray."

"Are you praying to the sun?" I asked, remembering that this was the "Sunrise Ceremony."

She looked at me sharply. "We believe in one G-d, and always have. We pray before the sun not to worship the sun but because the sun reminds us of the creator of the sun, which warms us and gives us life. We respect the animals and honor them because they're part of G-d's world and His creation."

We fell silent. I danced, looking at the girl in buckskin. She glanced in our direction and smiled, and in her smile I saw my own 14-year-old daughter's face. I prayed for both of them as I danced.

Across from us in the line were a man and woman about my age who were dancing with a particular enthusiasm. Judy nodded at them with her nose (Apaches don't point with fingers) and said, "That's her father and mother."

Her father was almost directly opposite me, and so I synchronized my dancing with his, praying for his daughter and my own.

The girl's friend was replaced by her godmother, an Apache woman in her thirties who I later learned works in the nearby hospital in Globe. The chant and drums began again, and we danced for another half hour, as the air became dusty and dry and the sun poured down heat on us like liquid fire.

The chant stopped and the godmother helped the girl down onto her knees. The girl kneeled and then rocked back onto her feet on the buckskin, and lifted her hands to the sky, holding them palms facing the sun, on either side of her head. The chant began again, and the girl rocked from side to side, moving with considerable effort, still bouncing with the beat as she did so, looking in the direction of the eastern horizon. This continued for a half hour or so, as we all danced with her; occasionally she'd begin to wilt but each time, just before she fell over, her godmother would bend over and rub her back and say some words to her, and she'd then go back to her motions with a new vigor.

The godmother then stretched the girl out, face down, on the buckskin. In a very ritual fashion, she massaged the girl, starting with the top of her head. The girl was laying in what in Yoga is called the "Cobra" position, flat on her stomach with her hands at her sides, but with her head, shoulders, and chest held just above the ground and her face lifted to face the sun and mountains in the east. It's a very difficult position to hold for more than a few minutes.

The chant was going again, and there was a recurring phrase: *Di stitkcthe lay*. The "tkcthe" sound is like a guttural back-of-palate sound that they have in German and Hebrew but for which there is no equivalent in English.

"What does that mean?" I asked Judy.

"*Di stitkcthe lay* means 'she will become strong," Judy said. "The godmother is giving the girl her strength, giving it to every muscle in her body. A woman can only be godmother to a young girl four times in her life because of this."

"Why is that?"

"After four times, a woman risks losing her own spiritual power. A person only has enough power, normally, to do this four times in her life, because much of this ceremony is the giving of the godmother's spiritual power to the girl."

After massaging the girl from head to foot with her hands, the godmother did it again, twice, with her moccasin-clad feet. The chant continued, and we kept dancing. I was experiencing pains in muscles I didn't even know I had, and was incredibly thirsty.

When we'd first arrived and I'd seen the people dancing, my thought was that it was a quaint and primitive ritual. Culturally interesting, from an anthropological point of view. I'd wondered why they kept it so simple and hadn't made it more sophisticated, like European ballroom dancing.

Now, dancing in the hot sun, I noticed that my consciousness kept shifting. The mountains seemed distant, then near. The sky was flat, then deep. The cactus and scrub brush around us seemed to shimmer as if glowing with an aura. Occasionally a bird would fly over and I could feel its life as if something warm and radiant had beamed from its heart to mine. I kept feeling waves of alternating joy and grief, and a lump welled up in my throat whenever I prayed for the girl and my daughter, whenever I caught the eye of her father across from us.

Then it struck me, a flash of insight. The beat of the drums was always the same for each chant: we were tuning our brains, and it was probably to the 10-hertz alpha brain-wave frequency or a harmonic of it.

I realized that this wasn't just some sort of primitive dancing: it was a form of mantra meditation, just like the Hindus do, and the Tibetans with their prayer beads, and the Catholics as they recite the rosary for hours on end.

They're inducing altered states.

In a cascade of insight, I saw how this ritual is really very sophisticated, and the early white settlers corrupted it by turning it into square dancing and making it "entertainment." Like the medicine man's comments the night before about tobacco "hurting" us because we've turned it into a commercial product, with dancing we've turned the sacred profane.

I also realized in that flash that we in white society have lost our rituals of adulthood, leading to gangs and other replacement-rituals. The closest things I could think of were graduation from high school, or, for the World War II generation, joining the army.

This ceremony is the bottom line for these people, the most visceral, the most real and connected to *life,* and the most powerful. Watching it, participating in it, I knew absolutely in my guts that our white culture has become a shallow joke about to self-destruct, with television leading the charge.

I shivered, a wash of cold from the insight, and continued my dancing.

Around noon, after six hours of nonstop dancing and the temperature now well above 100, the chants changed. The grandfather, and then the father, stood in front of the people and gave long speeches in Apache. "They're thanking us for standing with their child," Judy said. "And they're giving prayers, thanking God for this day and this ceremony and for all of us."

Then the medicine man took a large bowl filled with pollen to the far end of the lines, and all the men (except me) lined up. Each dipped out a small handful of pollen, then, one at a time, went up to the girl and the godmother, sprinkling it over them—a pinch each to the head, shoulders, and breasts, and praying over each of them. It was highly ritualized, and each sprinkling took a few minutes. Behind the men, the women extended the line, and it took more than an hour for every person to go up and bless the girl and her godmother. Throughout it all, the chanting and dancing continued.

When Judy returned from her line, she told me to meet her here at 7:00 in the evening to see the Crown Dancers. I left and drove back to my hotel to recover from the morning and type up these notes.

The sky was so black it seemed hollow as I drove up to the area of the Crown Dancer ceremony. There was a bonfire the size of a small house in the center of the ceremonial area, flames leaping 20 and 30 feet into the air, the night sky stuttered with flecks of orange-glowing embers and smoke.

Around the bonfire were hundreds of Apaches. The drummers and medicine singers were going full blast, and most of the crowd was dancing, the left-right-left-right foot-lifting with hands just above the waist that I'd seen earlier. Judy and I joined.

After about 20 minutes of this, four men wearing six- or eight-foot antlers made of wood came running out of the darkness in the willow trees to one side of the area. Their heads were covered with black hoods, and they were naked other than a buckskin cloth around the waist and moccasins. Their bodies were painted with gray, white, and black clay.

Carrying staffs and spears with bells on them, they danced with a frenzied fervor around the fire, then turned and danced at members of the crowd, who fell back before them. All the while the dancers were jingling their bells and making loud animal noises.

"Their job is to scare away evil spirits," Judy said. "My boys are so afraid of them that they won't even come to the ceremonies." She chuckled. "Probably they should, though."

Behind the four Crown Dancers was a fifth man, painted in white, wearing a white hood, with a two-foot cross attached to his head. He carried a triple-cross, sort of like the old Easter Seal logo as I recall.

"That's the Grey One," Judy said, nodding at him with her nose. "He is the one who has the power. People think that he's just a fool, but he's the truly powerful one."

The Grey One carried something on a four-foot-long string that he twirled through the air. It made a loud buzzing sound like "Ooooooowwwwaaaaaammmmmmm" that reminded me of those signals the Aborigines of Australia use. Bull-roarers, I think they call them.

The Grey One went out of the circle for a moment, and returned with the girl, her friend who stood with her, and the godmother. He herded them into the area of the Crown Dancers, and they all eight began to dance around the circle. I had a disposable camera with a flash in it with me, and as they came around toward us, I took a picture. The Grey One ran over to me and shook his triple-cross at me, making sounds like an angry animal. The man next to me said, "If the tribal police see you take a picture they will arrest you and destroy your camera. This is a holy ceremony, not a spectacle for tourists."

I apologized and stuffed the camera into my back pocket. The Grey One danced on, the Crown Dancers and the women in his wake.

I'd assumed that the Crown Dancers were like the musicians at an Anglo wedding: they worked for money. When I asked Judy about this, however, she looked appalled.

"Nobody even knows who they are," she said. "To be a Crown Dancer is a sacred thing, and after the ceremony they don't bathe for four days to leave the sacred mud and markings on their bodies. They wouldn't accept money for this and there's no way to communicate with them because nobody knows who they are. You just hold an event, and they always show up. In the old days, they'd come down out of the mountains for things like this."

The dancers took the two girls and the godmother and danced them in a ritual fashion through a large double-arch made up of four pieces of willow, about 20 feet high, with boughs stuck from the top.

Judy leaned over and said, "This is the climax of the actual ceremony. We should leave now, as it's going to get pretty wild and you may not be safe."

We walked to our cars and I drove back through the night, the sounds of the chants still echoing in my mind.

The next morning my alarm brought me up out of a long dream about the Apaches, how they were chased and hunted and how even today, even this moment as I write these words, white men are still trying to take away more of their land from them (specifically the University of Arizona with their telescope project, joined by other universities, the Max Plank Institute in Germany, and the Vatican).

I got up, showered and dressed, checked my messages on CompuServe, and left.

♦

Driving through the desert darkness, I turned on the radio and found the station of the Navajo Nation, a few hundred miles to our north and west.

"Here's our historical thought for the day," the woman DJ said between country-and-western songs. "When Columbus blundered by accident onto our lands, he claimed them and all our people and all our wealth for the Pope and the King and Queen of Spain. His first order was to assemble all the local Indians and demand that every person over the age of 14 bring him, the next day, one handful of gold. The next day, all those who came with less than a handful, or were unable to bring anything, were hunted down and one hand was chopped off. Thousands lost their hands that day.

"Then Columbus took as prisoners as many Indians as he could jam into the holds of his ships and sent them back to Spain to be sold at the auction block as slaves. Most died during the journey, as they were kept in the hold of the ship, awash in their own excrement, with food thrown down to them when the sailors felt like it, but those who survived made the trip very profitable for Columbus. He made several trips back to take more slaves and cut off more hands.

"This is the man we're asked to honor on Columbus Day."

As Merle Haggard began to sing, I had to make an effort to unclench my hands from the steering wheel.

A Walk in the Woods

Touching and Being Touched
by the Power of Life

And that is the reason why I want you to read from Genesis this, at home, you see. Now it proves to you that God was it. "It" is the whole world, the expression of the God Mind—all His Mind. The way the Earth is, is only created by the God Mind.

—MASTER KURT STANLEY

Shortly after my visit to the Apaches, I went to Stadtsteinach for a few days to see Herr Müller.

The day I arrived was cold and there were a few inches of snow on the ground. The gray clouds hung low over the city and the air was clear and sharp. Herr Müller suggested we take another walk along the prophet's way, and so we headed up the back side of the mountain behind the Salem complex.

As we walked along the narrow trail on the side of the hill, I had a sudden feeling of remorse. Twice I'd left the Salem work to go back "into the world" and that was where I was now, with a business in Atlanta.

Thinking back on this, I said to Herr Müller, "I want to apologize for having left your side two times. I feel like I've wasted much of the 18 years I've known you."

He turned and looked straight into my eyes with a tenderness and ferocity that I've rarely seen. "You are right," he said, his voice thick with what could have been either anger or sadness. "You have wasted much of your life and mine pursuing money. I know that you thought it was best for your family, that you needed to provide for your children, but it was a mistake."

I started to protest, to point out that during all that time I'd used the money I'd made from those companies to fund my travels for Salem, and that I'd visited him several times every one of those 18 years, that I'd taught and touched hundreds of people in my classes and hundreds of thousands with my books, and that every Friday night I sent him a Shabat Shalom fax as a way of staying in touch: I was not completely disconnected from him or his work. But he held up a hand to still me.

"Thomas, we are standing at the edge of a vast ocean. All of humanity is here with us on this shore." He gripped my arm hard, and waved his other hand at the distant mountainside across the valley. "Over there, across the sea, is a golden, shining isle. It's a place of safety and salvation, the home of our Lord. Some of the people sense its presence, most are totally unaware of it."

He pulled me closer to him and put his face a foot from mine, looking me straight in the eyes. His voice became strong, commanding:

"Your destiny, Thomas, is to save those people. To show them how to reach that shining isle. If you fail to do that, you have failed in your life."

He let go of my arm and started to walk ahead of me. I was trembling, filled with grief for the years that I knew he felt I had abandoned him. "Of course, you are always welcome to go back into business," he said. "Or write some more books about ADD, or about anything. That is all important, and I will never tell you what you must do, you know that. But," he turned, and looked at me, "I tell you now, I have little time left, and no time to waste on people who are merely curious or merely friends. If you are with me, you must be with me totally, and if you are not, then leave my sight."

I had never, in my life, heard him talk like that: he'd always been totally nonjudgmental and left me completely free to make my own decisions.

"I am with you," I said without hesitation. I could feel a swelling in my throat, my heart beating faster. My voice was breaking.

He looked at me hard, his eyes sparkling. "Are you? If so, then I give you all of my spirit, all of my power, all of my blessing. If not, then get behind me. It is now *ja* or *nein*. Yes or no. If you are lukewarm, I spit you from my mouth." And he spat on the ground, turned, and continued his walking.

I ran to catch up. "I am with you!' I shouted. My eyes were filled with tears and I stumbled on the path.

He turned and hugged me. "I know, Thomas," he said, his eyes also shining with moisture. "You have always been with me, even when you yourself did not know it. Now," he pointed again at the distant horizon, "you must begin your real work. And it will mean that you shall encounter tribulations and terror and pain—as well as joys and insights—such as you cannot imagine. It will push you to the point of thinking that you can no longer stand it. It will test your physical and spiritual powers in ways that the average person would not survive. Perhaps you shall not survive it. It will be your greatest challenge, but if you persevere then you shall sit with me and Him at the feast."

"What shall I do?" I said. I did not want to hear these words: they aroused in me a primal terror. And yet I also stood straight as I spoke to him, and, so standing, knew that inside me was the will and the strength to withstand the tribulations of this future.

"Listen and pray," he said simply. "G-d will tell you what to do. You will feel it in your heart." He turned and began walking again, saying over his shoulder, "And finish writing that book you are working on." He was referring to this book which you are reading.

We walked a mile or so up and around the side of the mountain to the secret stone on which he had inscribed the tetragrammaton. His marking was now covered with moss, but we both knew it was there: this was where he had first anointed me with oil more than a decade earlier.

As we walked, I continued to wonder what type of work I should do to "create peace," how I could step out of the business world, and where I should do it. Should we move to Germany again? Should we start another children's village? Or a natural health center, like the clinic at Salem Stadtsteinach? I knew from long history that Herr Müller would not "tell" me what to do: he absolutely believes that each person must determine their own destiny, and that the role of a teacher and mentor is to help people along the path of their own choice, not to choose the path for them.

When we got there, he put his right hand on my forehead and said a blessing in Hebrew, and then put his right hand on top of mine and we put them both over the stone. "Say a prayer that will help you know what to do," he said, so I said the Lord's Prayer, with particular emphasis on *Thy will be done.*

"Now wait and remain open," he said. "Look, listen, and feel. You will know when the answer comes."

"Do you think this book I'm working on is my work?" I said.

"It could be," he said. "I have hidden these things from the world for years, only sharing them with my little flock. But now the world is on the precipice, and it is time that more people must hear about my life and this work. Then they will learn to know G-d and be inspired to begin to do as we do."

I was already making an internal and increasing commitment to the book. It was consuming more and more of my time, and I was pushing other things out of the way for it.

So, I asked him if he'd write down some of his thoughts, teachings, or stories, and he agreed. A few weeks later we received over a dozen typewritten pages from him in German, some in English.

Here is one of them, a short story about the walk he and I took during that November trip. He told it in my voice, probably with the assumption that I'd use it as a skeleton to write a more detailed story, but it's so exemplary of how he speaks and thinks that I'm printing it intact. While I always refer to him as "Herr Müller," in this he wrote his own name as "Gottfried," which in his Germanic culture was his way of expressing how close he felt to me:

November in the Franconian Forest, cold, frost, icy roads, fresh snow.

Gottfried walks next to me, step by step, thought by thought, word by word. The sun is shining. The forest gleams, gold, yellow, covered with glistening crystals.

Suddenly Gottfried stops. Right before his foot a long worm wriggles across the icy street, twisting itself in the snow. Gottfried bends over, lifts up the small creature with a gentle hand and carries it to the curb and with his free hand scrapes away snow, ice, leaves and dirt, making a small hole in the ground and lays the worm carefully inside. Then he covers it with fresh soil and leaves and says:

"There, my dear friend, now you will be warm and cozy and must not die."

We go on in silence. Suddenly Gottfried stops, looks at me, and points to heaven:

"You know," he says to me, "someday, when I stand before my judge up there, then the worm will stand next to me and say, 'Lord, be merciful to my friend Gottfried, because on Earth he was merciful to me, saved me from death, gave me a warm hole in the Earth, so that I could escape the cold, frost, and being run over. Lord, I love him, my friend Gottfried, because he loved me. Please requite him with love, which love he gave to me.'"

We continued on, turned off the road onto a narrow forest path, man behind man, I ahead, Gottfried behind me. After a while, Gottfried stopped, put his arms around a large, tall, and wonderfully beautiful fir tree, patted it lovingly on the bark, laid his face on its trunk, and said:

"You, I love you, and I thank you, that you are standing here, and through your beauty my eyes find joy and my heart peace. May G-d preserve and protect you, so that you will live for a long time and can be a friend and companion to us men."

I followed his example, put my arms around the beautiful and strong fir tree, thanked it and wished it a long life.

"You know," Gottfried said to me, "**everything** comes from G-d. We are all children of G-d, even the plants, the grasses, flowers, shrubs, and trees. As we, they have souls, and as we, they are happy when they are loved and when we demonstrate that and tell them that. Then they are so happy, that they stand straighter and healthier and more beautiful that they may serve us and please us."

The path became steeper, narrower, as wide only as our feet; it was slippery, icy, we had to be careful. We went on in silence—Gottfried ahead of me.

To the left of the path were stones carefully placed in a pile. Gottfried stopped. Took my hand, laid his hand on the stones, put mine on the back of his, and on top of that his other hand. "This," he said, "is my altar, at which I always pray when I come here."

He lifted his face, looked towards heaven, and spoke in Hebrew the great benediction:

"G-d, make your face shine upon us and give us your peace. Amen!"

What Herr Müller didn't know during our walk, at least as far as I knew at the time, was that I had noticed that he was limping slightly, and that his lips were becoming blue. So I put my hand on his shoulder and silently prayed, "Lord, if he is suffering, let me take some of his pain and burden."

The next week something inexplicable started happening to me. I would sit down to a meal, chew and swallow a few bites of food, and then feel like it was stuck halfway down my esophagus, just above my stomach. It wouldn't go all the way down. The first time it happened was during lunch while I was teaching a seminar on writing, and I ran out of the room to a bathroom, where I threw up what was stuck in my esophagus. Every day for the rest of that week, it happened almost daily. This wasn't any kind of flu or illness: there was something weird going on with my esophagus and diaphragm (which the esophagus passes through on the way to the stomach) that was mechanical in nature.

A few days later Louise Richards called me and asked if I'd heard that Herr Müller had gone into the hospital.

"What's wrong?" I asked.

She wasn't sure, but said she'd get back to me.

Very concerned, I called Salem in Stadtsteinach and reached Ursula, who said that, yes, he was in the hospital and would be having surgery the next day, but that it was nothing to worry about. She couldn't describe the problem, however, because of her limited English and my lack of knowledge of German medical terms. I called my travel agent and booked a flight to Germany for the next day, went to have lunch, and ended up throwing up again.

The next morning I reached Ursula again and told her that I was flying to Germany, and she asked me not to, saying that his surgery would prevent him from having visitors. She said that Louise Richards, who speaks fluent German, could explain to me what his condition was. He'd be going in for surgery in just a few hours. I called Louise, who said that Herr Müller was having surgery on his diaphragm, that somehow there'd been a hernia or tear from the war years that was temporarily repaired 40 years ago, but he'd never had permanently fixed. It interfered with his ability to swallow food.

I was both startled and gratified. I wondered if a prayer had been answered, or if I'd taken some energy or injury from him when I put my hand on his shoulder. I wondered (and still wonder) if my doing so lessened his pain and suffering until his surgery, or if it created some sort of psychic connection between the two of us, or both.

After his surgery was over, I stopped having the near-daily problem swallowing.

Similarly, when my father had open-heart surgery in 1996, I put my hand on him and asked that I could take on some of his pain and give him healing from my body. For the next month, I experienced regular angina-like pain, while he was experiencing a crisis from an infection he got during surgery, and then from a subsequent heart attack he had which the ER physician misdiagnosed. As he recovered from these, however, the pains in my own chest diminished. Again, I don't know if it was psychological, physiological (in some homeopathic way), or spiritual, or a combination of all and maybe even more.

What I learned from this is that, at least for me, moving around other people's energies is something to do carefully and only with specific intent. Healing by sending light and through prayer seems to be drawing G-d's power down and through, whereas healing by moving a person's energy risks distorting or disturbing our own energies. There may be times when this is desirable, but it should be done only with great care.

This also fed into my question of what I should be doing next, how I should fulfill my obligation—that by now was absolutely clear and real to me—that I should somehow work to help others come to "that shining shore" of self-realization and a better future for the world.

I'd been thinking of getting back into the healing arts, as when I'd founded The Michigan Healing Arts Center, taught classes, and had a small practice in herbology and homeopathy. Increasingly, though, I was coming to know that I should not be involved in a medical-practice type of environment, but instead in a teaching work.

But where? And teaching what? And how?

The Flaming Sword
Learning and Receiving Tools
for the Coming Times

*Knowledge with love is truth, perfection, and the true
light, which comes from G-d and leads to G-d.*

—ABRAM POLJAK

Working through the process of clarifying and writing down insights
about cultures, consciousness, and religion was both exhilarating and
painful. While reviewing my and Herr Müller's lifetimes' worth of
insights and work, I was also experiencing a crisis-like time of change
that began virtually the week I started compiling this book. I'd resigned
as president of my company, and my personal life was going through a
radical transformation. I felt as if I were under attack, and yet at the
same time it was one of the most intensely spiritual times of my life.
Insights of the seamlessness of reality, the power and constant presence
of G-d, and the true nature of my own soul and destiny alternated with
wrenching and powerful pulls back into the world. I was prepared to
head to my tipi again, or enter a monastery, or take on a new Salem
work. I'd been too long not "living on the edge," and also could feel
with an urgency I'd never known before the spiritual and physical
changes that are looming on the world's horizon.

So I booked a flight to Germany for a few days to visit Herr Müller.
When I told him all the details of everything that was going on in my
life, he smiled compassionately and told me stories from his own life
that made my dramas seem minuscule. But he never minimized what I
was going through: in fact, instead, he said that it was the portent of
something very important and that I would need a special weapon for
a coming battle.

"Weapon?" I said. We were sitting alone in the kitchen of his apartment in one of the buildings at Salem. His sons were off somewhere and Ursula was in Africa. We were eating bread baked in the Salem bakery from wheat grown organically on the Salem farm, with slices of fresh vine-ripened tomatoes grown in the Salem greenhouses, and drinking beer brewed in the next town over, Kulmbach. The sun was setting and the sky was a deep crimson through the kitchen window next to the table.

"*Ja*, weapon. About 1960, I was at a small castle on the border of Swabia and Bavaria. It was about four in the afternoon, and I was walking alone on the castle grounds. And a man approached me, and I knew he was an angel. He was carrying a flaming sword."

"A sword?"

"Listen. I was shocked! I backed away from him, but he gestured for me to come to him. I stood there for a moment, and then held my chin up and walked toward him. 'What do you want?' I said. 'I am here to give you this flaming sword,' he said. I looked at the sword and now was very frightened, 'I cannot take that,' I said. And he looked amazed. Big eyes, very emphatic. And he shouted at me, 'You will take this!' And so I took it from him, and from that day I have carried with me this flaming sword."

I was astounded. "What did you do with it?"

"I cannot tell you," he said. "Except that it is the second most powerful weapon I have."

"And the most powerful?"

"To do small deeds of mercy and compassion."

I nodded my head; it was what I'd expected to hear him say. I'd been hearing about that for 18 years, and practicing it myself.

"What happened to the man who gave you the sword?"

"He vanished. He simply vanished, right in front of my eyes. And in that moment, I recognized him as an angel: a good angel, an assistant to Archangel Michael."

I took a drink of beer, boggled by the idea.

"Thomas, I have been ordered to give you a flaming sword," he said in a loud voice.

"What?" I said, starting to rise up out of my chair.

"Thomas!" His voice was a bark. "Sit down! Be quiet and close your eyes!"

I did so.

"Now, put out your right hand, with your fingers curled to receive this sword."

I put out my hand, and felt his go into it, as if in a handshake but at a different angle. And then his hand in mine became cold and hard like steel. It was a sudden and sharp transformation: it felt as if I was holding a piece of very heavy and very cold steel.

"Now," he said, "draw in your breath."

As I did so I felt the steel become warm, and then hot. I could hear a crackling sound, like fire, and see bright lights dancing through my closed eyelids. I could feel the weight of the sword in my hand, and feel its heat.

We sat like that for a few minutes, then he withdrew his hand from mine. I could still feel the weight of the sword, although it quickly diminished after he'd withdrawn his hand.

"Open your eyes," he said.

I did so, and saw my right hand out in front of me, curled around empty air. I pulled it back, and noticed that it was trembling.

"Never use it in anger: always use it with love and compassion," he said.

The experience affected me strongly: since that day I have often felt the weight of the sword in my hand.

I looked through a Bible for references to flaming swords, and found only one, which raised even more questions in my mind. It was in Genesis 3, right after Eve's run-in with the serpent and the apple:

> And the LORD G-d said, Behold, the man is become as one of us, to know good and evil: and now, lest he put forth his hand, and take also of the tree of life, and eat, and live for ever: Therefore the LORD G-d sent him forth from the garden of Eden, to till the ground from whence he was taken. So he drove out the man; and he placed at the east of the garden of Eden Cherubim, and a flaming sword which turned every way, to keep the way of the tree of life.

The reference to the sword was interesting, but the LORD G-d (the most common translation of the JHWH in the old Hebrew text) speaking of "us" was even more interesting. I'd often wondered if the creation story in the Bible had come to the Hebrews from some earlier tribe, perhaps one they conquered in their early history, one that was an older culture.

In any case, the flaming sword is still with me. And, I suspect, if you visualize and feel it strongly enough, you can bring one into your own hand, too.

Try it now, as we consider how real any physical matter can be.

Consciousness and Transformation

Our Hope for the Future

> *Standing on the bare ground . . . a mean egotism*
> *vanishes. I become a transparent eyeball; I am nothing;*
> *I see all; the currents of the Universal Being circulate*
> *through me; I am part or particle of G-d.*
>
> —RALPH WALDO EMERSON

Recent scientific studies show that matter and the mind that perceives it are not as separate as Aristotle, Descartes, and our modern culture have believed.

Around the turn of the century, physicists realized that the traditional Newtonian model of the way matter and energy worked and interacted wasn't complete: it didn't explain certain phenomena having to do with the transmission of heat.

This led theoretical physicists to postulate that energy didn't just move in waves, but also in little packets, which they called quanta. The system by which the movement and transitions of these quanta are measured and predicted is called quantum mechanics, and is no longer considered just a theory, but a practical way of describing the behavior of subatomic particles and energy.

But as physicists began performing experiments to test the concepts of quantum mechanics, they began to observe strange things. A particle split in two, for example, would send two parts spinning away from the split-point in opposite directions with opposite spins. However, if the spin-direction of one of the half-particles were changed, even thousands of miles from the point where it originated, the other half-particle would instantaneously change its spin as well.

At first the idea of this was ridiculed, because what it implied was that there was no such thing as time or distance when working with bits of matter/energy/reality this small, even though they may be separated by millions of miles of distance. Such a concept calls into question all of our notions of reality.

When it was demonstrated over and over again in the laboratory, however, this weird behavior of subatomic particles came to be accepted and was given the name of nonlocal phenomena or nonlocality.

But the plain-language description of the implications of this research, named the Copenhagen Interpretation by Danish physicist Niels Bohr, is even more mind-boggling. Bohr proposed that quanta could behave as either particles or energy (which was already known), but that only one thing determined whether they manifested as particles or energy: whether they were being observed *by a conscious being.*

In other words, the entire universe exists only as energy, as a mathematical wave of probability, until a conscious being observes it. In that moment of observation—instantaneously and faster than the speed of light—the wave of energy being observed snaps into physical reality and is measurable.

At first this idea, too, was ridiculed. But then at the University of Texas in 1977, George Sudarshan and B. Misra showed theoretically that an unstable particle's decay would be suppressed by the act of observation. Like the watched pot that never boils, so long as a person is observing an atom's disintegration, atomic disintegration is suspended.

Because we observed it, it continued to exist.

In 1990, David Winehead and colleagues proved this by actual observation in an experiment performed at the National Institute of Standards and Technology in Boulder, Colorado.

Suddenly, physicists were talking like priests from the most ancient religions in the world.

Many physicists now assert that this is how all of creation is: so long as we sense it, it exists. (Certainly the *personal* reverse is true: before we existed, when we are unconscious, and possibly after we die, this physical world will cease to exist for us.) In any case, there is a clear and solid connection between matter and consciousness, proven now in the most sophisticated physics laboratories in the world. Without consciousness to observe it, it seems that the entire universe of matter would dissolve back into energy!

This is consistent with the philosophy that I developed during my year in the tipi: that the entire physical universe could be a dream or thought in the "mind" of G-d, and that we are the eyes, ears, and senses of G-d.

It's unfortunate that in English we only have the word *consciousness,* because most people think of consciousness as "thinking," and that is absolutely not what I mean. A closer term is the German expression *Bewufste Wahrnehmung,* although an English dictionary will only translate that into "conscious awareness." A German, however, knows it has a different meaning. When I asked Herr Müller to describe what it really meant, he popped his eyes open and opened his mouth and took a sharp breath. "That is it," he said. "Oh!"

"Oh?"

"*Ja.* There is no equivalent English word."

So we're stuck using a word to describe something that hardly does it justice, because we're lacking the real word. In Sanskrit it's *ananda.* In Japanese it's *satori.* But in English we don't have the word, so I'll have to use the word "consciousness."

Please remember, though, that I'm not talking about "thinking," and every time you instinctively translate "consciousness" into "thinking," step back and correct yourself. It's referred to in the Bible as "I am that I am" (the phrase G-d used to describe Himself when Moses said, "Who are you?") which is actually a pretty clear and solid way of saying it. Some would call it bliss, but that implies that there is a not-bliss as well, that it's part of some continuum. It's not; it's beyond "from here to there": it just is, all at once.

It is the source and wellspring of the soul.

This, then, raises an interesting question about human consciousness, taking us back to the earlier chapters on this topic. What if our thinking mind, our likes and dislikes, our opinions and fears—our *thoughts*—are not tools to help us connect with consciousness, but instead they *keep us from it?*

This would explain why when a person dies (as we learn from people who have near-death experiences or NDEs) and their thinking brain shuts down, they suddenly experience light, bliss, and something for which they tell us there is no word in English: what I am calling consciousness. "The entire universe is filled with the fire of life," they often say, "and I realized in that moment that I am part of it, seamlessly."

Aldous Huxley, in *Doors of Perception,* proposed that the mind serves as a filter, shutting out most of our awareness, closing the "doors of perception" so we can *think*. If we're fully aware, we can't think; when we're thinking, we are by necessity somewhat unaware!

This fits with the observation that so many religious traditions emphasize techniques which shut down or short-circuit the thinking brain to get to *consciousness*. These range from saying the Rosary for hours, to meditation, to wild physical activities (like the whirling dervishes, and singing and dancing in churches), to the use of sacramental plants such as peyote and pscilocybin mushrooms. What all these do is alter the neurochemistry and function of the brain to the point where the "receiver" changes channels.

I suspect that thinking is not here to bring us closer to G-d or consciousness: it's here to keep us *from* G-d and consciousness, so that our species will be perpetuated. Thinking is an artifact of our animal bodies, our mammal brain, and functions to help our physical bodies survive and procreate. This is why we can see so many of our thinking processes mirrored in other animals, as any dog or cat owner will tell you.

Assuming for a moment that this is true, and that the ancient prophets and saints were aware of it, then and only then do the traditional religious concepts of sin begin to make sense.

When Jesus said that looking upon a woman with lust was the same as sleeping with her, I believe he was referring to the danger of thinking— of separating ourselves from the created world by our thoughts. Instead, he said very clearly at the end of the Sermon on the Mount and in other places, *just be.*

All the "primary" sins cataloged in the world's major religions then are seen as things which increase *thinking* and *wanting*, pulling us away from *being.*

This is why they're warned against.

But those messages have been twisted over the years into rules and power grabs, because they've been viewed from the younger culture perspective instead of the older culture viewpoint where they originated. They've been taken from the mouths of mystics (where they were positive suggestions for self-realization) and put into the mouths of the religious equivalent of police who then used them to lord over their subjects.

Younger cultures value thinking. In Western civilization, *cogito ergo sum* is a mantra: I *am* because I *think*. And thinking leads to wanting, to conquest, to war, to oppression and exploitation, to the utter separation of human from human and from the life around. In Sanskrit, for example, the word "war" translates into "desire for more cattle."

Younger cultures value conformity. This became even more true with the advent of mass production, which demonstrated that it's more efficient if all ingredients are identical. There may be less soul put into the work, but that's consistently seen to be an acceptable trade-off in younger cultures.

Not surprisingly, younger cultures view variations in thinking styles as deficits or disorders. It's not uncommon for some "deficits" to disappear if you change the setting, but the diagnosis persists, with the presumption that chemicals should be added to the patient's brain, or at least some sort of psychotherapy.

Older cultures view this as presumptuous, and place a high emphasis on *being* instead of thinking. They honor those who have touched the "kingdom of heaven within," who have awakened out of thinking and *into* consciousness.

When a person lives in this place, tiny acts of compassion become part of and, in fact, create awareness of moment-to-moment life. They are love in expression, and have the effect of transforming our thinking mind into a conscious mind.

When we realize that the entire world around us and within us is made from the stuff of G-d which we can experience as love, then the entire world becomes sacred.

Every act of life is sacred.

Every bit of creation is alive and vital and sacred, and touches us with love.

And the idea of fouling the planet, of destroying our environment, of exploiting or stealing from "them" to the advantage of "us," or even of labeling another human being as "disordered," is seen as the younger culture *poverty of consciousness* and the excess of thinking that it represents.

Next Steps Along the Prophet's Way

Thou must be emptied of that wherewith thou art full, that thou may be filled with that whereof thou art empty.

—MEISTER ECKHART

Herr Müller always asks me, "What is the next step?"

I remember back in 1981 when he came to New York and gathered a small group of us together and told us that we should begin to prepare for some very specific things to come. Water supplies would become unreliable, electricity sporadic, food contaminated, and three days of darkness would cover the Earth. We must have supplies, from water and food to candles, he said.

Even more important, however, he told us that over the next few decades we must create communities—and encourage others to do the same—that would be places of transition and survival into the next age. These places should be self-sufficient for the time when that is necessary, yet also catalytic: they'd be places of inspiration and education for those who would learn. Like the monasteries of old, they'd be places of spiritual light, which would touch the entire world whether it knew of them or not.

Such places could be called Salem or not, be affiliated or not, accept his ideas or not: they just should come into being, for the future of the human race.

"We are not trying to create a cult or sect or religion," he said. "Anybody of any religion is free to do this in their own way. Because what we are doing is not an organized religion, it's a personal spirituality."

I have seen in my travels around the world, heard in the pained cries of starving children, felt in my heart and gut, that the world is in trouble. The planet is being damaged by the blindness of our conquering, dominating, disassociated-from-life younger culture, and that damage is threatening all of humanity.

From this, I've learned that in order to save ourselves and our planet, we must change more than the simple stuff of our behaviors: we must transform our consciousness, our culture, and our spirit. As long as our thinking dominates, and we don't realize that we're all part of the same existence, there will be no reason for the behaviors to change.

This change can only happen at the most fundamental level of society: individual by individual. It will either happen voluntarily (e.g., we'll all begin to wake up before it's too late) or involuntarily (e.g., we'll find ourselves being swept aside by changes such as massive disruptions in our food, power, water, and communications systems in the years soon to come).

Some already see this, such as the Hopi Elders who three times went to the United Nations to try to tell what their prophecies say about the coming times, or the Confederation of Small Island Nations which has petitioned the UN to enforce the international laws against increasing greenhouse gas emissions. But most of us are blissfully unaware, more concerned with the storyline of this week's TV shows, or the made-for-TV politics and news.

You can help.

Employ the techniques in this book to change from a younger culture perspective to an older culture one.

See G-d everywhere, keep a Sabbath, send light, eat vegetarian foods as much as possible, meditate and pray, build an altar both in the world and in your heart, commit random acts of mercy, and share *your* insights with others.

With or without such large physical changes as starting or going to live in a rural or spiritual community, consider your everyday life as it is now, and how you can change yourself, and *through that* how you might change the world. This is where real transformation happens: one person at a time. Consider changing your life so you more often live in the sacred *Now* and, through tiny acts of mercy, transform your future.

Every moment of every day is part of the eternal *Now*. As you're reading these words, glance around you and see and hear and feel the presence of the place you're in.

Notice the empty spaces around you.

Feel your connection to the Earth, and your sense of time, of the presence of this *now* moment.

Notice your thoughts and how easily they pull you away from *now,* from *consciousness,* from *love.*

This *now,* beyond thought, is the Mind of G-d, the Only Moment, the True Reality.

If you simply pause a few times each day to experience this meditation, your life will be changed. You, in turn, will change others around you, and they others around them (even if they don't realize they're doing it).

And thus begins our transformation of the world, and perhaps even our saving of the Earth and its inhabitants.

Afterword

Herr Müller celebrated his 90th birthday in April 2004. Salem programs in Russia and Uganda have become substantial and extraordinary undertakings, and programs have sprung up in new countries as well: there have been challenges, problems, and miracles along the way, many of which are chronicled at www.saleminternational.org on the internet.

Here in the United States, the New England Salem Children's Village has grown substantially under the extraordinary care and guidance of Jane Merrithew and an amazing and dedicated staff. We've also started a school for ADHD children on the property (called The Hunter School after my theory that ADHD kids are "hunters in a farmer's world") and it is becoming a model for education of "learning disabled" kids around the world. The Salem Children's Village in Maryland is still strongly running under the guidance of Louise (Sutermeister) Richards.

The original edition of this book has brought much-deserved recognition to Salem and Herr Müller. In part because of it, I've also been invited to visit, meet, and talk with His Holiness Pope John Paul II and His Holiness the Dalai Lama (invitations I accepted), and could probably fill another book with stories, although it seems it's now time to leave that to the next generation.

In my younger years, although I had been active in the movement against the Vietnam War, I largely felt that politics and spirituality were very different things. After this book was first published and Louise and I moved to Vermont, we found in the attic of the old house we'd bought a tattered and mildewed 20-volume collection of the complete writings of Thomas Jefferson, published in 1903. Reading his autobiography, his Notes On Virginia, and thousands of his letters led me to realize that Jefferson, like most of the other Founders, was a deeply spiritual— although totally non-religious—man. He would have nothing to do with any church, yet he saw the presence of the Creator everywhere, and felt that bringing democracy to the United States was a profoundly spiritual work.

Reading Jefferson in depth has broadened my view of the ways we can help change the world, leading me to write several books about democracy and to start a daily talk-radio program that deals mostly with the topic of democracy. This, to me, is another dimension of the path of the Prophet's Way.

What follows is the experience of one of the people who was motivated to travel to meet Herr Müller in person and participate in the work of Salem International as a result of reading the 1997 edition of this book.

Epilogue

The Work of
The Prophet's Way

by Andrea Lomas

At the fifth Prophet's Way conference in November 2003, Thom invited me to write an update on the conferences that came about as a result of this book, and the continuing work of Salem International. In the following pages I have tried to do justice to the myriad "points of light" which have been encouraged to shine around the world and help alleviate suffering as a result of Gottfried Müller's commitment to a life of peace.

I "woke up" in the summer of 1999, at age 30, when a book about G-d fell on my head. After that other books started appearing in odd places, leaping off shelves and turning up in handbags. As a result of the trail they enticed me to follow, I took a leap of faith, chucking in the career I'd worked hard to establish for ten years, leaving behind friends and family, and moving hundreds of miles in search of a group of like-minded individuals who wanted to put their spirituality into practice and who didn't look at me like I'd just stepped out of a flying saucer.

One of the key books that influenced me was Thom Hartmann's *The Last Hours of Ancient Sunlight*. I had moved to Scotland to start a business with my partner Seth, and at the meeting where we were pitching a new Web site for a global peace event known as Spirit Aid, I noticed the book peeking out of a bookshelf above our heads. It had been listed as a "must-read" by Neale Donald Walsh in his *Conversations With God* trilogy, and I had been trying to track it down for months. At the end of that meeting we were awarded the contract; introduced to Kenny, Spirit Aid's Information Technology (IT) expert; and received a copy of *The Last Hours of Ancient Sunlight* to take home.

The book had a profound effect, inspiring me to take personal responsibility for my lifestyle choices, give up meat, and look for environmentally sound alternatives to the way I'd been bumbling about my daily existence.

Hungry for more of this wisdom, I turned next to *The Prophet's Way*. It was like finding the Holy Grail. Here was a book that epitomized my search for spirituality in action and by the time I was halfway through, I'd decided I wanted to meet this guy; his books had a way of speaking directly to my soul. So, unaware that I was unleashing a chain of events that would lead to me writing this epilogue two years later, I logged onto Thom's Web site and asked how I could become involved in Salem International's work.

Thom replied immediately, providing me with the name and e-mail address of his UK contact, a Kenny MacDougall, who lived "somewhere in Scotland." He also informed me that Kenny was in the process of setting up the first Prophet's Way conference in Germany that October, giving people who'd read the book a chance to meet Thom and Herr Müller and walk the Prophet's Way together.

Terribly excited, I dropped a line into the cyberpond. Nothing came back but I jotted down Kenny's name and popped it into my handbag anyway.

The following week I was invited to a fundraising talk by the Spirit Aid team with my friend Pamela. The first speaker was announced as Kenny MacDougall. As Kenny walked to the front, Pamela found her knee in a vicelike grip with a shrill maniac by her side babbling "He's Kenny MacDougall! He's my Spirit Aid IT man!" We could hear the angels chuckling and decided there and then to travel to the Germany conference together with Kenny in October.

This was not to be Kenny's first trip to Salem's headquarters in Stadtsteinach, Germany. Having read *The Prophet's Way*, he'd attended a talk by Thom in Scotland, who'd encouraged Kenny to go to Germany to meet his teacher. Herr Müller, delighted that someone had traveled from the UK to meet him, said, "I will give anyone my blessing but first of all they have to be here."

The deep sense of peace and serenity that Kenny carried home from Salem inspired some of his friends to read *The Prophet's Way* and they traveled with him on his return visits to Germany. On one of these visits he met Olga from Salem Russia. Some months later Kenny received a letter from Herr Müller saying, "I think it's important you go to

Russia" so he and a friend, Hamish, traveled out to help Olga and Gerhard Lipfert, who were opening the first Salem house in Kaliningrad. Kenny has since helped to further projects in Ecuador and Uganda.

Having experienced some of Salem's work firsthand, Kenny volunteered to create a Web site for the organization. As he was linking the site to Thom's, he noticed that Thom's speaking engagements would bring him to Glasgow, Scotland, the following summer for a Spirit Aid event. Kenny had finally found a group of like-minded souls in his own city!

Kenny and his colleague Jane, Pamela, Seth, and I became a group for the first time on the flight to Germany for the first Prophet's Way conference. Jane and Pamela were hastily rereading *The Prophet's Way* on the plane, marveling at the fact that they were going to meet the key "characters" in the book in the space of the next twenty-four hours.

We arrived at Salem at twilight, just as the Shabat ceremony was beginning and were ushered into a room scented with the aroma of freshly baked apple strudel. Herr Müller was instantly recognizable—a bearded, smartly dressed bundle of dynamic energy, with the face of a prophet, an angelic smile and blue fire in his eyes. As he punctuated his reading of the Bible with animated arm movements and the odd "Ja!" turning occasionally to his younger companion (Thom) for translation, his wife, Ursula, stood by, ready to light the seven ceremonial candles. The air was charged with destiny and we had to keep pinching ourselves to make sure we hadn't walked into a dream.

The following is an excerpt from my journal, written at the end of that first timeless weekend:

Imagine a place, cradled in nature, set high above the cares and concerns of your daily world. A place where trees replace television, home-nurtured organic feasts replace mistreated chemical-laden food and peace pervades the air. A place your soul calls home before your mind even has a chance to acknowledge it.

Then add a small family of people bearing gifts of friendship, who you have always known, loved, and respected though you haven't met before. Sprinkle with a golden dusting of sacred rituals, timeless wisdom, and the presence of a truly inspirational holy messenger and you have the perfect recipe for a new world.

This place exists. Set on a hill above Stadtsteinach in Bavaria, it has become the flagship of Salem International, a material manifestation of a lifelong relationship with a loving G-d. As soon as you arrive, you are struck by the holistic harmony of the place, wooed by its simplicity. You feel as though you are suspended above time; the whole world could grind to a halt and Salem would continue, weaving its threads of peace.

This weekend it was the setting for the first Prophet's Way conference, a small gathering of people from around the globe who'd been inspired by Thom Hartmann's book and wanted to experience its magic for themselves. Together we walked the Prophet's Way, benefiting from the wisdom of a man [Herr Müller] who speaks with G-d every day.

When we reached Herr Müller's shrine we stopped and, after a worm had been carefully removed from our path, were anointed with holy oil. As Herr Müller said the Aaronic blessing in Hebrew, a profound silence settled over us and the universe seemed to shift slightly. It was as if in that one moment everyone allowed the peace that is Salem into their hearts and souls. Many contemplated their divine purpose, some making radical alterations to their life plans. Some committed to extending Salem's network of peace, others decided to "be the change."

It is Herr Müller's magical mix of sober piety, focused energy, and childlike glee that make him a joy to be around. He seems to approach life with the precision of a German engineer, the mindfulness of the Buddha, and the wonder of a child, combined.

One evening during the conference the dining room was full of life and buzzing with excited conversation. This was the "last supper" before the Prophet's Way conference would disperse and the international family that had formed such strong links over the weekend would head back to their respective corners of the globe. Everyone was brimful of inspiration and unwilling to leave the warmth of the circle so there was a great deal of hugging, crying, and swapping of personal details going on.

Standing at the back of the room, I was about to lift my jacket from its hook, when I noticed a figure transposed against the mêlée. Slightly stooped and wearing his customary tweed jacket and hat, Herr Müller had slipped through the front door and was standing quietly at the top of the steps. I watched curiously as he single-mindedly picked his way through the tables toward one of the large picture windows that look out onto the hills. He seemed to be utterly and very seriously absorbed in his inner world, as unaware of the other people in the room as they were of him.

At that moment the scene became two spools of the same film. The chattering, technicolor crowd of departing guests slowed down, their babble slightly muted, while the silent deliberate strides of Herr Müller became the single point of truth in the room. Lit by an inner purpose, he reached his destination and, with the utmost care, cupped a trapped fly in his hands, opened the window and released it. A huge, joyous grin spread across his face and as the soundtrack came back on; he turned towards me and winked, before vanishing into the crowd!

I focused back on the room, unsure whether I'd just imagined the whole scenario. Nobody else seemed to have noticed anything so, vaguely unsettled, I went to join the rest of my friends.

Later that afternoon, as we were saying our goodbyes, Herr Müller gently touched my arm. "G-d's smallest creatures," he whispered with a smile.

On another visit in January 2003, Kenny and I were fortunate to spend some private time with Herr Müller and his family and felt deeply honored to be invited to his home for the Friday evening Shabat celebration. We read together the parable of the sower (Matthew 13) and Herr Müller started to recount the story of G-d's latest miracle.

Louise, a young Australian pregnant with her first child who had been inspired by one of Thom's talks in Melbourne, read *The Prophet's Way* and decided she must meet Herr Müller. As a deaf-mute since birth, lone travel in a foreign country was a challenge, but her determination and faith saw her through and she arrived on Salem's doorstep in Stadtsteinach in September 2002. She had a three-month visa and managed to communicate her desire to help the Salem cause however she could. The Müllers took her in, unsure of what the next step would be, but certain that it would be revealed to them when the time was right.

Two and a half months later, a group of German guests arrived for the Christmas celebrations, one of whom was reading a book about dolphin healing in Florida and shared some of the stories with his fellow guests. One of these stories told of the miraculous healing of someone who also had Louise's same condition.

As Herr Müller opened his Bible to begin his nativity reading that Christmas, a check fell to the floor. It had been donated some time ago by a close female friend of Salem who insisted he would need that exact amount one day. He had tucked it into his Bible and promptly forgotten about it.

The check was for 2,500 Euros, the exact amount that would be needed for Louise's treatment in Florida. The trip was arranged and on her return to Salem Louise spoke her first words to Herr Müller asking him to bless her unborn child.

As he told this story, Herr Müller pointed to a plaque bearing the inscription "With G-d, anything is possible." His eyes filled with tears, as did our own. I found it touching and humbling that a man who had witnessed and been part of so many miracles had not become immune to them.

On another memorable visit, Herr Müller was standing solemnly surveying the guests from the top of the steps that descend to the dining room, looking every inch the elder statesman about to deliver a life-changing speech to the gathered masses. Fixed by one of his piercing gazes mid-way between my chair and the buffet table, I stopped. The gaze continued for several very long seconds. His expression was so intense, so serious, that I was sure I was about to receive some kind of divine transmission.

With the utmost gravitas, he inclined his head and reached up to remove his hat. "This must be really important," I thought, knees starting to tremble. Then, quick as a flash, he threw his hat straight at me like a Frisbee. Caught by surprise I only just managed to leap up and grab it without dropping my plate. Gottfried Müller, sparkling eyes belying his 89 years, threw back his head and chuckled with delight.

Over the course of the past five Prophet's Way conferences, a tradition has grown up. In the evenings we gather around the fire to share stories, songs, tears and laughter, dissolving our cultural differences in a celebration of unity. Sitting in a candlelit circle, singing songs of peace with people from Russia, Germany, Australia, New Zealand, Switzerland, Ecuador, Canada, Portugal, Britain, and the United States are memories I will cherish forever. If only the UN were as effective!

This sense of unity represents to me what Salem International is all about. Although the format of the conferences always changes, the message remains the same and each time the circle round the fire gets larger and louder. The following are just a few of the stories from people I've met who were profoundly affected by walking the Prophet's Way.

Richard came to the first conference from Florida, aged 18, his fresh face and startling baby-blue eyes a direct contradiction of his spiritual maturity. Two years later he is an integral part of the Salem organization, living at the headquarters. He has mastered the German language and traveled extensively around the Salem projects, helping out where needed.

Charlie was working as a financial consultant in Germany wondering where his life was taking him. After reading *The Prophet's Way* he contacted the Müllers, visited Stadtsteinach and in no time at all became a trainer for Salem's neurofeedback program. Together with Samuel, the Müllers' eldest son, Charlie has gone on to develop a community tree-planting initiative, a model since transplanted to other Salem projects around the world.

Hilary from Eastbourne, England, had been acquainted with Salem's work since the 1970s. The need for spiritual refreshment and new direction brought her to the third conference in November 2002. She had been working to free herself from her role in commissioning, planning, and project management within community NHS services and had sold her house and most of her possessions in preparation, but had no idea where life would lead her next. The following January she was asked by Salem to help out in Uganda and in April 2003 took up her new role as technical and management advisor on the project management team. Her calm, unflappable nature has been crucial in the rebuilding of the Ugandan village after a recent fire destroyed property and vehicles.

After Adam's third visit to the Prophet's Way conference he took the leap of faith and packed in his job as a successful manager of a chain of American electrical retailers to train as a vegetarian chef. Hilary already has him earmarked for Uganda!

Jane left behind a successful television acting career to pursue her spiritual path and is now a qualified Sundoor master and firewalk instructor, helping people to face their fears and find their own spiritual paths. She is hoping they will become an exciting addition to future conferences.

Lilo and Bruno, a social worker and teacher from Switzerland, were inspired to leave their careers, sell their house and move to Salem Ecuador where they are now project coordinators. On their second visit, daughter Conny accompanied them. She has since been active in bringing her "peace dove" campaign to the attention of the Swiss people and their government.

Pamela shocked her family when she left behind a very successful career in the Scottish film industry to retrain as an herbalist. She recently spoke at a Salem bio-conference in Russia.

Seth discovered the meaning of "letting go and letting G-d" on a recent trip to Salem Uganda. The moment he left his career behind, his expertise in media and child development were immediately called upon and put to good use assisting the self-determination of Salem villages. This experience has strengthened his commitment to furthering the Salem cause. Seth, Kenny, Pamela, and myself are already drawing up plans for Salem Scotland.

And who could forget Olga Sholmova, a Russian goddess and first-class lawyer who, assisted by the ever-ebullient Gerhard, has brought into existence Herr Müller's dream of a bridge of healing between Germany and Russia. Having overcome seemingly endless cultural, bureaucratic, and financial difficulties (Gerhard would call them "situations"), Salem Russia now stands as a model of excellence in a country seeking to reinvent itself.

Salem is alive and growing. Many of us keep in touch on a regular basis via e-mail, sharing stories, messages of support, and weekly Shabat greetings. Herr Müller really is the guy that Thom wrote about and then some. He just passed (on April 10, 2004) his ninetieth birthday and spends most of his time in a state of union with G-d, quietly inspiring people from around the world with his life's work.

The lessons in *The Prophet's Way* are not just empty words, they are wisdom lived, which is what inspires so many people to find out more. We invite you to join us and touch the power of life.

For more information visit www.thomhartmann.com or www.saleminternational.org

Appendix

Lessons from Abram Poljak, Herr Müller's Teacher

A teacher affects eternity; he can never tell where his influence stops.

—Henry Adams

On a trip to Germany in June of 1996, Herr Müller shared with me the story of being arrested in Germany in the 1950s. He had built a substantial multi-city organization of homes and refuges for prisoners, alcoholics, prostitutes, and street people, and the authorities of one of the states where one of his homes was located concluded that he must be doing it in order to get rich.

They were also upset because he was donating ten percent of his fundraising revenue to Jews in Israel, and so labeled him a "friend of Jews" (which is no longer a crime in Germany but in the 1950s was still dangerous to be accused of) and "not sufficiently patriotic" because he was sending some money overseas to Israel.

Because German law doesn't have the same "innocent until proven guilty" provision as American law, they arrested him and then began their investigation. When they were unable to find any evidence of financial improprieties, they sent him to a court-ordered psychologist to find out if he was crazy.

The morning of his trial, the psychologist stood up and testified, "This man believes he has been personally told by G-d that he should do this work. He may or may not be right about that, but I find no insanity in him. In fact, if more people were like him, this would be a better nation and a better world."

The astonished judge ordered Herr Müller released from the jail.

From there, he went to the funeral of Abram Poljak, his mentor and teacher. When he told me about this decades later—that Poljak had died while he was in jail, and that the "miracle" of the psychologist had gotten him out of the jail just in time for the funeral, his eyes glistened with tears. He then gave me a well-used little chapbook of Abram Poljak's writings in German, which Poljak had given to him. "This is my gift to you," he said, tears now escaping from his eyes. "I know you will respect it and learn from it."

I was particularly interested to read this, as I'd heard many stories from Herr Müller over the years about Abram Poljak. How he emerged from the Holocaust to become a famous evangelist across Europe. How he'd grown up as an Hasidic Jew and had studied under a man who'd studied under a man who'd studied all the way back to the Baal Shem Tov. How he'd taken Herr Müller on as a student in the early 1950s and they'd traveled together for years across Europe teaching and preaching in churches and lecture halls. How he'd performed miracles of insight and ancient knowledge, and given his blessing and anointing to Herr Müller.

So on the train ride from Stadtsteinach to Frankfurt for my flight home, I typed into my computer some of the passages that Herr Müller had underlined, and then ran them through the translation program on my computer. This is just a very small snapshot of some of Poljak's writings, and I'm sure you'll see and hear and feel in them how he influenced Herr Muller's world view . . . and how he then influenced mine.*

Je mehr Licht der Erkenntnis wir bekommen, um so einsamer werden wir An dieser Einsamkeit können wir zugrunde gehen, wenn nicht zum Licht der Erkenntnis em höheres Licht, das vollkommene, kommt: das Licht der Liebe und der Demut.

The more light of knowledge we get, the more lonely we become. We can be destroyed in or by this solitude if to this light of knowledge is not added a higher light, the perfect light: the light of love and humility.

---

*I include the German text first, because they were never translanted during Poljak's life and he didn't speak English in any case, so he could not and has not "cleared" my translation; for those readers who understand German, you will find often-subtle and multiple meanings in the original German which cannot translate into English.

Alles Licht, das wir erhalten haben, strömt aus Seiner Gnadenhand. Er gibt es uns nicht, damit wir hart werden und jene verachten, die weniger Licht haben als wir, sondern damit wir uns ihrer erbarmen und ihnen dienen.

All the light we have received streams from His merciful hand. He does not give it us so that we become hard and scorn those who have less light than we, but so that we will have compassion for them and serve them.

Es ist die Aufgabe des Sehenden, den Blinden zu führen, mild und sanft, ohne ihn zu stoßen und zu erschrecken. Stilles Dienen wird von uns verlangt, heiliges Schweigen. Räume den Blinden die Steine aus dem Wege und beschütze ihn vor jenen, die aus seiner Blindheit Nutzen ziehen wollen!

Christus aber sagt: Ich gebe dir mehr Licht—nicht damit du jene verläßt, in deren Kreis du jetzt gewesen bist. Ich habe dich reich gemacht—nicht damit du dich von den Armen wendest, sondern damit du ihnen hilfst. Ich habe dir Erkenntnis geschenkt, Klugheit und Verstand—nicht damit du hochmütig und selbstsüchtig wirst, sondern damit du jenen hilfst, denen Klugheit fehlt!

It is the task of the seeing to lead the blind, mildly and softly, without pushing them or frightening them. Quiet service is demanded of us, sacred silence. Take the stones out of the way of the blind person and protect him from those who would take advantage of his blindness.

Christ however says: I give you more light—not that you would leave the one in whose circle you now have been. I have made you rich—not so that you would turn away from the poor, but so that you help them. I have given you knowledge, understanding, and discernment—not that you would become haughty and selfish, but so that you would help those who lack discernment!

Weisheit

Wahres Licht leuchtet nicht nur, sondern wärmt auch.

Erkenntnis ohne Liebe ist haltes Licht, ein Irrlicht, das in den Abgrund führt.

Erhenntnis mit Liebe ist aber Wahrheit, Vollendung, das wahre Licht, das aus Gott kommt und zu Gott führt.

"Gott ist Lieb, und nur wer in der Lieb bleibt, bleibt in Gott und Gott in ihm." (1 Johannes 4:16)

Wisdom

True light not only lights, but also warms.

Knowledge without love is cold light, a false light which leads into the abyss.

Knowledge with love, however, is truth, perfection, and the true light, which comes from G-d and leads to G-d.

"G-d is love, and he who dwells in love dwells in G-d, and G-d in him." (1 John 4:16)

Gnade

Ja, auch wir haben das Gericht verdient. Daß es uns nicht traf, ist unverdiente Gnade. Für Gnade muß man danken, unaufhörlich danken. Wenn man nicht dankt, jagt man die Gnade fort. Wir können wählen zwischen Gnade und Gerechtigkeit. Wählen wir die Gnade und danken wir für sie, Tag für Tag und Stunde für Stunde. Nehmen wir das Gute in Unserem Leben nicht als selbstverständlich hin, sondern nur als Gnade und als Prüfung, als Prüfung unserem Dankbarkeit.

Denken wir daran jeden Tag, im besonderen an Tagen, die Gott ausgesondert und uns zur Zeit der Besinnung gesetzt hat—wie die Tage des Advents, der Weihnacht und des Jahreswechsels. Es sind Tage der Liebe und Dankbarkeit, der Versöhnung und des Friedensschlusses. Wir sollen Frieden schließen mit Gott und mit Menschen und mit uns selbst. Im Lichte der Advents- und Weihnachtskerzen sollen wir die Jahresbilanz ziehen und erkennen, wieviel Gutes uns erwiesen wurde von Gott und von Menschen. Erkennen wir es und schreiten wir dankbar durch das Tor der Zeit—in das neue Jahr.

Mercy

Yes, also we each deserve judgment. That we did not receive the judgment is undeserved mercy. For mercy one must thank, continually thank. If one does not thank, one chases the mercy away. We can choose either mercy or justice. Let us choose mercy and be thankful for mercy, day by day and hour by hour. Let us not accept the good in our lives as a matter of course, but only as mercy, and as a test, a test of our gratitude.

Let us think about this every day, in particular on those days which G-d has set aside and given to us as a time of reflection—like the days of the Advent, Christmas, and the new year. There are days of the love and thankfulness, of reconciliation and peace. We should make peace with G-d and with men and with ourselves. In the light of the Advent and Christmas candles, we should evaluate our past year and recognize how much good we have received from G-d and men. Let us recognize it and proceed gratefully through the gate of time—into the new year.

Eins ist notwendig

Eins ist notwendig, wenn der Herr vor der Türe steht und anklopft: Alles liegen lassen, Ihm öffnen, Ihm zu Füßen sitzen und zuhören! Die Arbeit wird nachgeholt werden—mit Hilfe der Engel, die jedem helfen, der zuerst nach dem Reiche Gottes trachtet.

One thing is necessary

One thing is necessary, if the Lord stands before the doors and knocks: let everything go, open your door to Him, sit at His feet, and listen! The work (you left behind) will accomplish itself—with the help of angels who help each person who aspires first to the Kingdom of G-d.

BOOKS OF RELATED INTEREST

The Edison Gene
ADHD and the Gift of the Hunter Child
by Thom Hartmann

Walking Your Blues Away
How to Heal the Mind and Create Emotional Well-Being
by Thom Hartmann

The Biology of Transcendence
A Blueprint of the Human Spirit
by Joseph Chilton Pearce

From Magical Child to Magical Teen
A Guide to Adolescent Development
by Joseph Chilton Pearce

The Crack in the Cosmic Egg
New Constructs of Mind and Reality
by Joseph Chilton Pearce

Matrix Meditations
A 16-week Program for Developing the Mind-Heart Connection
by Victor Daniels and Kooch N. Daniels

Radical Nature
The Soul of Matter
by Christian de Quincey, Ph.D.,

The Way of Beauty
Five Meditations for Spiritual Transformation
by François Cheng

Inner Traditions • Bear & Company
P.O. Box 388
Rochester, VT 05767
1-800-246-8648
www.InnerTraditions.com

Or contact your local bookseller